AF580047

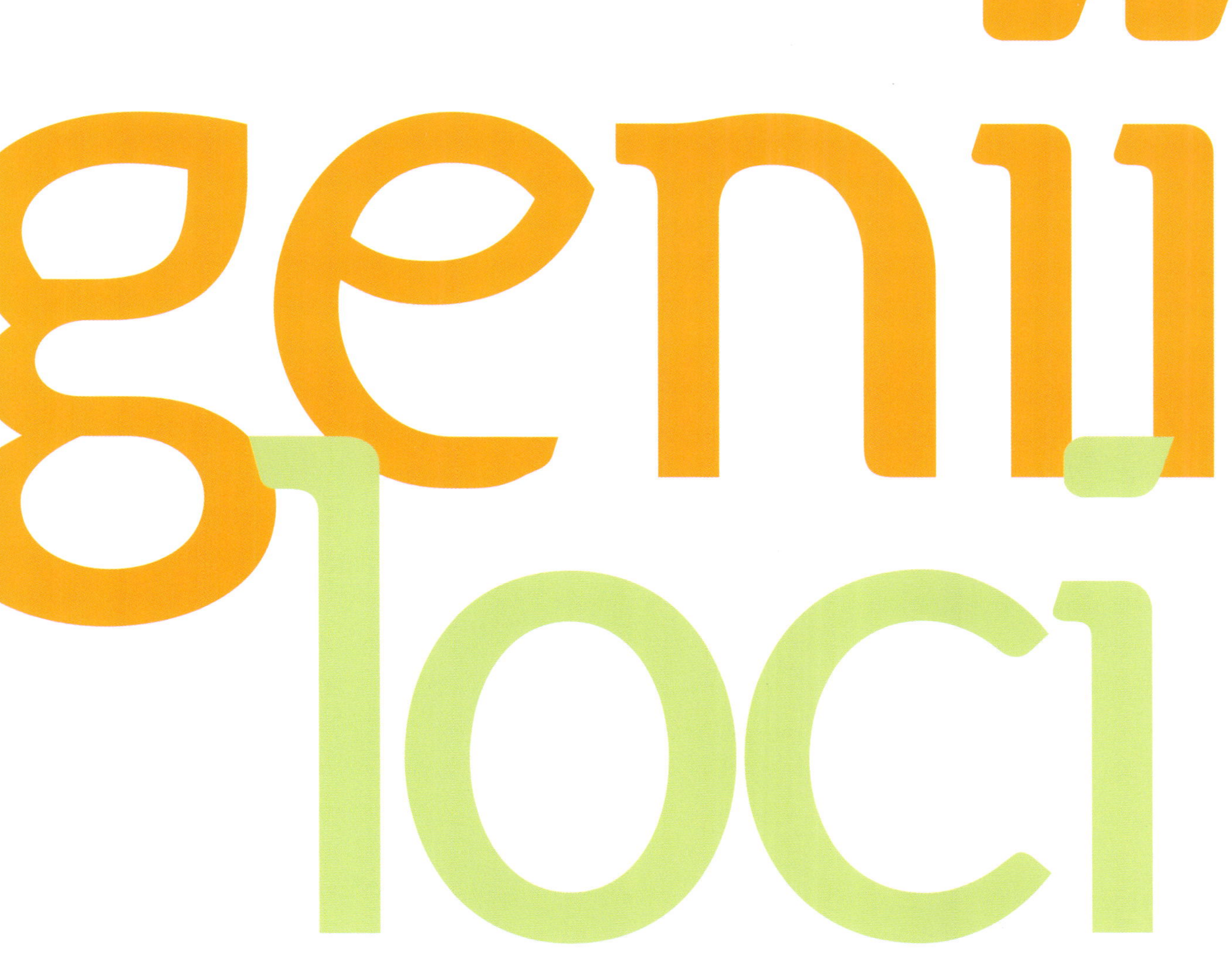

Karen Knorr

genii loci

The Photographic Work of Karen Knorr

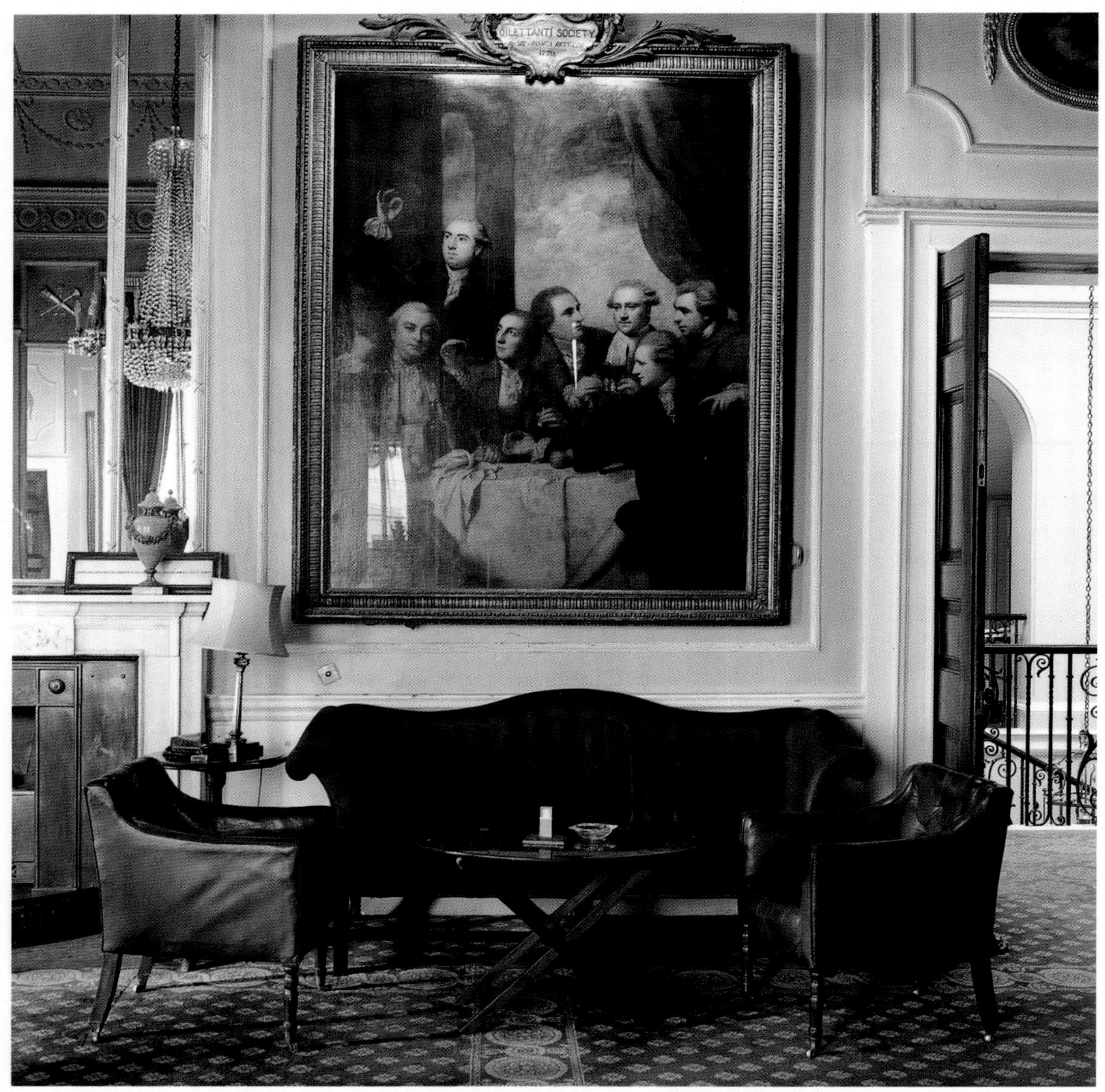

Lawrence disapproved.
Knight's critical judgement
was thoroughly warped
by Sensualism.
How anyone could favour
the flabby Luxury of a Rubens
to the linear Chastity of a Raphael
God only knows.

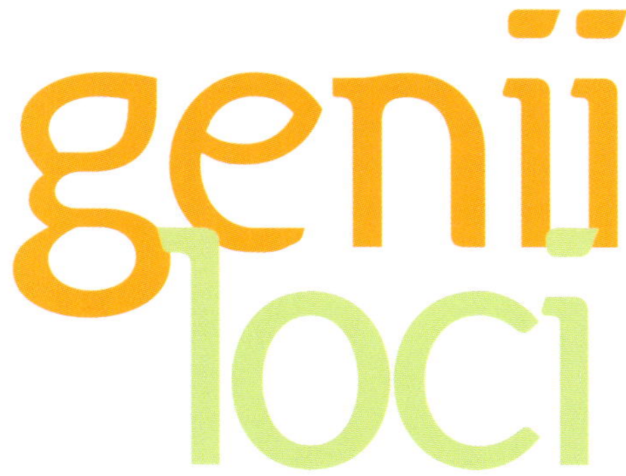

contents

Antonio Guzman

Rewind and Fast-forward: Photography, Allegory and Palimpsest

from volksgeist to zeitgeist

Since the late 1970s, the photographic work of Karen Knorr has developed through seven major series: *Belgravia*, 1979–1980; *Gentlemen*, 1981–1983; *Country Life*, 1983–1984; *Connoisseurs*, 1986–1989; *Capital*, 1990–1993; *The Virtues and the Delights*, 1993–1994. This development continued with *Academies,* a long series which she began in 1994 and highlighted with the *Sanctuary* exhibition at the Wallace Collection during the summer of 2001. The *Spirits* work, also from 2001, is still too fresh to say how it shifts or confirms this development.

The first steps in this itinerary are already sufficiently well documented and discussed elsewhere, so that it will be unnecessary to go back over them in detail.[1] Here it will be more interesting to deal with the evolution and the continuity of the work over more than a twenty year period, between what it has retained, what has been left aside, and what has been added, attempting in this way to define its current situation.

It is precisely in this sense that *Connoisseurs* appears as the series which no doubt most clearly marks the distinction between the origins of Karen Knorr's work and her approach today. It is obvious that with *Connoisseurs* Knorr abandons the abstract formalism of black and white photography and undertakes the exclusive practice of colour. With this colourist decision, the work moves technically toward a more directly interpretative vision of the subject; the saturated luxury of colour takes the place of the economical stippling of black and white and of the modest (but precisely coded and often fetishistic) pleasures of the gray scale, just as positive processes replace the reversed, phantom archive of the negative (Cibachrome for *Connoisseurs*, C-print for *Academies*). Physically, these changes of support medium and photographic material after the first three series are accompanied by a change of format and object.

The prints of the series *Connoisseurs* measure 39.5" x 39.5", those of *Academies*, 39.5" x 39.5" or 40" x 40", by comparison to the 24.5" x 20.5" format of the previous series. They are framed by a black strip with a fixed width of 2" or 2.5", a new codification of the work that persists up to and beyond the oblong and rounded framing of *The Virtues and the Delights* of 1993-1994. The square format replaces the rectangular, and–change of reference for change of referent–the work is referenced to painting and more precisely to picturesque painting, with the *Sanctuary* exhibition as the ultimate pictorial example, whereas the works of the preceding series referred to the printed photography of published image and typeset text. This is why, among other indications, the tight semantic relation between image and text in the earlier works is loosened; the text is no longer on the same contiguous plane as the photograph, nor on the same support medium of paper, but has shifted to the form of the traditional brass plate where the engraved text now takes on the role of the title of the print.

More fundamentally than these questions of form, this series clarifies the rhetoric of the work and identifies it as belonging to the domain of allegory. A work like *Shattering an Old Dream of Symmetry,* 1988, informs us about the choice of this figure of thought and discourse. Here we see a beautiful young woman in a black pant-suit, standing in the frame of an open door. Soberly dressed, with simple hairstyle and make-up, she holds an arrowless bow in her hand. One also sees a window and a staircase behind her, with two chairs placed symmetrically on either side of the threshold of the open door; but we primarily remark the classicising decorative motifs of the mural reliefs.

The mannerist prolixity of the giltwork highlights the severity of the contemporary young woman's black suit, if not the reverse. In any case, they are two different registers. On the other hand, the bow as an accessory partakes of the same mythological register as the painted decor; it shares in the same iconography as the nymphs in their drapery, the mythological figure of the sphinx with a woman's breast and the body of a winged lion, the oil lamps, vases and three-footed Etruscan urns, linked together by polychrome motifs of garlands and arabesques of foliage, all against a compartmentalised polychrome ground and above a frieze of Neronian fans. These elements were elaborated in Italy from the mid sixteenth century onwards; their classicising codification of vocabulary and syntax constitutes the language of the *grotesques.*

Another example from the *Connoisseurs* series is *The Analysis of Beauty,* 1988. The setting of this scene is very different: a gallery of paintings. This time, two male figures in suits and ties study the paintings of a tightly packed display, arranged in tiers of different levels. They use numerous instruments of astronomical and maritime optics (compasses, sextants, telescopes, and spy-glasses, among other accessories), as though the paintings were located at a great distance. Engravings and half-opened books are arranged around them and at their feet, in the manner

The Invention of Tradition
1988

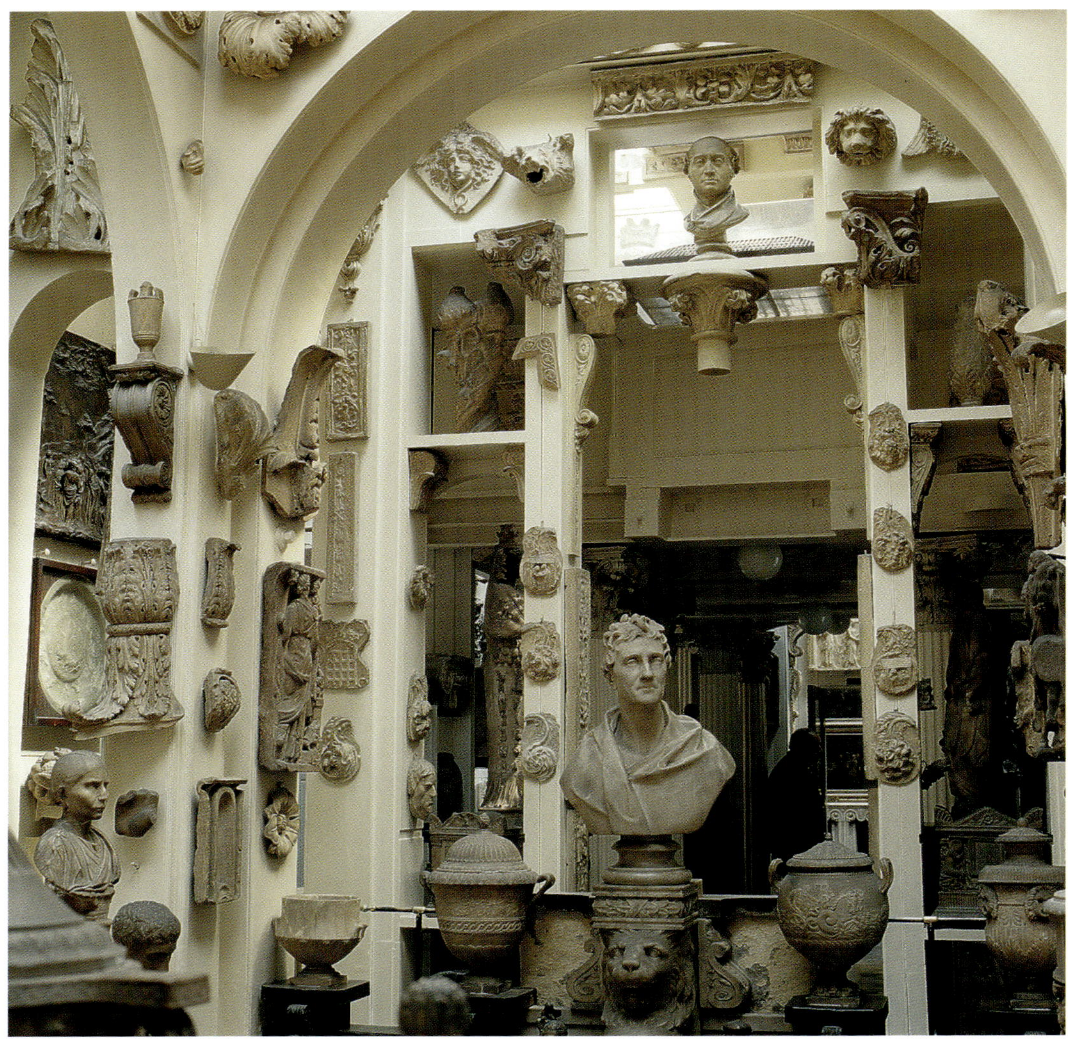

of a *cabinet d'amateur* or *tableau de collection* scene, as though a great investigation or process of research were underway. (More than ten years later, *Sanctuary* will return to the motif of the collection and re-exploit it, as we shall see further on, as both site and situation).

Although the taking of the pictures poses no strictly photographic question, the examination of these two examples suffices to note the deployment of a dense iconographic approach in the series. It also serves to isolate several important orientations in the work's iconicity, namely, the fact of photographing in architectonically charged spaces, the decision to use contemporary figures in these significant surroundings, the choice of heteroclite objects to be represented, the staging of the two (figures and objects), and finally, the text engraved on the brass plate fixed to the black frame, serving henceforth as a discursive, but enigmatic and often ironic title.

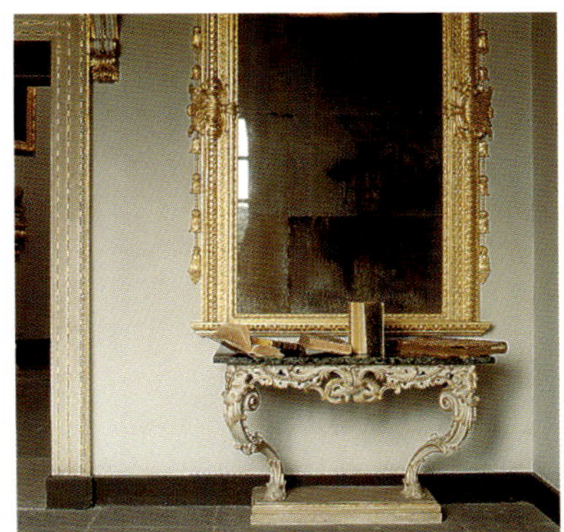

The Dictionary
of Received Ideas
1986

the topographic index; locus classicus

Beneath our gaze, the series of *Connoisseurs* moves from ceremonial chamber to pompously decorated hall and back again. From palace to exhibition gallery, and then from library to museum, from *topos* to *logos*, an indexical design repeats and ultimately makes itself explicit in the series. Such a wealth of gilding and molding, so many Doric columns and Ionic pilasters, entablatures, friezes and cornices, such an abundance of statuary and painting–the whole forms a *summum* which finally situates the style and period of the referent as eighteenth century neoclassicism.

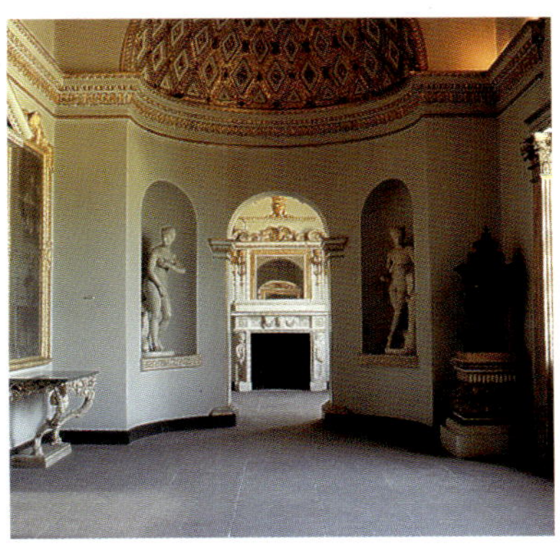

Antiquity as a
Guide to Nature
1986

In its turn, the gaze of the continental spectator can miss the specifically British localisation of the places chosen as the work's setting, scene, or background. The continental viewer may not know that in *Connoisseurs*, Knorr has photographed at Chiswick House (Middlesex, 1725), at Osterley Park (Middlesex, 1761–1780), at the Dulwich Picture Gallery (London, 1811–1813), at the Sir John Soane Museum (London, 1782–1837), and in the cast courts of the Victoria and Albert Museum (London, 1873). Or that she photographed *Sanctuary* entirely in Hertford House (London, 1776–1778).

The work circles around and stalks through these places. It literally turns in space, like cinema, and sometimes the photographs are only new angles and new viewpoints of the same site, making these locales into full-fledged figures of the work. The same spectator (whether British or continental) may be unaware of the meaning of these great private mansions, which have today become public historical monuments and national museums. But one cannot ignore the fact that the work is situated, literally and *figuratively*, in a particular place, which is furthermore a place of heritage, nor that it appropriates the decor and the architecture for quotation and situation.

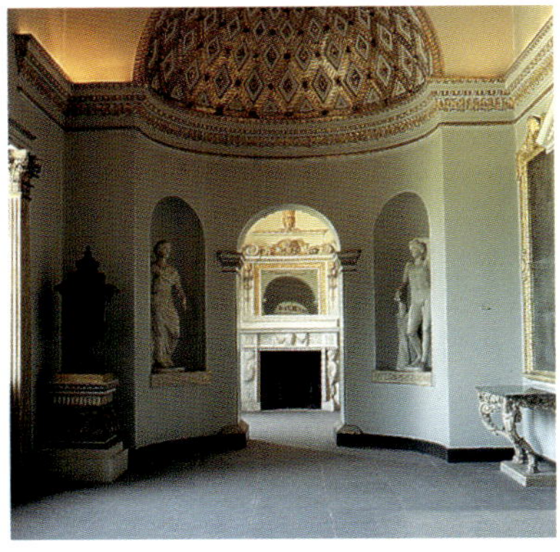

Nature Ennobled
by Reason
1986

Thus the work designates (even if this may not be apparent at first sight) certain outstanding personalities of the time: Lord Burlington, Sir John Soane, and Robert Adam. Architects above all, but also art collectors, patrons, *grand tourists* and great travellers to Italy, academy members, and finally, men of taste. These three are among the *congoscenti* to whom the series of *Connoisseurs* refers. They are also associated with the political and social theorist Edmund Burke and the parodic poet Alexander Pope, among those who together invented a century by reinventing classical antiquity.

From site to historical and classicising site, Knorr revisits the eighteenth century like a ruin, like the emblematic image of a human project and a cultural edifice brought low by history, predestined to be ultimately reabsorbed by nature. Within the heritage of this ruin of an enlightened century, repaired, restored, and rehabilitated, but forever incomplete, the work travels from Burlington's Palladianism to Soane's neoclassicism, with side trips through Adam's Hellenistic ornamentation, Pope's English garden, and Burke's sublime. The topographically indexed historicism is a measure of the work's photographic realism; the real displacements are its guarantees and the photographs are its documents.

This realistic siting or topographic indexing is not new in the work. On the contrary, it is rather a constant. Already, the series of *Belgravia* and *Gentlemen* in the late 1970s and the early 1980s are clearly situated in a well-defined urban perimeter: that of the eponymous district of old London in the first case, and in the second, the traditional men's clubs in the Saint James district, still in London. More bucolic, as its title indicates, the series *Country Life* situates less a fixed or particular place than a generic pastoral lifestyle. More recently, in the series *Capital,* 1991-92, the spheres of influence of international high finance are photographed in-situ, in the very restricted perimeter of the Anglo-Saxon *square mile* that delimits London's financial district, the City.

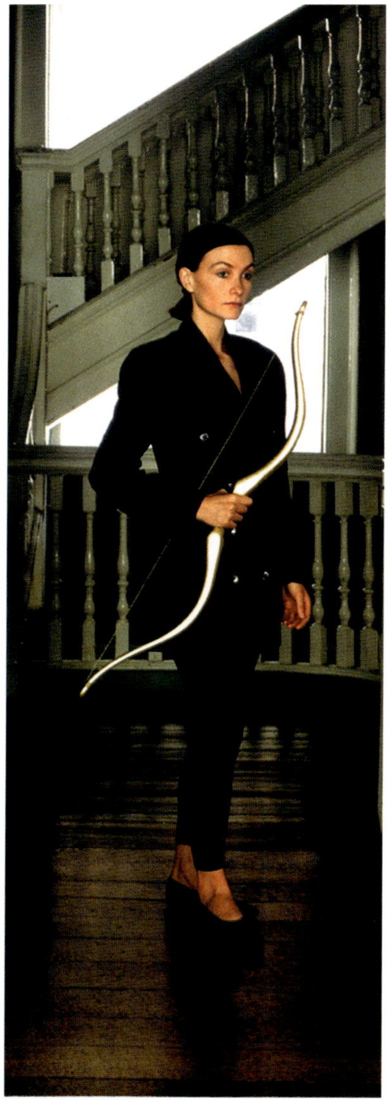

Shattering an Old Dream of Symmetry
1988
(detail)

After this, the indexing becomes less anglicised or anglomaniac. Given the homage rendered to the libertine and liberating thought of the eighteenth century (in historical and ideological opposition to the series of *Connoisseurs*), the series of *The Virtues and the Delights* was naturally treated at Ferney, the administrative seat of the canton at the Swiss border where Voltaire resided from 1758 to 1778. A more European and cosmopolitan series because of its subject, *Academies* takes the paths of a more itinerant project: Goldsmiths College of Art in London, but also The Royal Academy of Fine Arts in Stockholm, the Gustavianium Anatomy Theater of the University of Uppsala, the Ecole des Beaux-arts in Paris, the libraries of the Academy of Sciences and of the Royal Palace in Turin. As for the videos, they were carried out at the Victoria and Albert Museum in London (*Being for Another* and *Movement of the Soul*, 1995), at the Musée d'Orsay in Paris (*The Visitors*, 1998), and at the Jesuit Library in Valenciennes (*Readers: Portrait of an Artist*, 1998).

personages and figures: proscenium

It is in the sense of site specificity that the work is spatially realistic. It is contingent on the history of places. From series to series and from scene to scene, there is the same concern as from site to site: the work is faithful to its subject as documentary and its realism serves to reinforce the imaginary. Where the work deviates from reality is with the personages called upon to figure in the photographs. And in this respect too, the first three series of *Belgravia*, *Gentlemen* and *Country Life* share the same kind of scenic play to different degrees, while *Connoisseurs* marks a new orientation in the scenography of the figures.

In the first three series, it is plausible that the personages are at home. The men and women who figure in them, young or mature, are in their proper place. Nothing indicates the contrary, no gesture or posture, no piece of clothing; there is no intrusion on the places, nothing untoward breaks into the scene. As they are seemingly in their domicile, their club (or for the valets and other servants, their workplace), nothing distances the figures from the decor in which they appear. These series deal with the socially private domain; the personages take on roles within their immediate scope (wives, husbands, children of good families, members of clubs, or their retinue of chambermaids and butlers), apparently without any effect of change of decor or costume, in real life just like on the movie screen.

By enlarging the field of reference from the modern bourgeois private sphere to the public domain of heritage, *Connoisseurs* carries out a change of decor and above all of scale. The domestic interiors of the homes in the early works are replaced by the monumentality and historicity of this series (constituting both a scale and a dimension that will be pursued in the work all the way to *Academies*). In turn, the introduction of contemporary figures into these new anachronistic settings creates a gap: the personages are no longer at home, and for this reason they return to their initial and sole true role as figures. The gap results from the division of time and the telescoping of eras. As in the two works quoted as examples, the clothes of the figures distinguish them from the decor, while their gestures and postures tie them to it, now that from this point forth, and consistently, the figures are called upon to play a role and no longer merely to take their place as plausible personages.

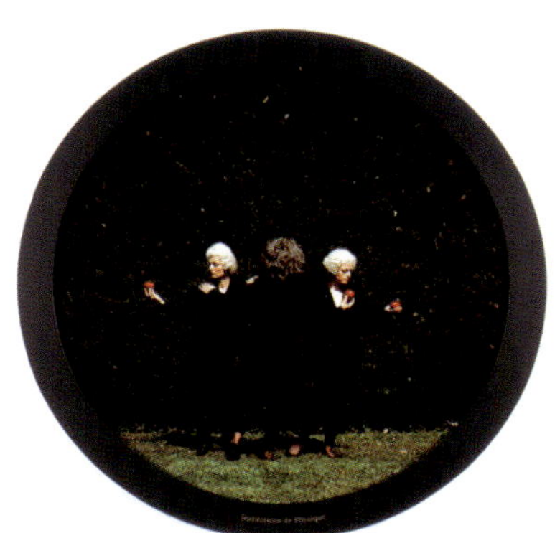

The Story of Juliette
Institutions de Physique
1992

Life in the midst of history, the contemporary in eighteenth century classicism: this is an anachronistic use of photography. There is also a return of the emblematic and of the rhetorical figures of mythological and cyclical time, erupting here into a linear temporality–unless it is not also a question of just the opposite, a question of remanence, of the persistence of the historical in the living, of neoclassicism in the contemporary, of the survival of ideological determinisms, the grip and perennity of myth in a Proustian lost time. This, in my opinion, is the meaning of the Artemis or Diana with the arrowless bow in *Shattering an Old Dream of Symmetry.*

She is the first feminine figure not to display a domestic or quotidian image. With her, the imagery of the matriarch at the hearth, of the kept woman, the ingénue or the housekeeper, is finished. Change of figure for a change of decor, if it is not, here once again, the reverse: from the commonplaces (in the strict sense) of the bourgeoisie to the non-normative topoi of classicism. For this mythological figure, at antipodes from the sweet charms of Aphrodite, is a huntress, a Saggitarian under the sign of the moon, a goddess of nature and mistress of wild animals, a vindictive and stormy virgin. She will be followed by a whole sisterhood of mythical, biblical, historical, and contemporary women, but the work will never return to the domestic figure or setting.

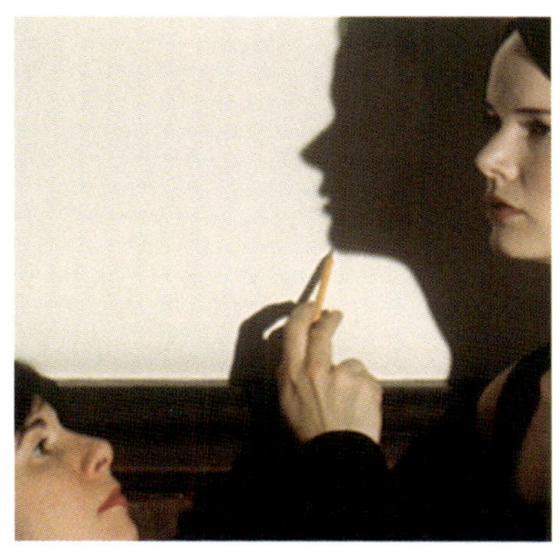

Butades' Daughter
1994
(detail)

This also holds for the series of *The Virtues and the Delights* of 1993–1994, which takes up and transforms the medieval moral allegory of the *vices* and the *virtues.* Knorr displaces the work to the Utopia of the Enlightenment's libertine garden, where woman tastes both delights and virtues without the moral condemnation of society. In this feminist reading of the emancipatory and egalitarian ideas of the eighteenth century, she quotes Condorcet, Sade, Voltaire, Emilie du Chatelet, Louise d'Epinay, Mary Wollstonecraft, and Thomas Paine, in opposition to the ideologies of class and privilege, blood and soil, as they had been exposed up to this point in the work (from *Belgravia* to *Connoisseurs*), but above all in opposition to the latent misogyny of Rousseau's historical legacy, which continues to attribute to women the role of men's *delight* along with that of *vestal* of virtue. This is why women are the only figures of the series and why they all wear masculine riding coats and powdered wigs, striking classical feminine poses, either as an odalisque or as a grace with three red apples in hand, in a series which stages various androgynous figures as Venus, Hera, and Athena, but without Paris–in reference to the paintings by Raphael and Rubens. (The motif of the choice between three different women embodying distinct types of beauty will ironically return in the *Judgement of Paris,* 2001, from the *Sanctuary* project, photographed before the 1754 painting of the same title by François Boucher, recalling Hubert Damisch's idea that this founding myth is the first *judgement of taste.*)

dramatis personae

The next series, the *Academies* of 1994–2001, confirms this option for the feminine gender in the work and generalises the disappearance of the masculine figure, with just a few exceptions (the man in a suit and tie whose skull is measured by a woman against a backdrop of painted portraits, in *Hårleman's Anatomy* of 1994).

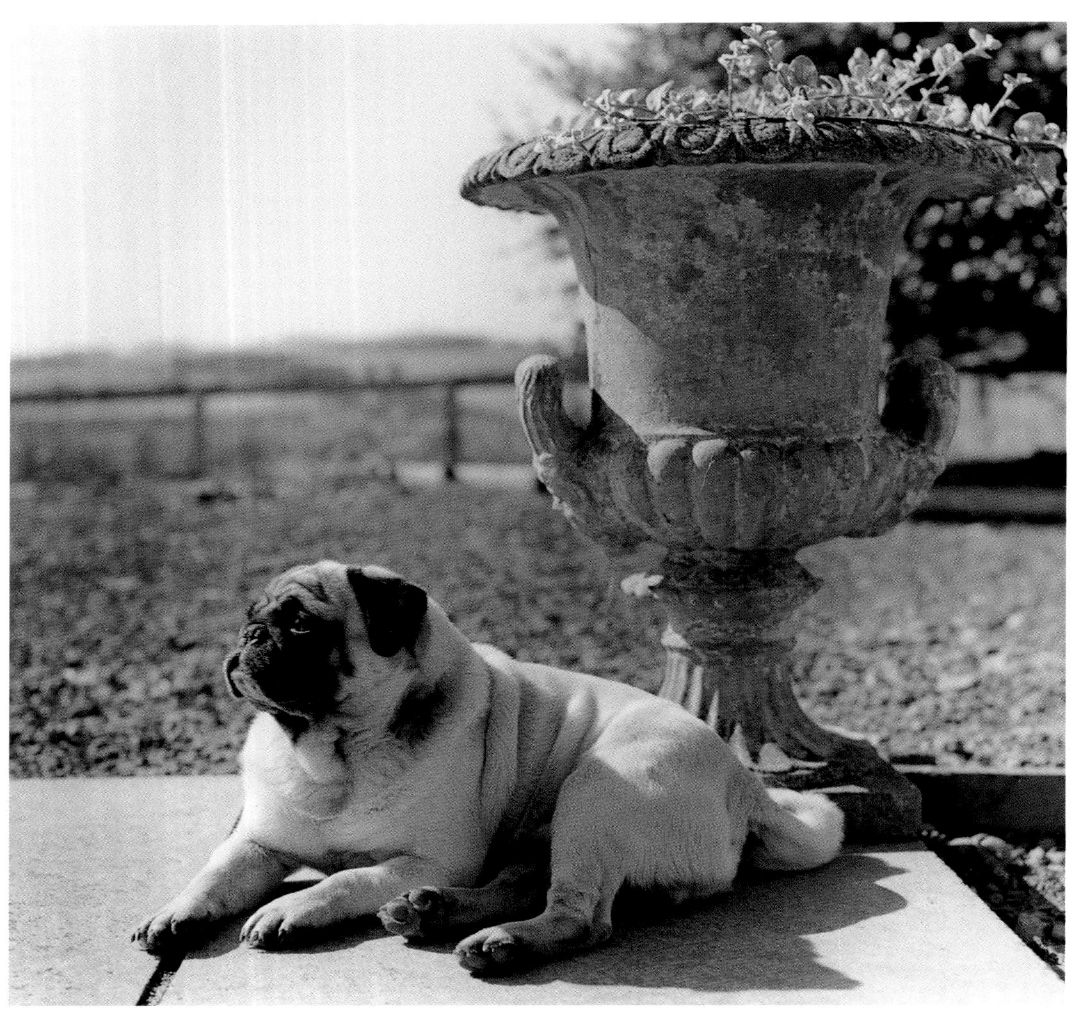

High Life

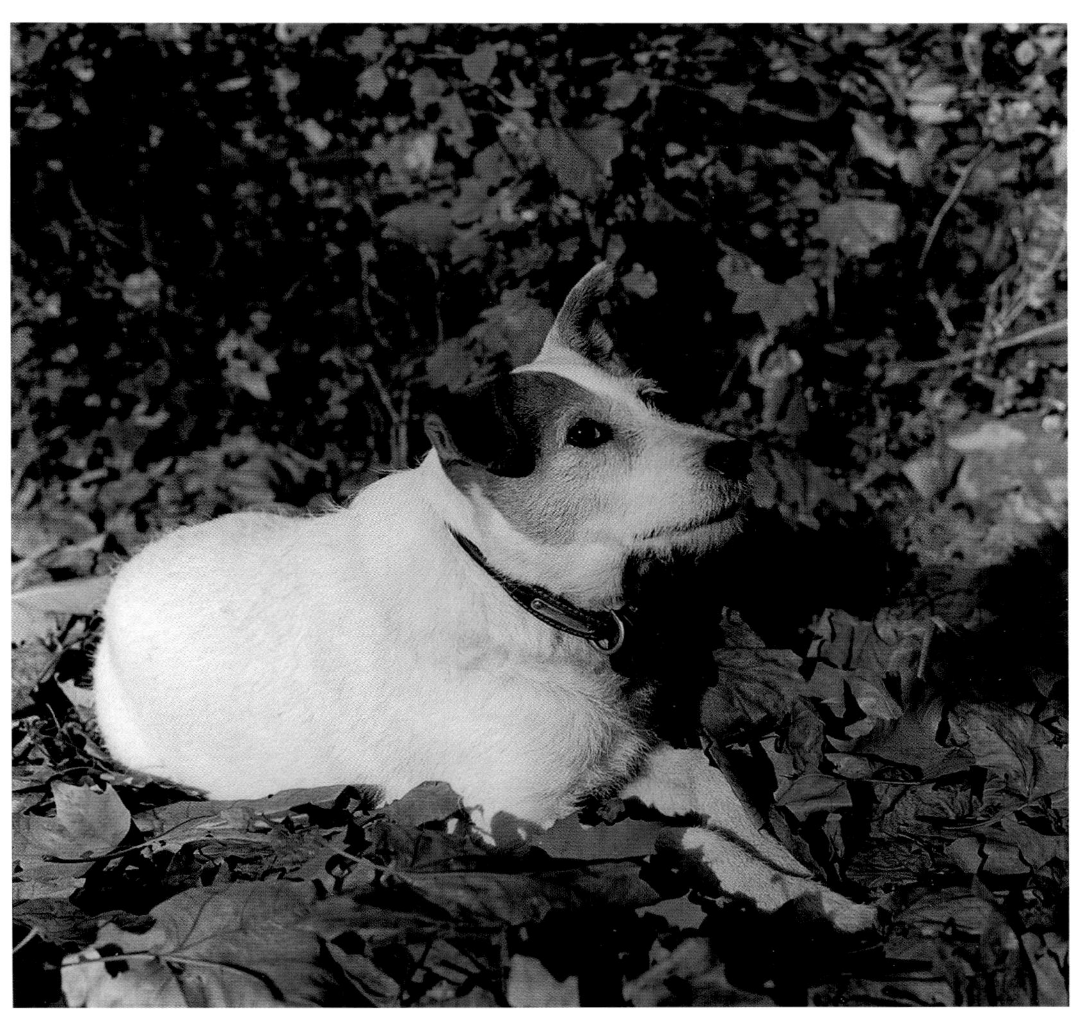

Low Life

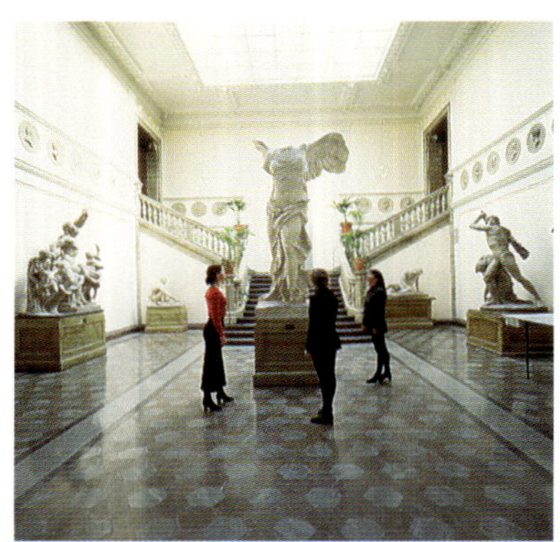

The Pregnant Moment
1994

As its title indicates, the series takes on one of the major institutional innovations of the eighteenth century, the art academies, which for centuries will govern the relations between the artist and society by a normalisation of pedagogical programmes and modes of production. This photographic cycle also goes all the way back to another of the founding myths of Western artistic creation, the myth of Butades of Sicyone, which it feminises in *The Pencil of Nature*, 1994. In this work, the figures of the father-potter and of the lover on the verge of leaving Corinth disappear; the potter's daughter, forever without a proper name (except that of "the daughter of the potter Butades of Sicyone"), and still enamoured of her young lover, traces on the wall the shadow of another girl, at the foot of one of the innumerable plaster casts of the naked Doryphoros. The reference between the title and the scenography of the work is double: on the one hand photographic, alluding to William Henry Fox Talbot and his book entitled *The Pencil of Nature,* 1844–1846, and on the other hand mythological (see Pliny the Elder, book XXXV of his *Natural History*). With a gesture of travesty included, since the paternity (sic) and the object of the creative act shift here from masculine to feminine. And it is from the grasp of this shadow–from the projection of myth and history, of the shadow of sculpture, painting, and drawing, but also the projection of the phantom, latent, reversed image of the negative, the cast shadow of representation and the play of shadows between presence and absence which photography retraces and rejoins, between figure and ground–that the 1998 Beauvais exhibition drew, I believe, its title of *Photography's Shadow.*

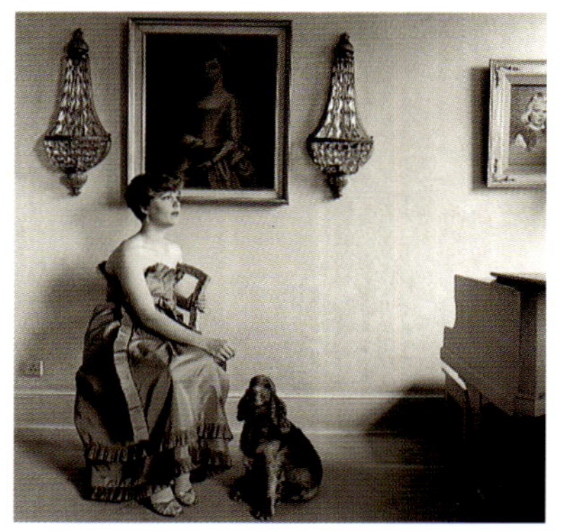

I am really looking forward to my Deb party.
1979

Apart from the example of the evident male attributes of the naked spear-thrower Doryphoros (cast in plaster after a Roman copy in marble of the original by Polykleitos, ca. 450–440 BC), even the statuary in this series is feminine. Woman here is either nymph or Helen, Eve or Mary Magdalene; she has many names, after either Canova or Knorr; changes of title, narrative and heroine parallel the changes of point of view. The identity of the women figured here is not biographical, fixed or stable, but mobile and interchangeable: these are emblematic, polyvalent signs, depending on the angle from which the same statue is photographed; they are denominative demonstrations of photography's very limited objectivity when it places a body in space (or frames a scene in architecture, as in *Connoisseurs* and the *Sanctuary* project). Elsewhere in the series, there is a plaster cast of the *Victory of Samothrace* (from a marble original, ca. 295–287 BC), without a rostrum, in the middle of the atrium of the Royal Academy of the Fine Arts in Stockholm, surrounded by three modern women with hieratic gestures and postures; or two young women in carefully measured poses engaging in a *rite of passage* on the threshold of an open door between two oblong masculine portraits. Or again, not to multiply these examples of the choice of gender, the case of the Baudelairean painter of modern life who is now represented by two young Asian girls, or that of the Joycean video-portrait of the artist who has here become a young, long-haired blond woman.

With this observation of the development of the female figure we can measure how far we are from the period of *Gentlemen* of 1981–1983, where the subject of the work was the closed, governing circles of the patriarchy, from which women are traditionally (and this is the issue) excluded. Which is to say that the work has become somewhat *misandrous*, revisionist, and more overtly political. It no longer deals with the simple photographic mimesis of its subject, with the restaging of banalities or the quotation of clichés, of cultural rumors, of persistent legacies, of received ideas or other old choruses and same refrains well known from texts or images, with the themes, conventional since Burke, of the social and natural order. Indeed, this was the way for the work to escape the stylistically conventional, immobilist, hegemonic, and doxical dead-end of the Thatcherist-Blairist ideologies of which it has been, since its beginnings, the voluntary and methodological

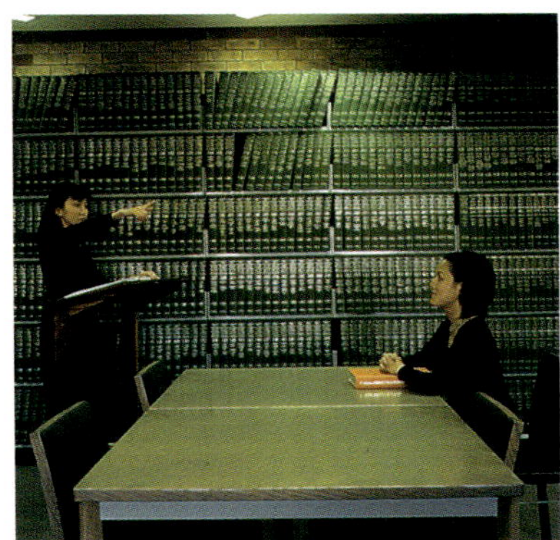

Study of the Canon
1997

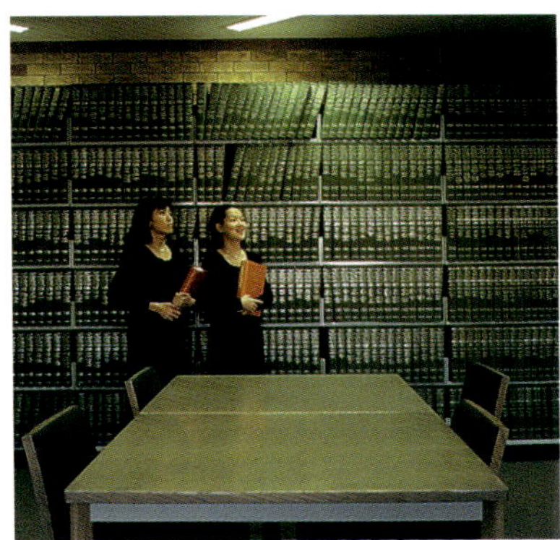

Liberation of Form and Content
1997

plagiarist, both textual and iconographic. Retrospectively, as one can remark in passing, the colourist option in the work in its reference to painting takes on a metonymical and feminine meaning, and this in the terms of the academic debate between the *ancients* and the *moderns*, the followers of Poussin or Ingres, Rubens or Delacroix–a debate in which drawing (or the graphic pattern of black and white) would be of the masculine domain, and colour (pictorial or photographic), of the feminine.

While the assumption and development of the feminine figure in the work can sometimes be a simple, economical matter of cross-dressing, it is nonetheless a little more complex than just parodying or travesting one figure for another. Women assail the insular machismo of the subjects being treated, but the presence of young Asian women in Western art schools in *Hanako's Colourful World, The Study of the Canon, Painters of Modern Life*, and *Liberation of Form and Content*, all photographs of 1997, and almost a sequence within the series *Academies*, more particularly undercut the Aryanism and Eurocentrism of these same subjects. The women are brought into the imagery and the normative institution of a sexually and ethnically territorialised subject, which they re-ethnicise at will. Referring to Charles Baudelaire as well as to James Joyce, but displaying the features and premises of another culture, they personify a double paradox: that of illustrating the contemporary multi-ethnicity of a post-imperial society, and showing the transcultural influence and attractiveness of another empire, that of the exponents of the academic canons. In the first case we see the effects of colonialism and of waves of immigration; in the second case, which is hardly better, there is the exotic effect of a touristic, Western sheen of surplus-value amidst cultural globalisation. In both cases one can ask what academicism, even in its most up-to-date forms, could offer of pertinence to these young women who have come from elsewhere, a little like Diderot asking *how the Ancients, who had no classical works, went about it.*

If Knorr takes up the theme of the *academy* in the most recent series, it is because the question is not so untimely at this turn of the century as it might first seem. Here again, the question is actually double. It is the question of the origin of the *academies*, most of which were founded during the Enlightenment from 1710 to 1810, of their disgrace and their decline into academicism, and finally their total discredit in the twentieth century; but it is also the question, still very current, of the transmission of artistic teaching. If today we are comfortably distant from the absolutism and centralising mercantilism that motivated Colbert to issue the decree founding the *Académie Royale de Peinture et de Sculpture* in Paris in 1663, within a system and a network of other academies in the service of the state, and if we are similarly distant from the spread of this grand design all over Europe, still the two sides of the question brought together form another paradox. It is the paradox of the dominant social and political expectation in matters of aesthetics, which is still academic (as a legacy of universal value, immutable and timeless, and as a cultural rank to attain in the climb toward bourgeois status). It is this paradox which contemporary artistic teaching must face when it organises studies (liberal as they may be, they are always somehow organised) and at the same time seeks to stave off the creation of a *neo-academicism*, as fashionable, trendy, current, or elitist as it may be (because history is there to warn us of that). Which is to say that Knorr, in this series, deals with the institutional roots and determinism of art, whether classical, academic, or contemporary, in a dialectic which is now that of an artistic practice at grips with its very *raison d'être*.

It is for all these reasons that the figure of the black man stands out in the series. While the first and only black man to appear before this point in Knorr's work was a valet with a silver tea service in hand, in a photograph from *Gentlemen* which reversed the conventional male and female roles, a second black man is introduced

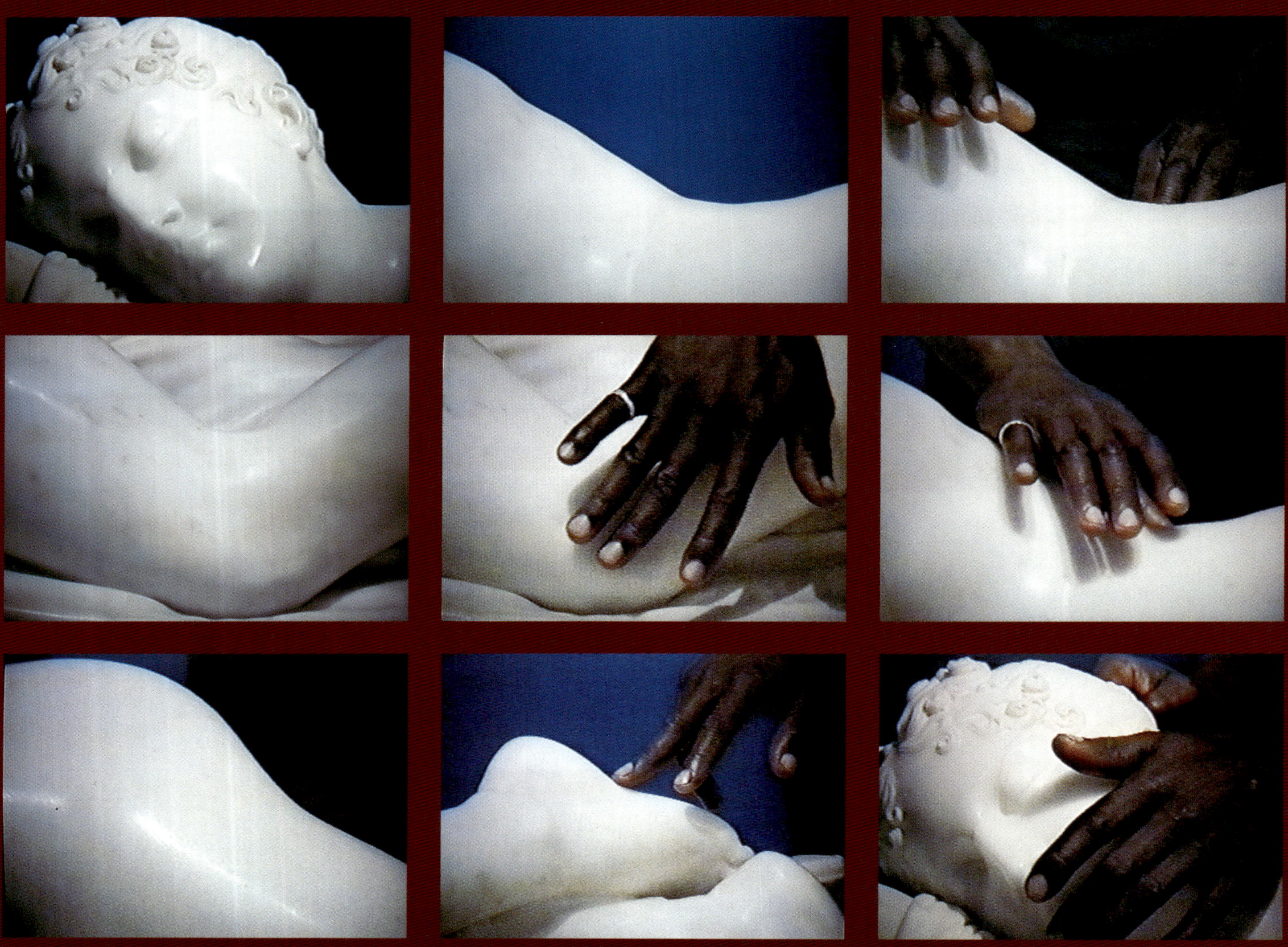

Being for Another
(video stills)

Nothing has a Spirit
that is ground within itself
and dwells in it,
but each has its being
in something outside and alien to it.

Hegel
The Phenomenology of the Spirit

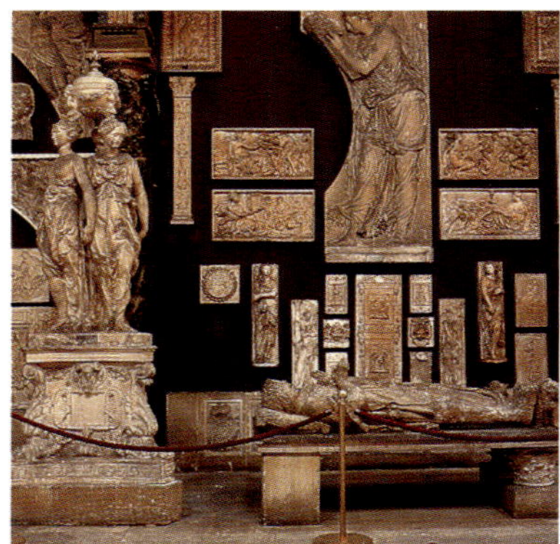

Comparison of the Ancients with the Moderns
1997

three times in the period of *Academies.* Crossing another threshold in the intentionality of the work, the role of the black man this time is to caress (and in the videos, ever so slowly) the statue of the *Sleeping Nymph* by Canova, which is now held at the Victoria and Albert Museum. With his caresses he transgresses several taboos: the institutional prohibition on touching the work of art in the museum, and the obviously racial prohibition on touching a white woman beneath our very eyes, even if this woman is a marble statue. One can wonder if these are not socially and erotically the same transgression. And yet the caresses are more chaste and modest than the languorous invitation of Canova's smooth, well-polished statue. Thus this photograph and the videos open up a more racial and equatorial, less *wasp* dimension and they confirm, in addition to the sexual and ethnic openings pursued in the same series, a more exogamous if not exogenous consideration, with respect to the Aryanism and ethnocentrism studied symptomatically to this date. Always with great economy of means, the photograph and the two videos organise several binary polarities between the statue of the white woman and the figure of the black man. Among them are a chiaroscuro of stone and flesh, cold and hot, disincarnation and carnation, lividity and pigmentation, inertia and movement, fiction and reality, where it is literally reality that touches the lie of classical representation's purity with its fingertips, and points out the fact that Antiquity was not so *white* after all, but rather gaudy and Levantine. It is in these effects of contrast, barely emerging from shadow or filtered light, that the black man is like a penumbra, belonging neither completely to the world in which he appears and figures, nor to that of the Victorian museum, nor to that of Canova's neo-classicism: he is a figure of the Other.

bestiarium, breviarium: kunst-und-wunderkammern

The work's extreme and ultimately recurrent figure of alterity is the monkey, introduced in *Connoisseurs* with the two versions of *The Genius of the Place.* Except for the live pet dogs that appear in *Belgravia* and in the 1984 diptych *High Life/Low Life*, for a peacock in a photograph from *Country Life,* the monkey is the first emblematic animal to be found in Knorr's work. It will be followed, over time and in the course of the evolving series, by a limited and selected menagerie of stuffed figures, including a crow, wolves, and various monkeys. Absent from the work for some time, it is in *Academies* that the monkey is asserted and exploited as a programmatic figure in many different pieces, to the point where it characterises another sequence within the series. With the monkey, questions of sexual gender and race are in their turn relativised by zoology, along with the questions of minorities, misogyny, and Euro- or ethnocentrism. Brought to the forefront by the bestiary, it is now a question of anthropocentrism and logocentrism, with the entry of the animal kingdom into so many erudite, scholarly, and cultural considerations, with the introduction of another kind of public into the museums, libraries, and great mansions of the work's topology. If the peacock is emblematic of wealth and vanity, if the black crow is a bird of ill omen, the wolf an indomitable spirit of forests and packs, earthly and fierce, a predator and psychomorph, the monkey is a friendly but foreign figure, strange and familiar. It is a *little man*, an anthropoid mammal, a hairy ancestor, in and outside the environment of the museums and heritage in which it is placed. Near and far all at once, a sub-order in the order of primates, related to us in the great divisions of nature, the monkey is physical, agile, and instinctive. It is a biological, buffoon-like figure that stands apart from the harmonious, well-ordered and civilised background in which it is staged. It is a partial mirror, a caricature, a hapless, decadent double of the civic, moral, and artistic humanism so amply documented in the work. The monkey is a Darwinian rejoinder to the creationism of so much pomp, an evolutionist reminder and regression amid so much circumstance.

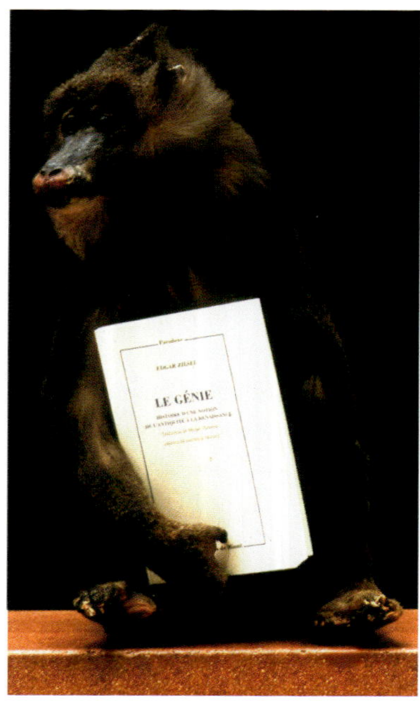

The Art Functionary
1998
(detail)

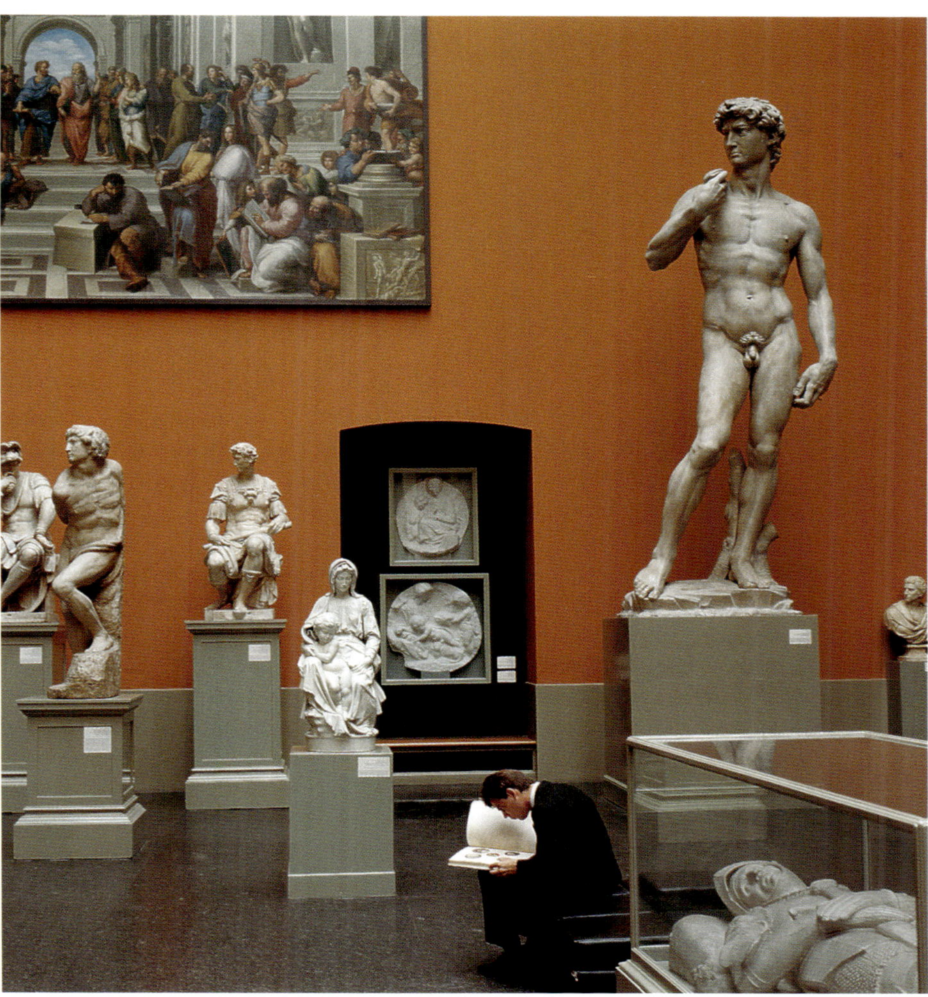

The Work of Art
in the Age of
Mechanical Reproduction
1988

The monkey stands out from an ecology which is not its own, and frolics in the gap that it opens and represents in this other environment. A light, parodic figure, allegorical and ironic, it does not respect the seriousness of the locales, the works, the discourses. Like the *simio gramático* of Octavio Paz, it contrasts its simple biology and noetic behaviour to human thought and language. A full-fledged and not necessarily inferior species, near but radically other and elsewhere, a real generic difference, a heterogeneous relation and an embarrassing relative, the monkey in *Academies* becomes a figure of first importance, a subject in itself. In the place of real personages and veritable actors, it plays all the best roles of the art world: in the central walkway of the Orsay Museum, devoted to French sculpture from 1840-1875, and provisionally empty of all visitors, the monkey is model, artist, art-lover, critic, functionary, and spectator, among the pale ephebes and generously endowed nudes on display.

By the time of the *Sanctuary* exhibition and the beginning of the *Spirits* project, that is to say the years 2000-2001, the menagerie in the work will be considerably enlargened and diversified. It will now include lambs, ewes, parakeets, parrots, a crane, a pheasant and an owl, in addition to wolves and monkeys. To the extent that there is no longer any human figure in either project, other than those pictorially (and not photographically) represented.

In 1998 the commission and the exhibition at the Orsay Museum, whose theme was the problematic of *photographing sculpture,* gave Knorr the opportunity to return to and (re)develop the simian figure; today it allows us to point to another

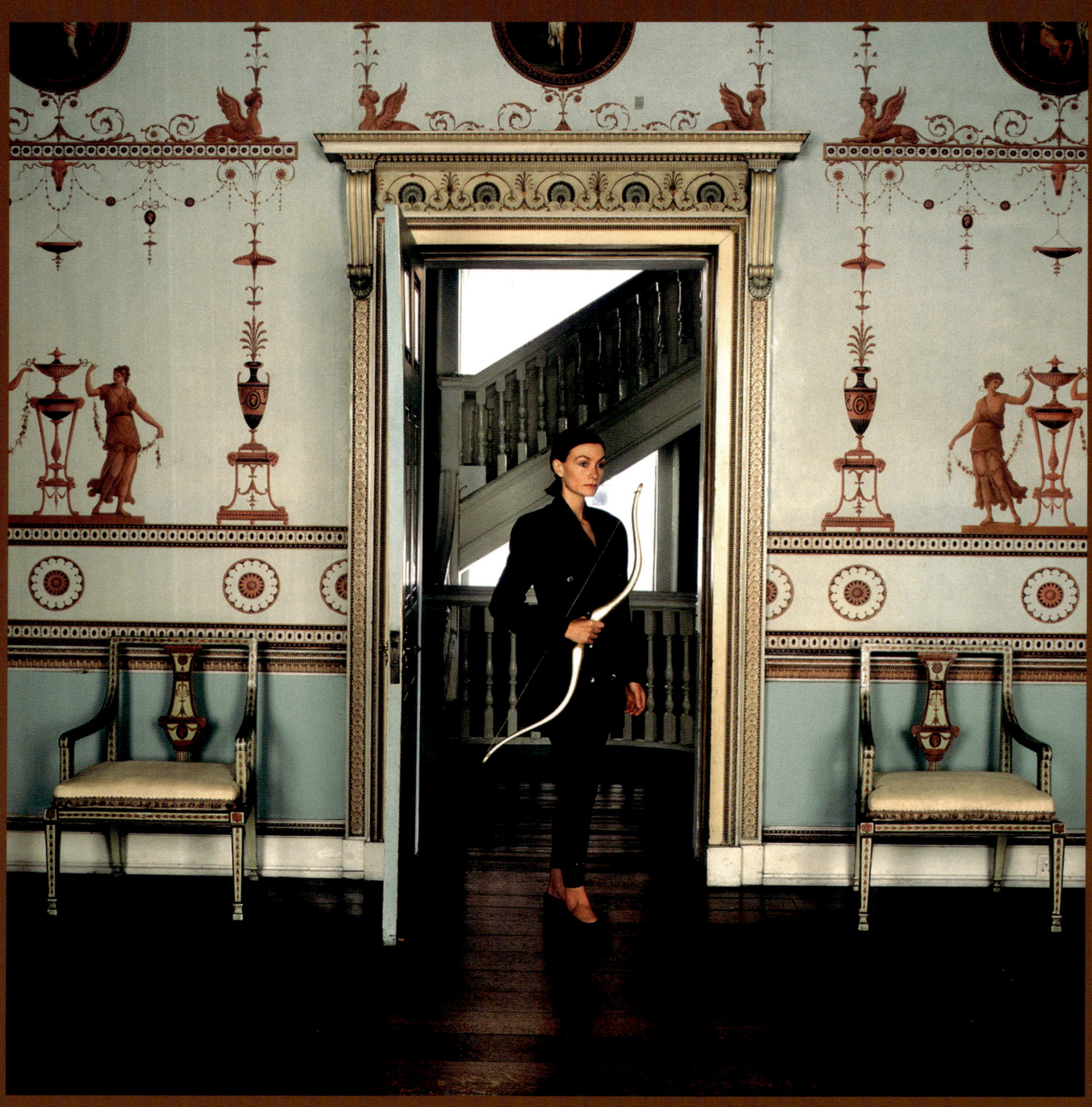

Shattering an Old Dream of Symmetry

I

Connoisseurs

The Genius of the Place

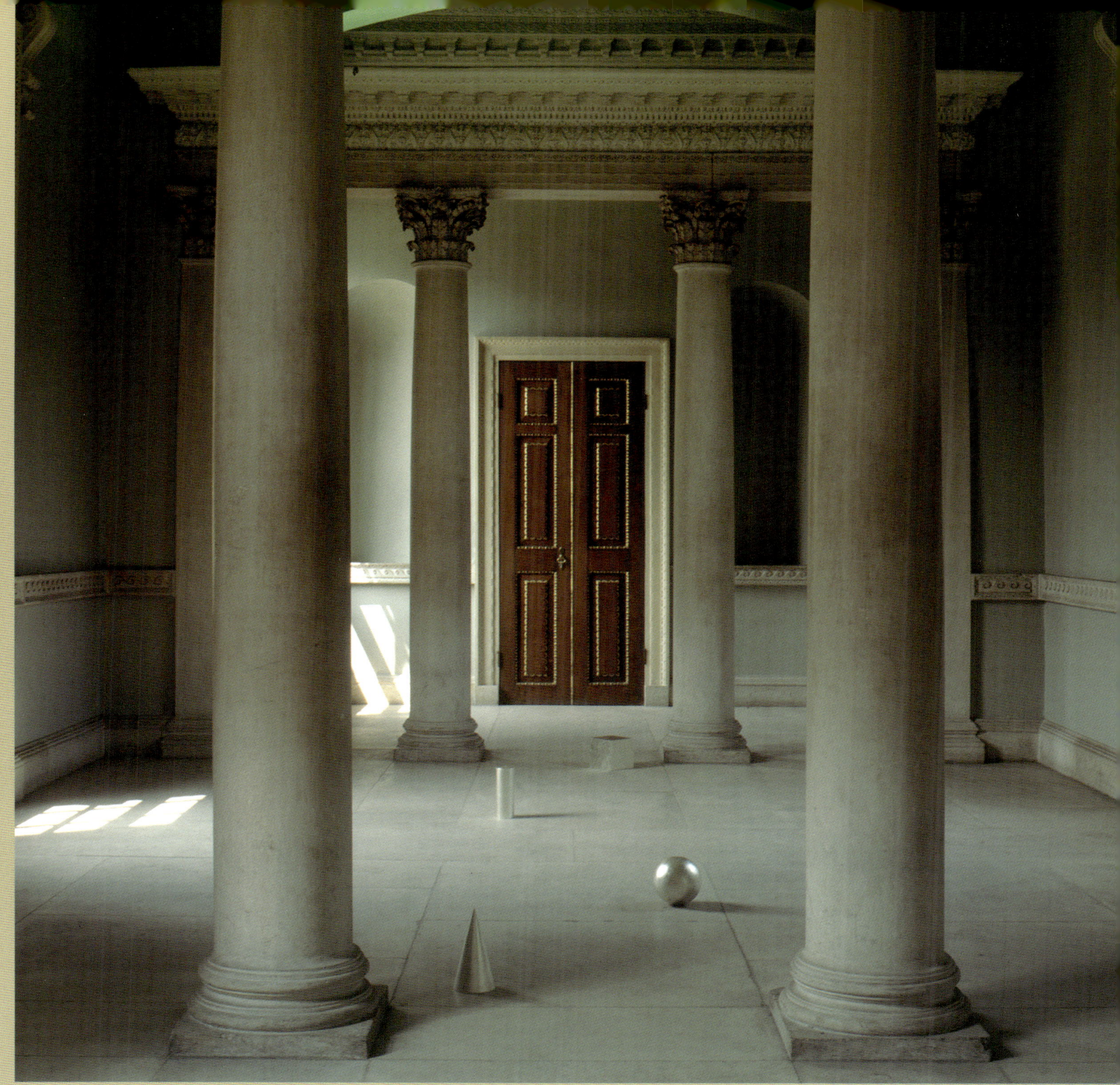

Contemplation of the Essential Forms

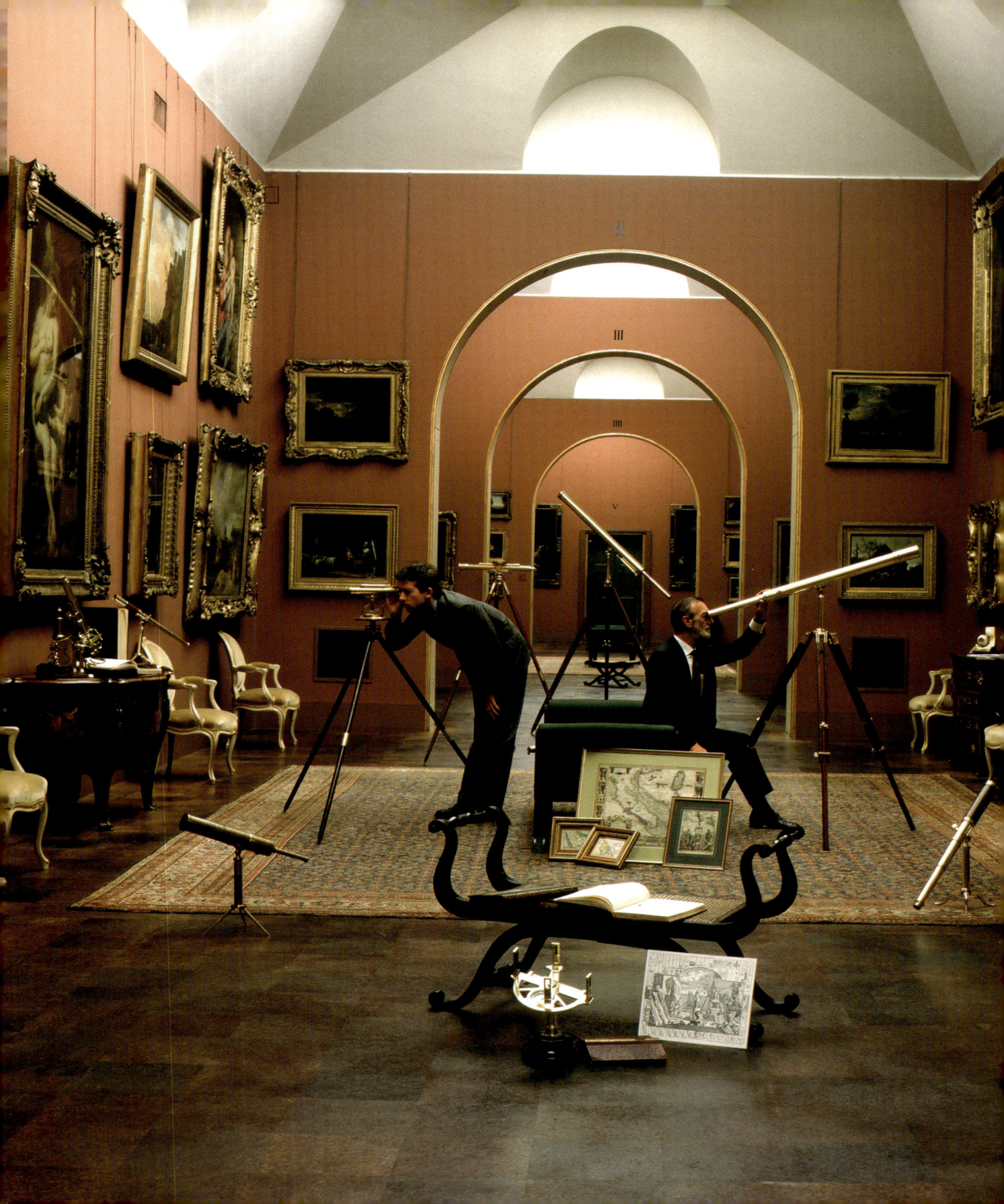

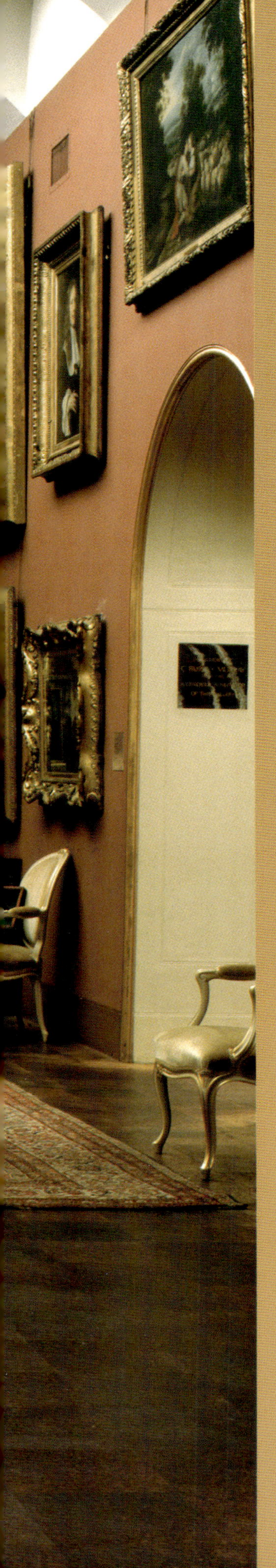

The Analysis of Beauty

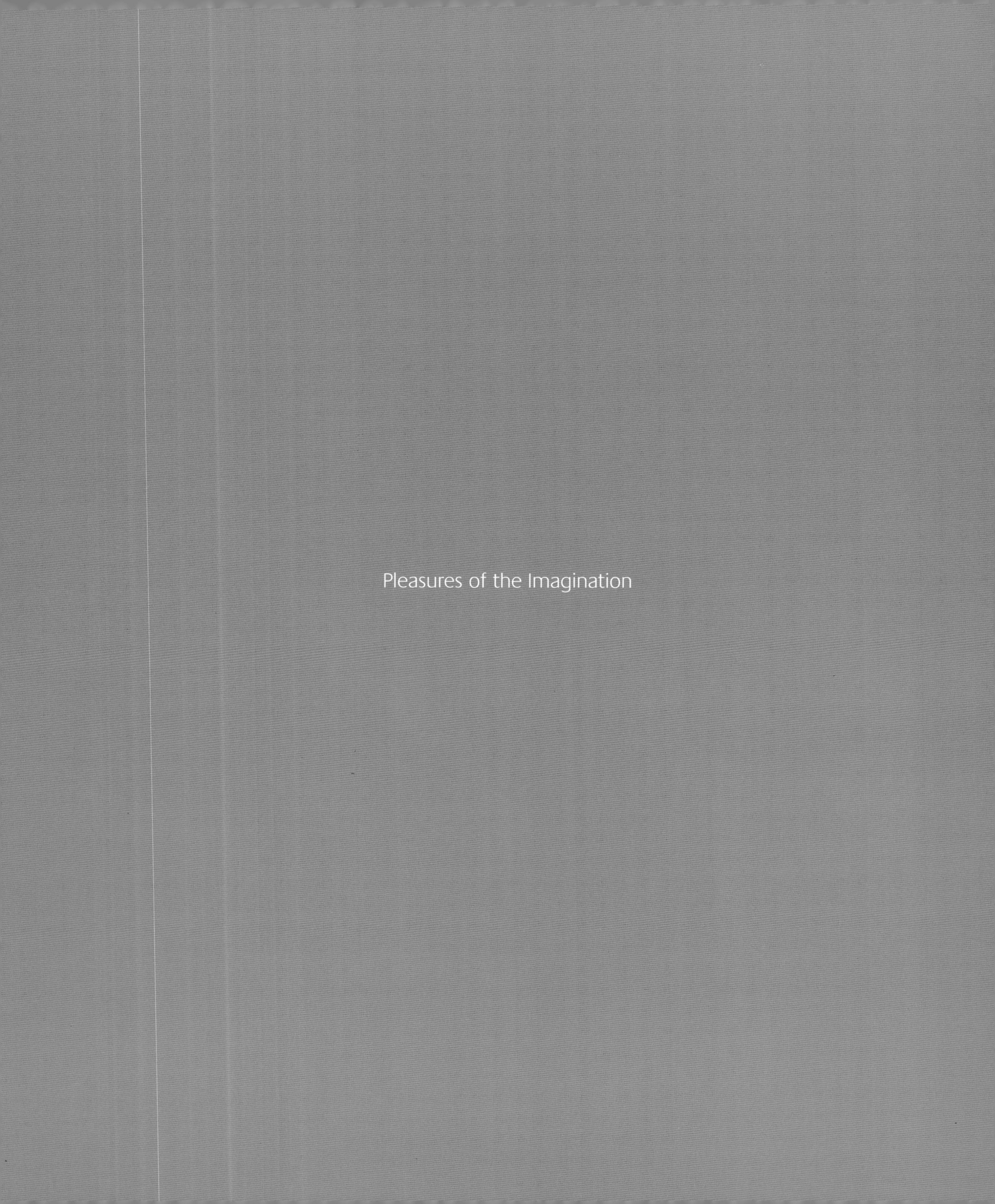

Pleasures of the Imagination

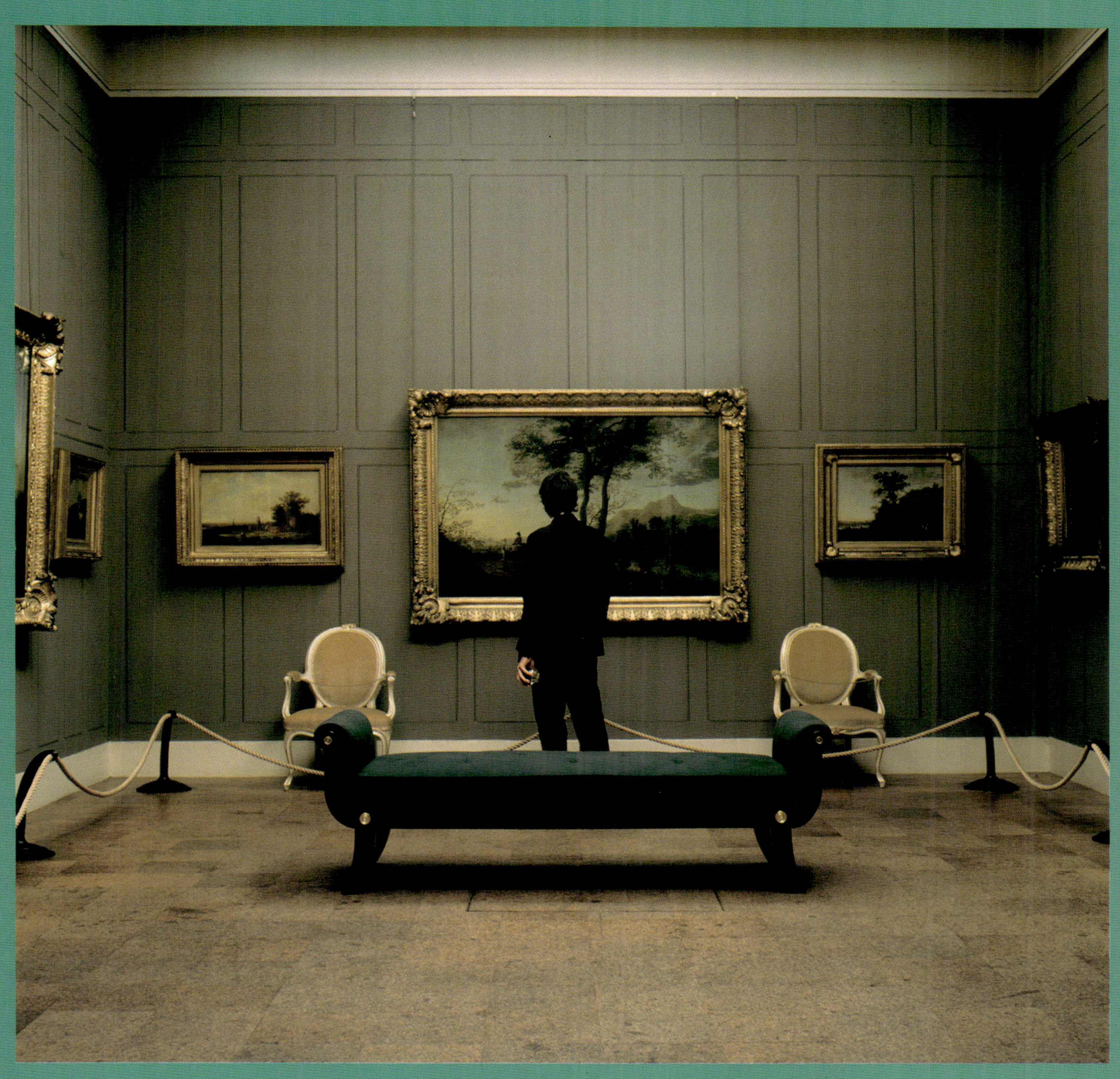

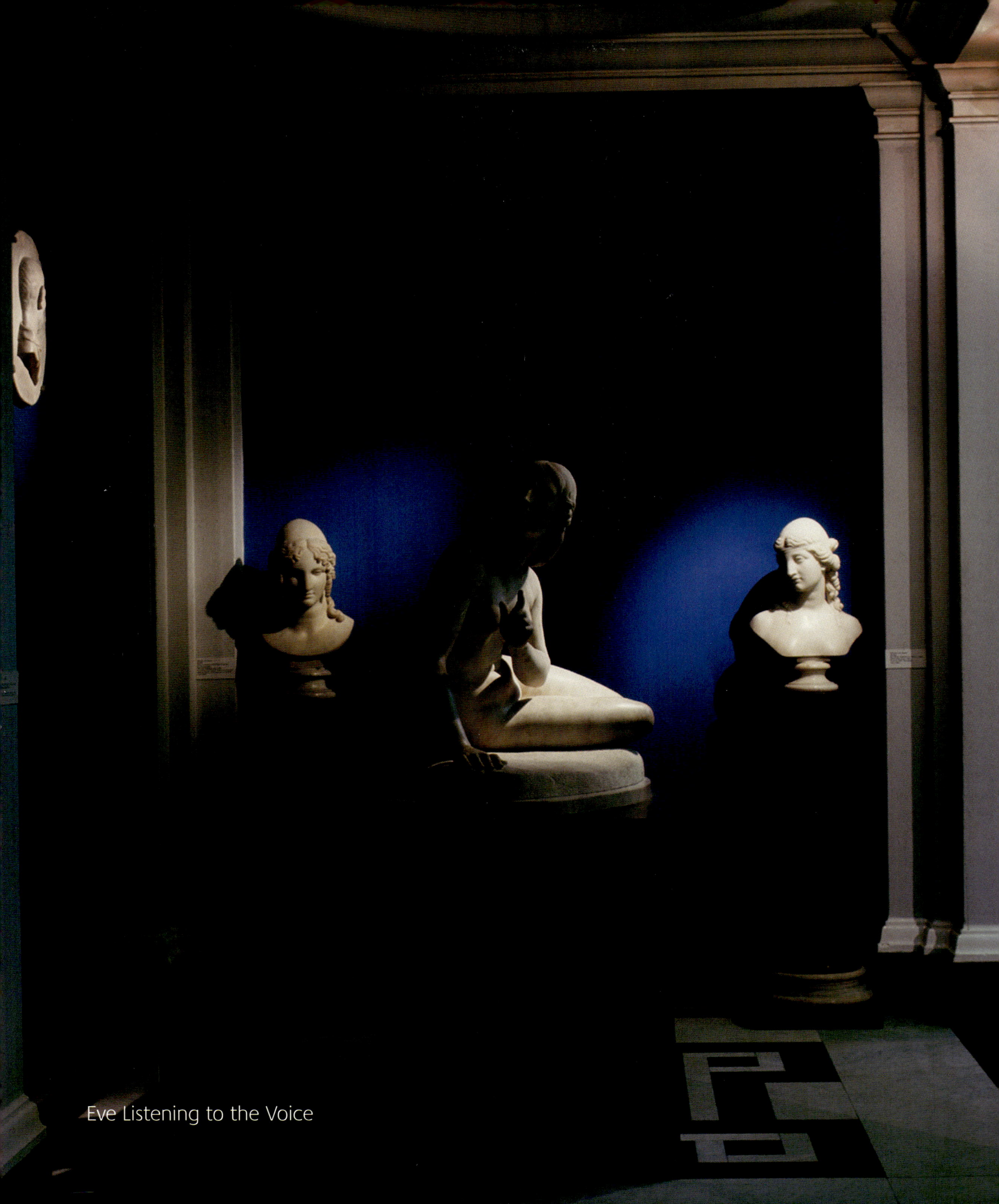

Eve Listening to the Voice

II

Academies

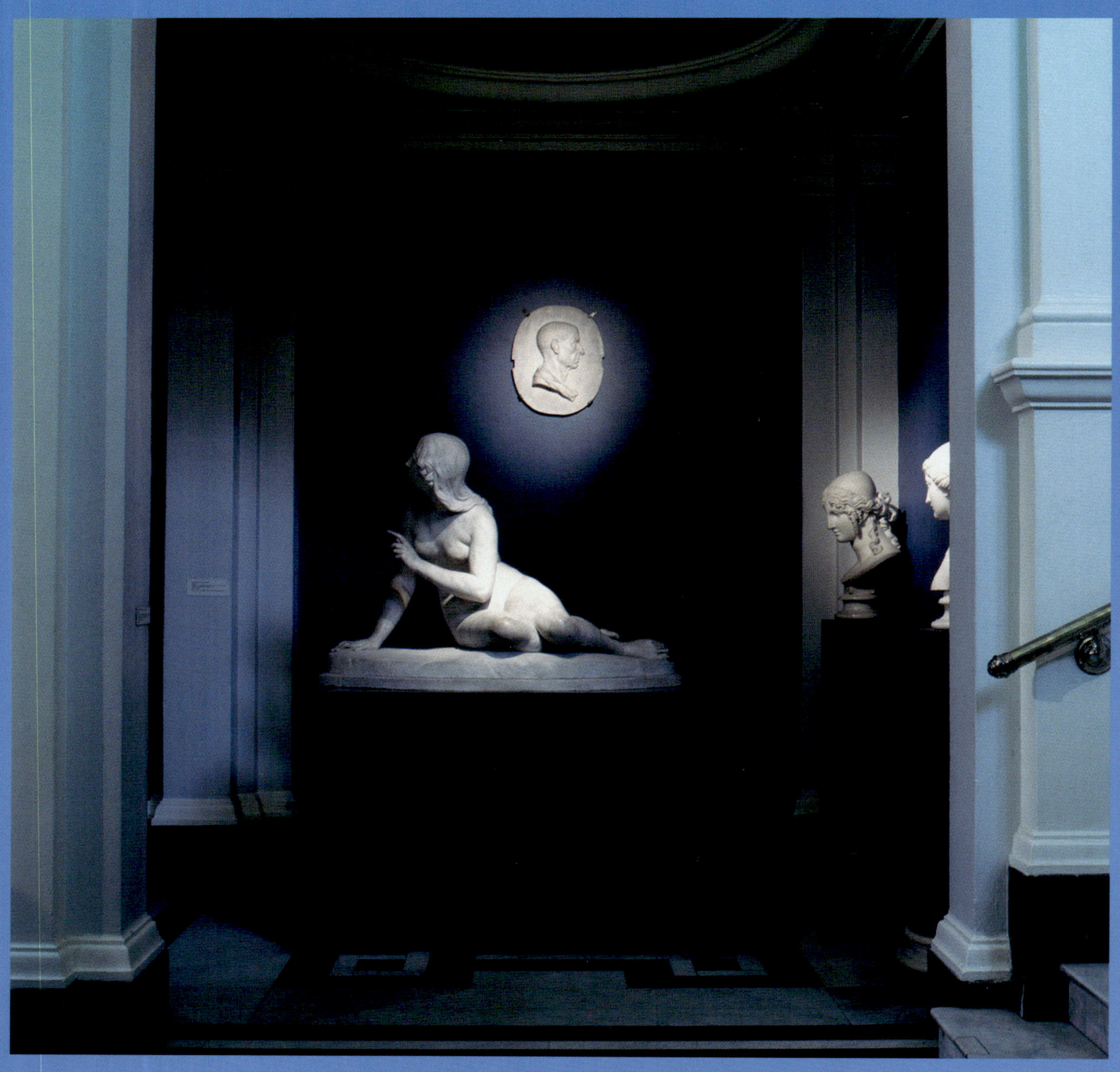

The Abduction of Helen

Movement of the Soul

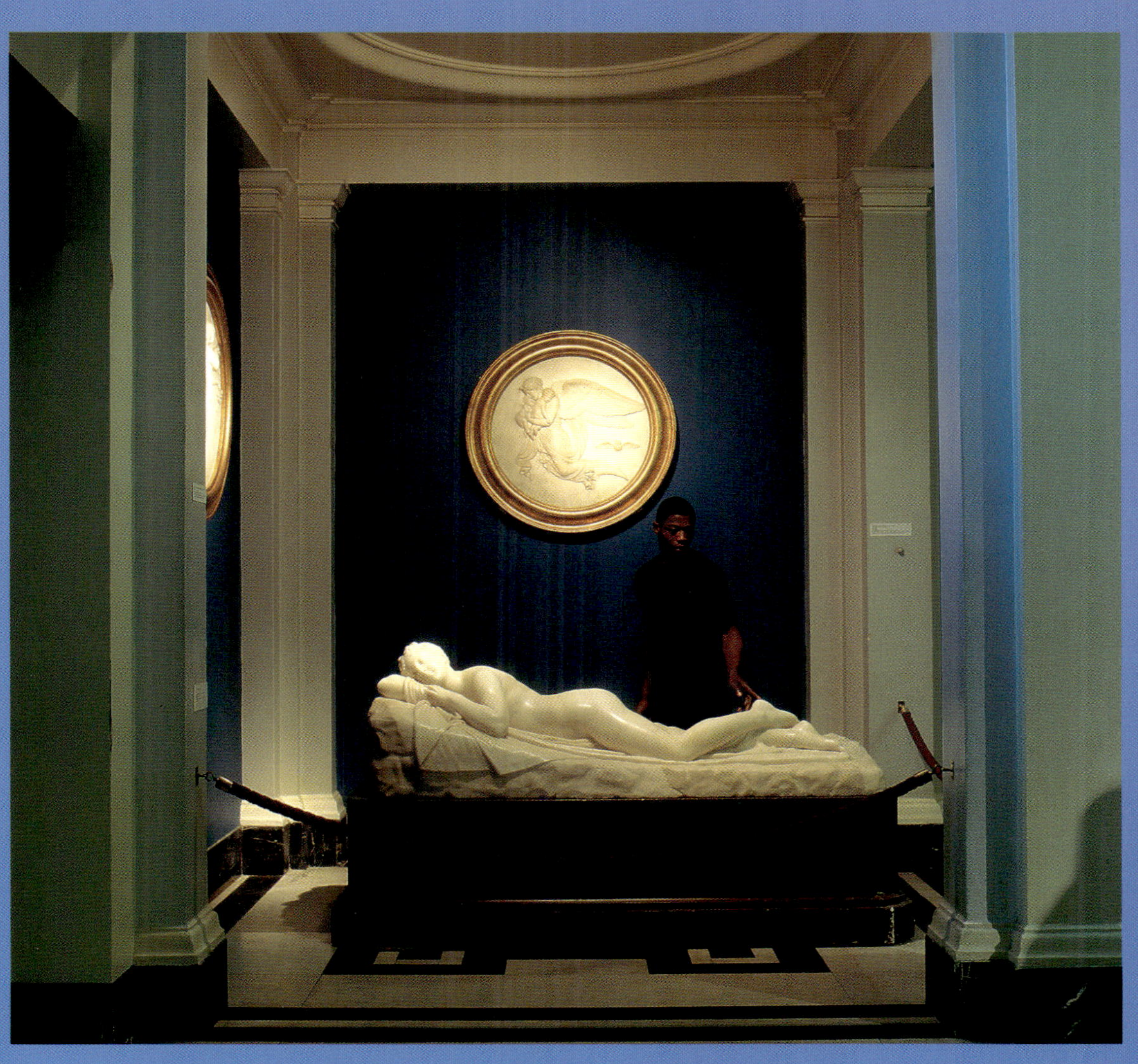

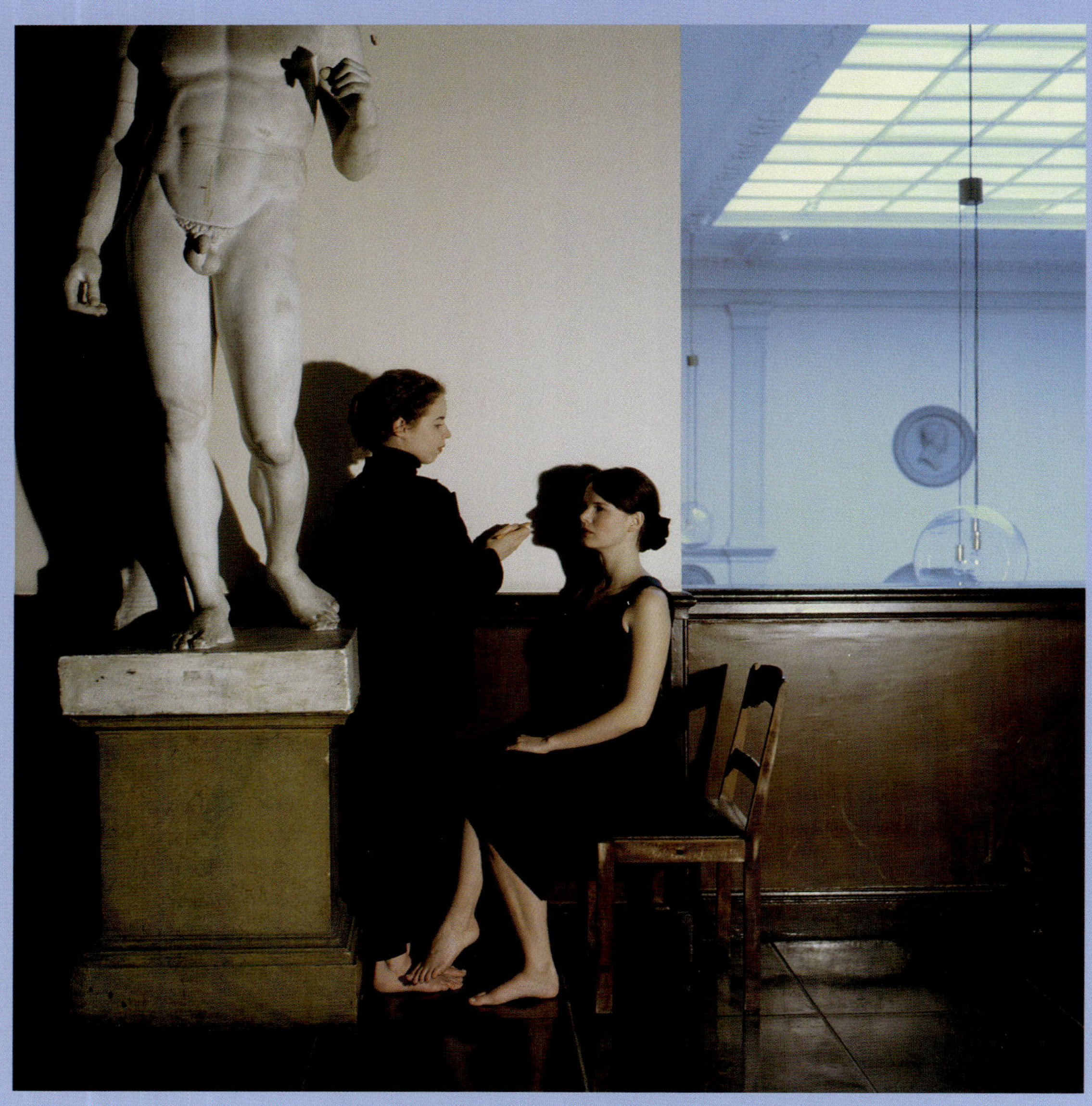

The Pencil of Nature

A Model of Vision

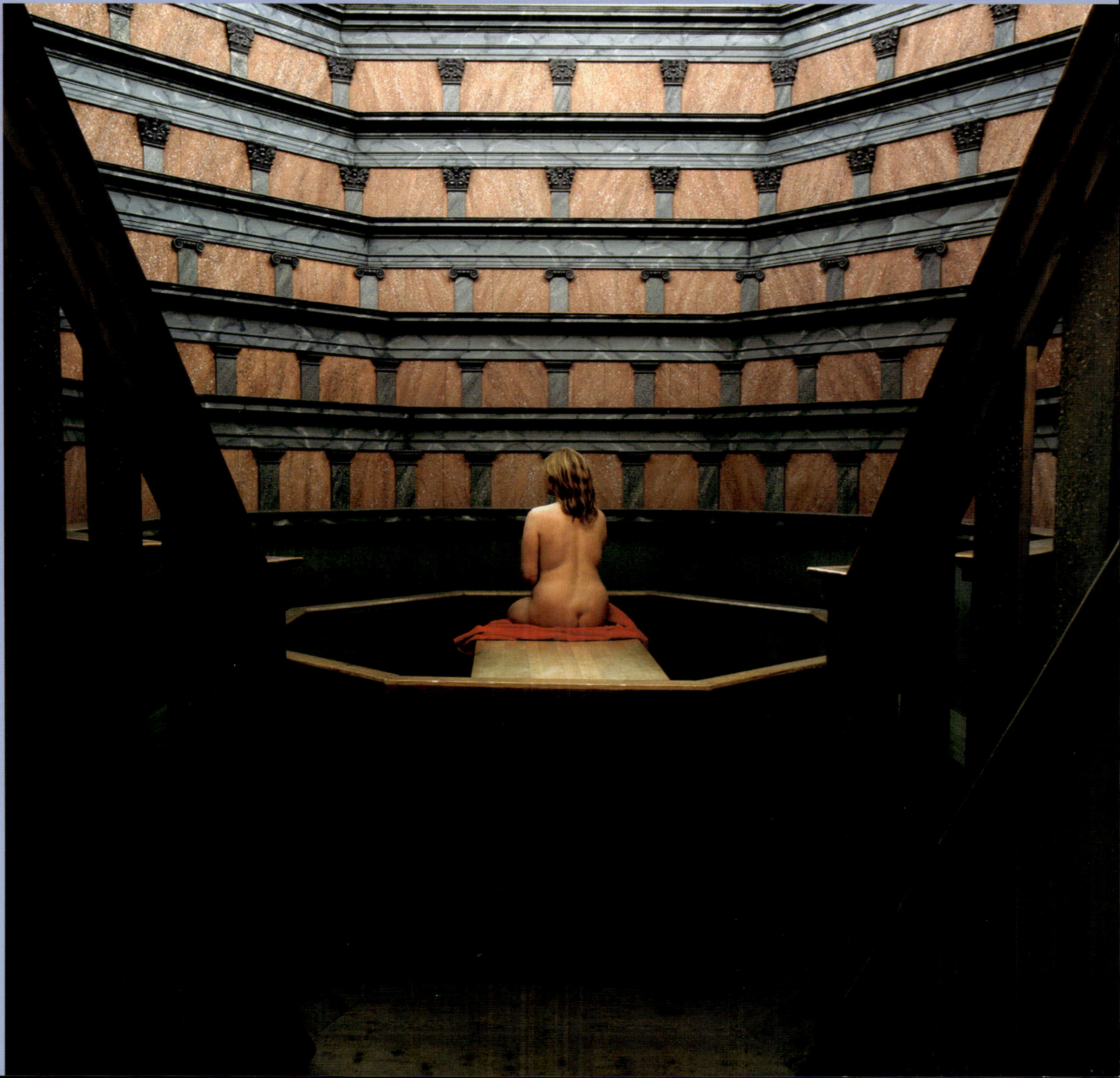

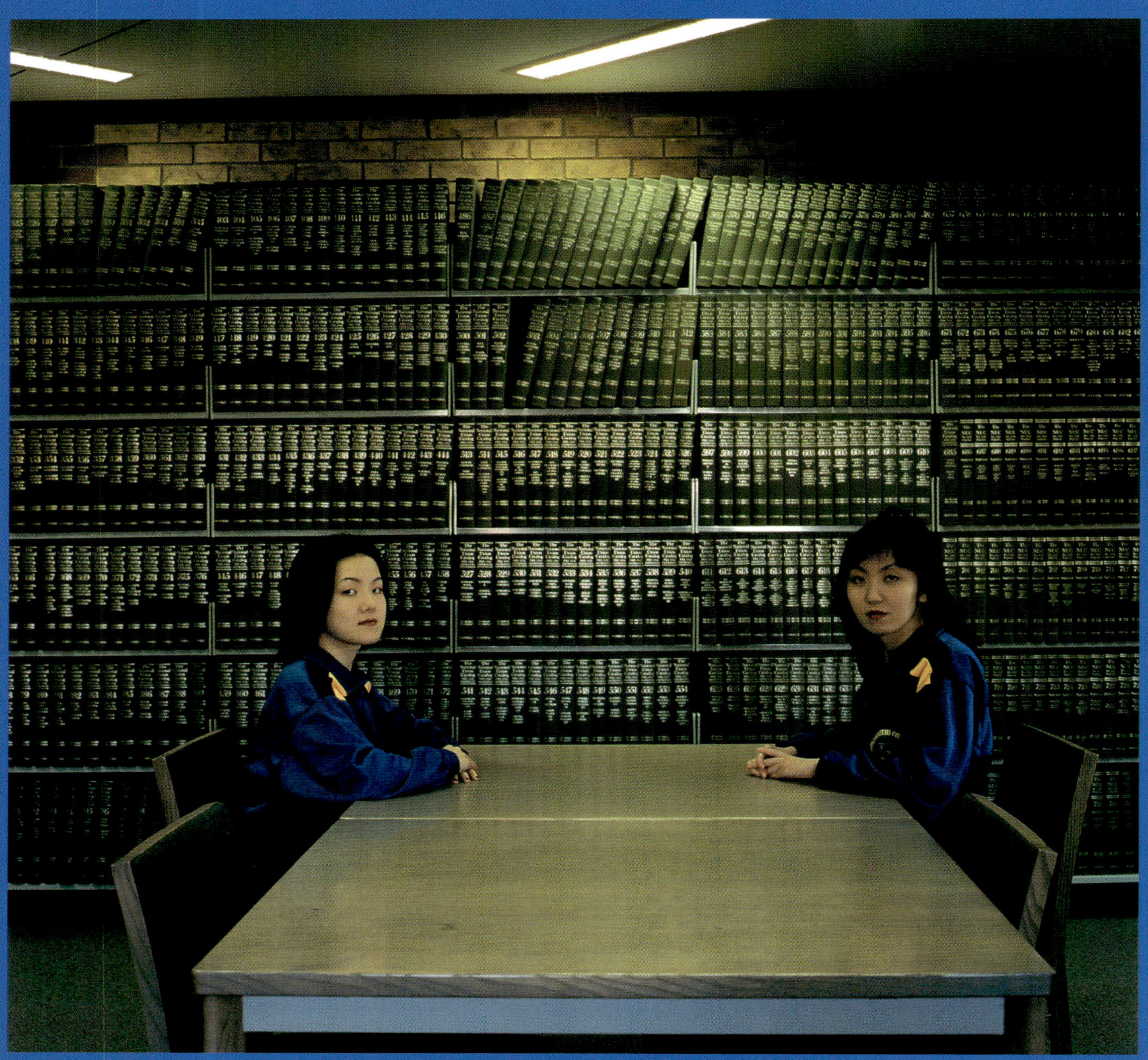

Painters of Modern Life

Hanako's Colourful World

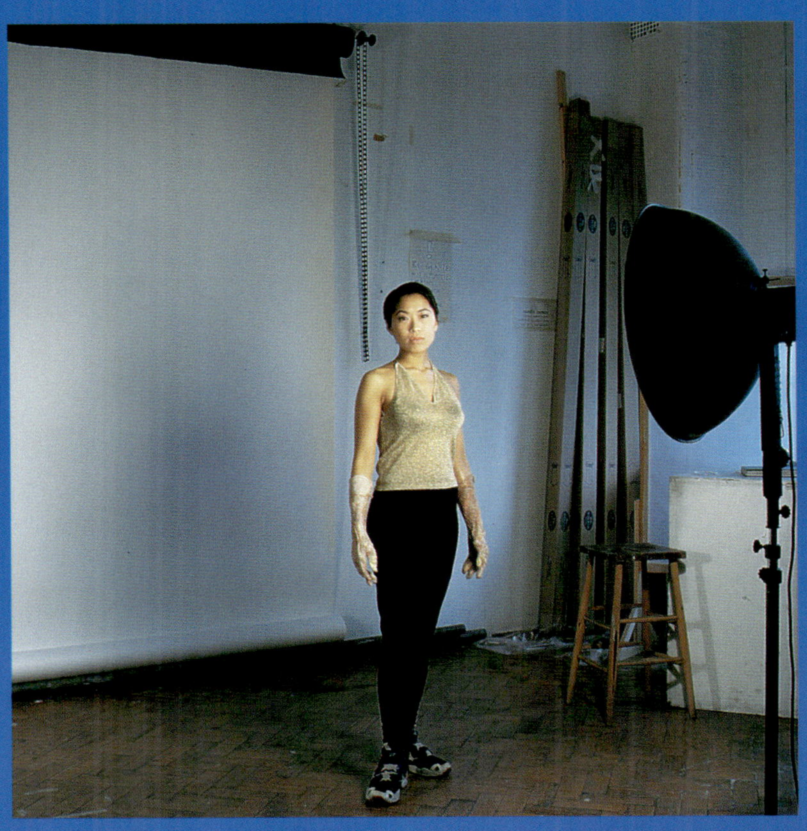

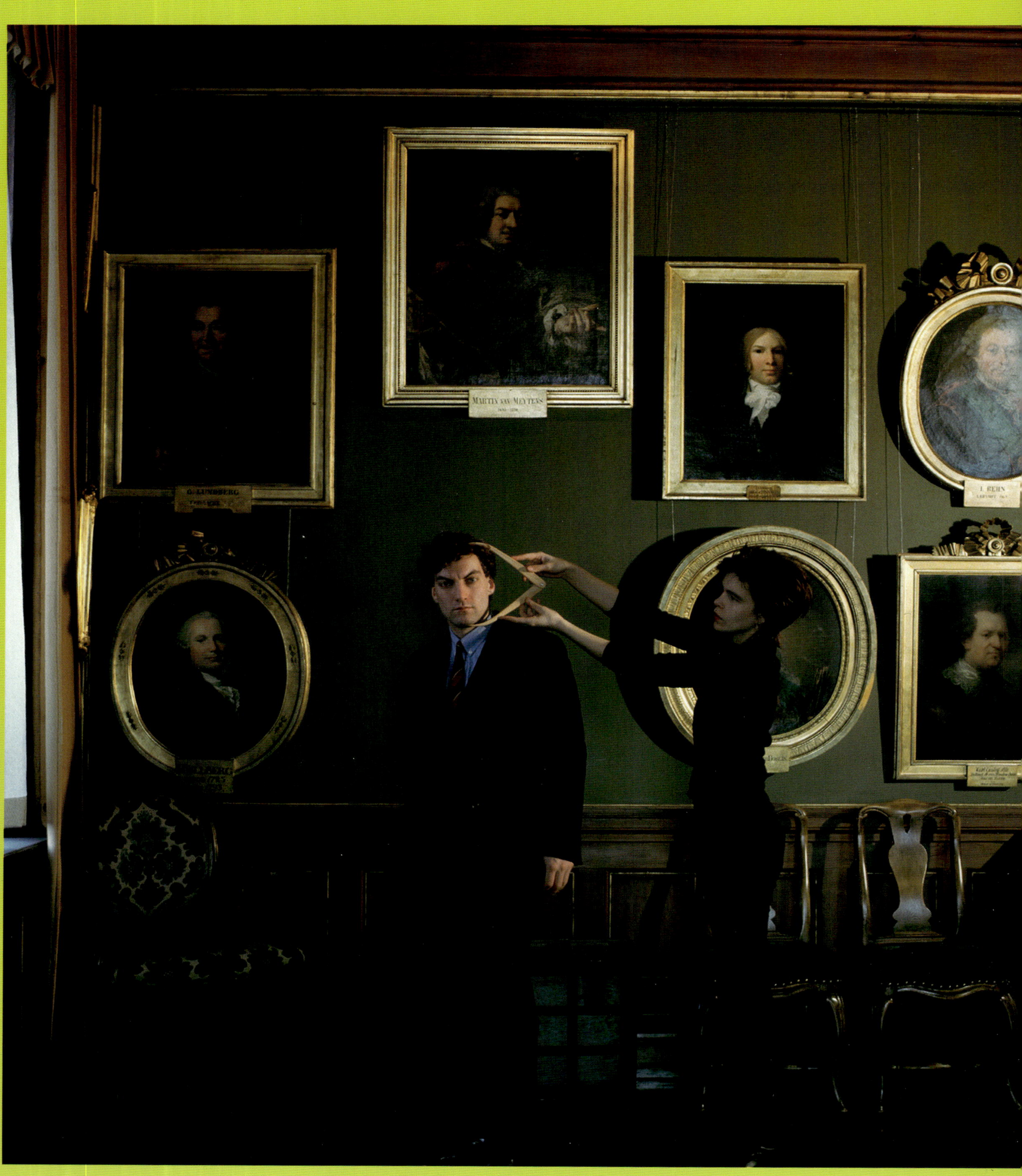
MARTIN VAN MEYTENS
I. BEHN

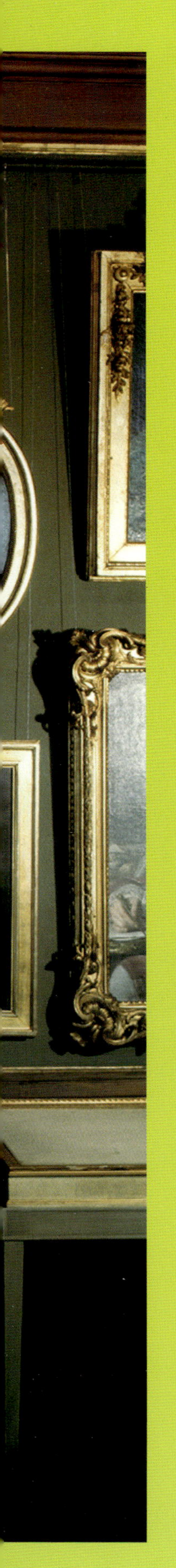

Hårleman's Anatomy

Lessons
(video stills)

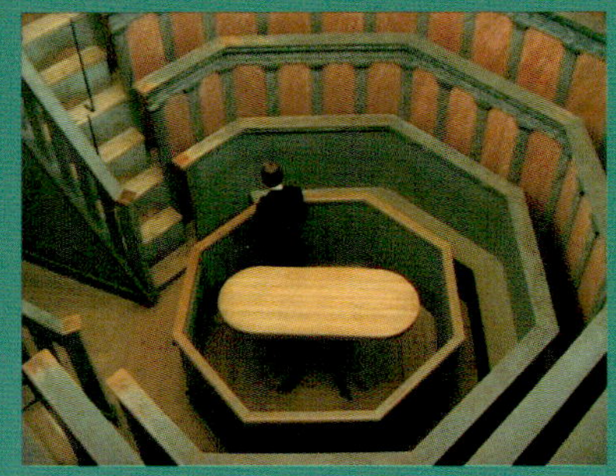

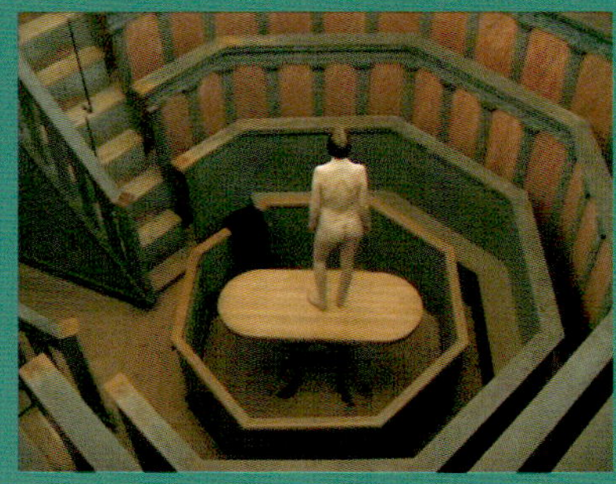

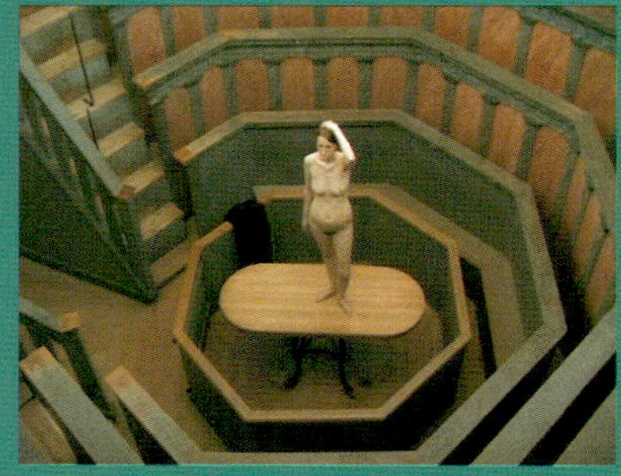

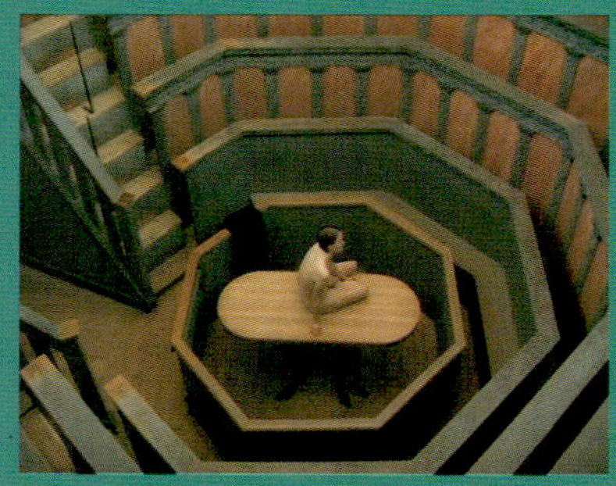

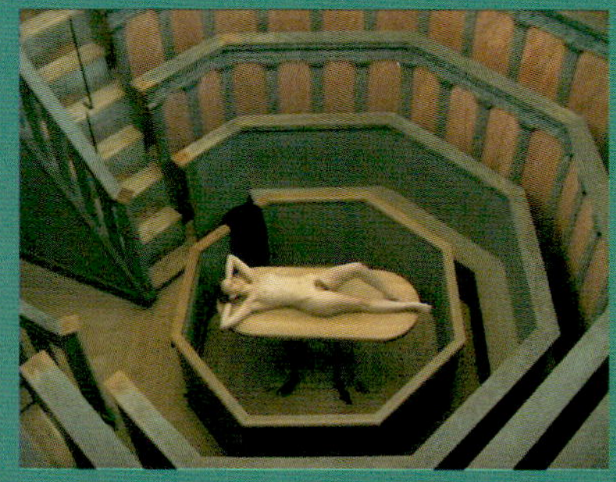

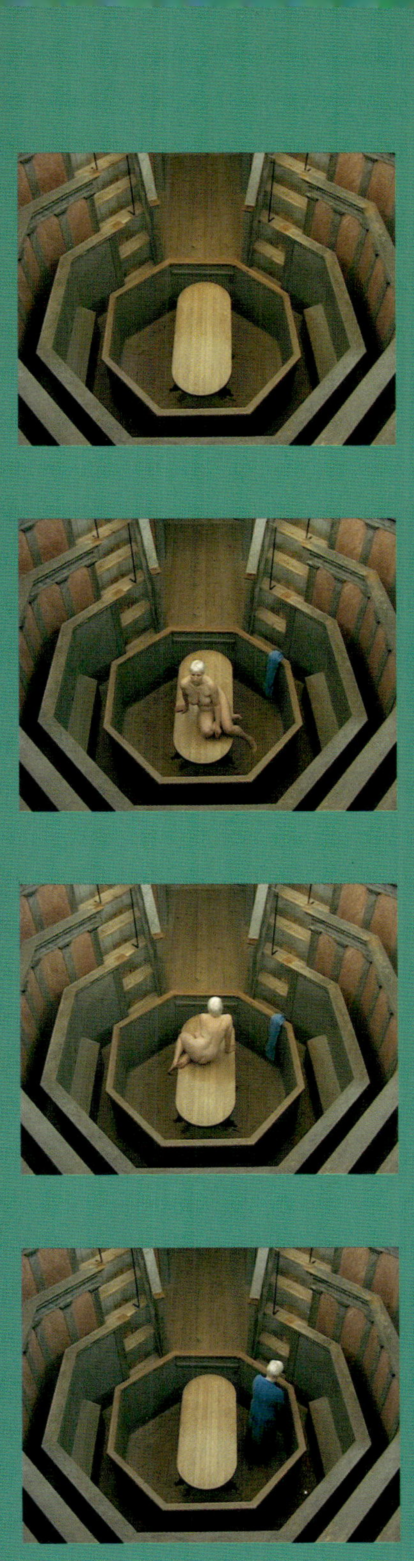

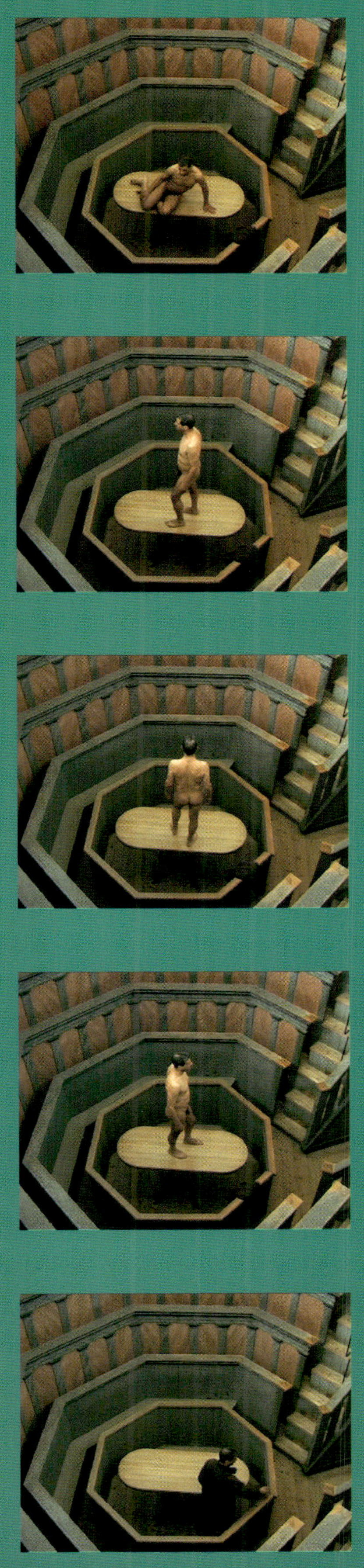

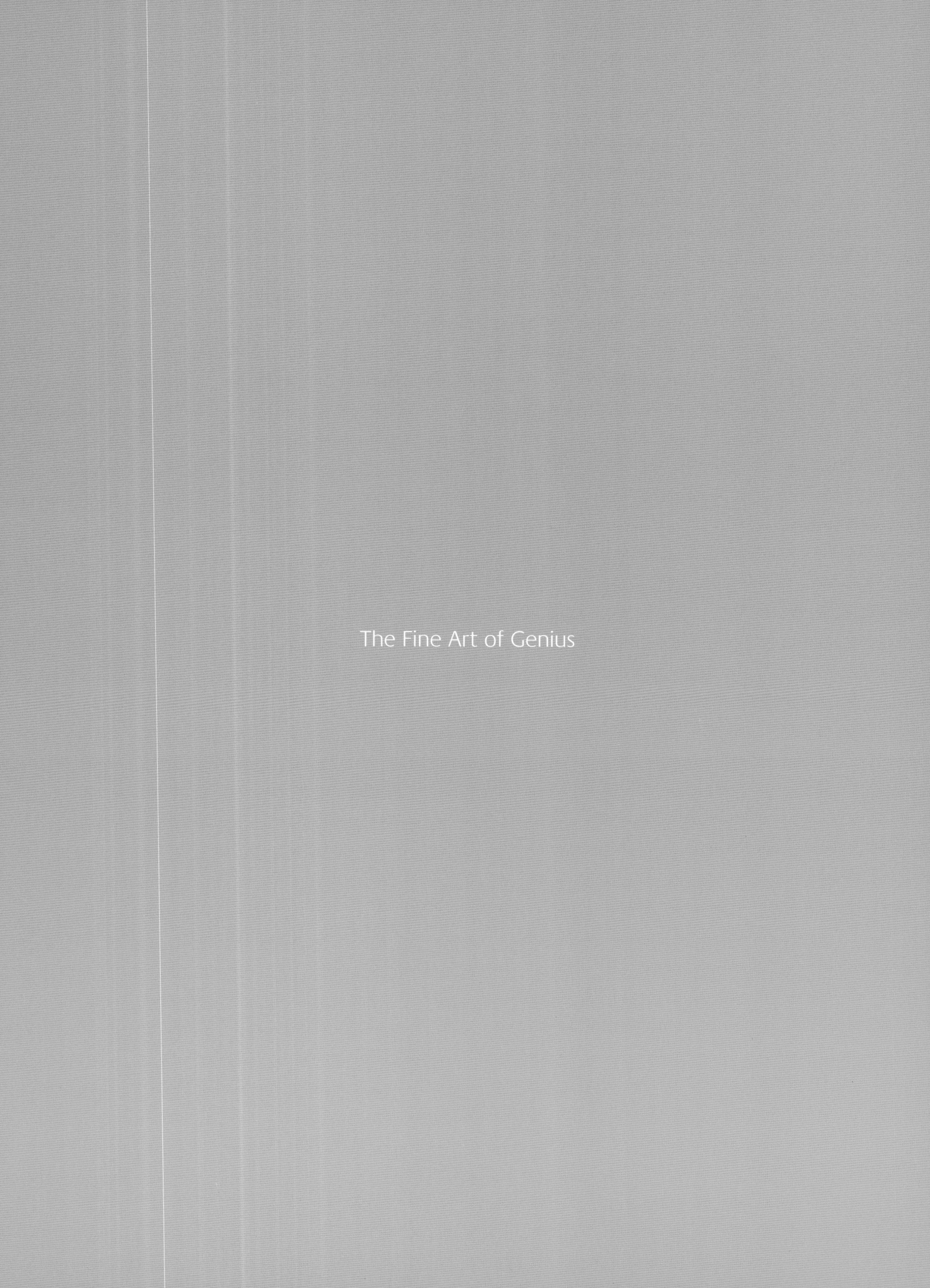
The Fine Art of Genius

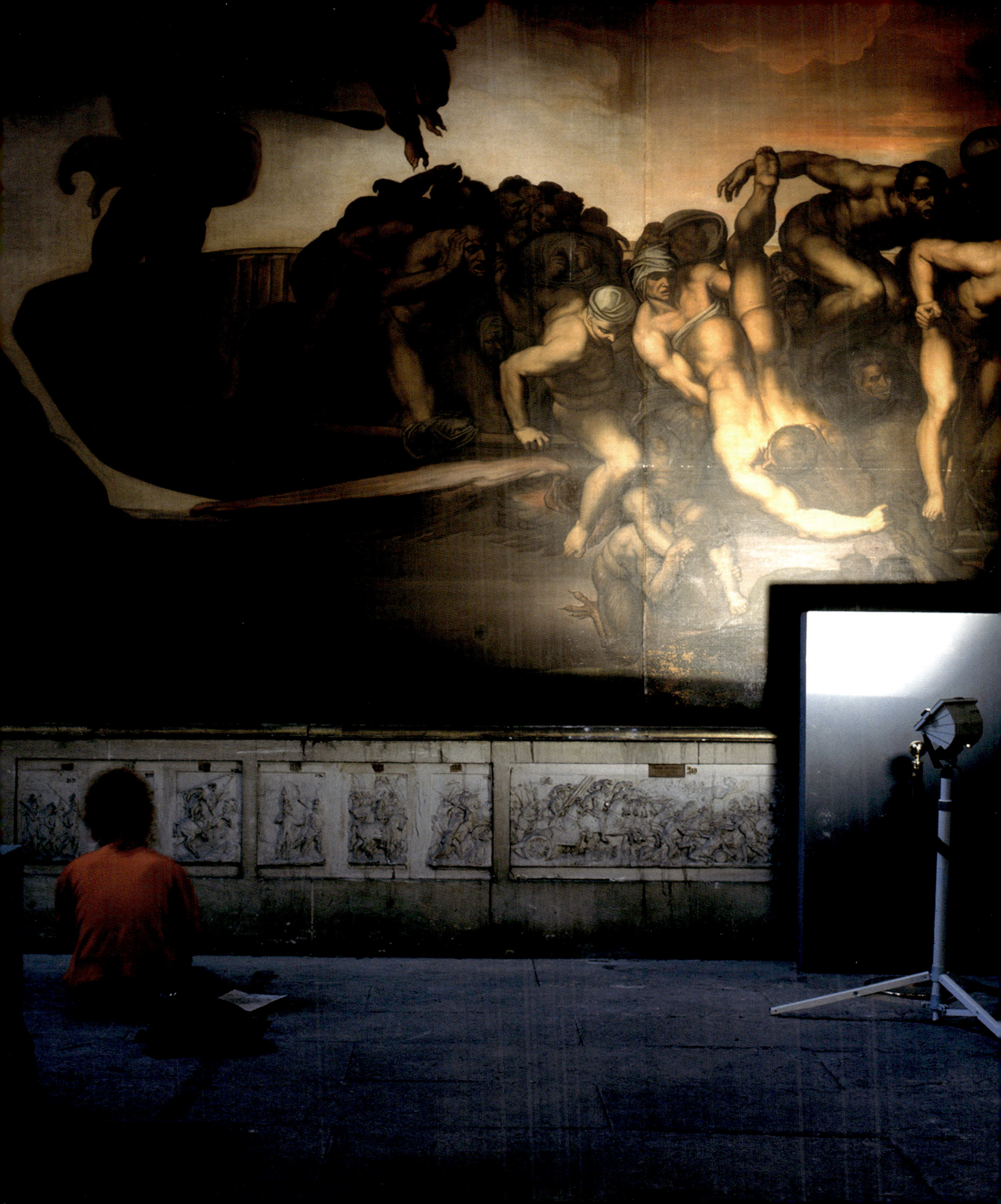

Natural Histories

Rebecca Comay

The following e-mail exchange took place over several days in January 2002, between Karen Knorr in London and Rebecca Comay in Toronto.

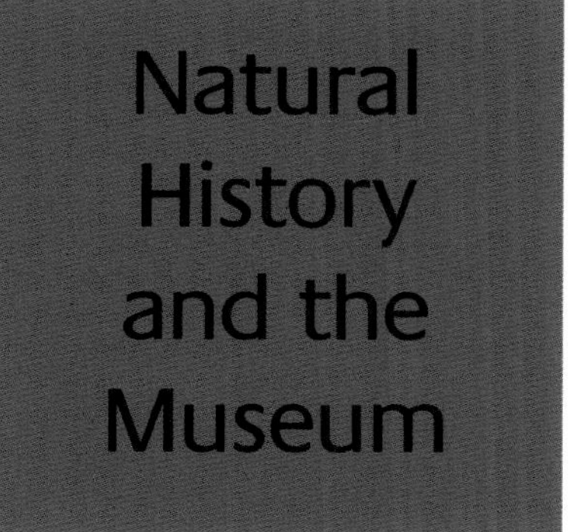

Natural History and the Museum

Rebecca Comay: *Between the sixteenth and the eighteenth centuries, the European cabinet of curiosity–successor to the medieval Church treasury, precursor to the modern museum–embraced in its collection both artificialia and naturalia. Without necessarily seeing the need to distinguish or classify these two broad categories of objects (although the day would soon enough arrive), it would array before the spectator the most marvellous specimens of both human and natural provenance– narwhale tusks and miniatures, gems and tapestries, exotic plant specimens and various ethnographic booty from voyages of discovery in the new world. The unity of the cabinet was underpinned by a theological continuity between the order of nature and the order of history–a continuity which would equally suture the gap between divine and artistic production (the latter incorporated within the former according to a doctrine of mimesis whereby man, created in God's image, would also produce images resembling the products of his maker: human creativity was thus a special case of divine creation.*

In the late eighteenth century–curiously, at the very moment when scientific ideas were forcing a revision of nature as static artefact and pushing towards an idea of nature as 'historical' in a robust sense (subject to mutation and decay, if not yet conceived in evolutionary terms)–the institutional separation between natural and historical artefacts begins to set in. The museum in its modern form begins to take shape, with a clear demarcation between the art museum and the natural history museum. A classic instance is Gottfried Semper's twin museums in Vienna, the Kunsthistorische Museum and the Naturgeschichtliche Museum, erected side by side on the Ringstrasse under Franz Josef in 1890, at the height of imperial power, architectural mirrors of each other (the symmetry both underscored and weakened by the awkward approach to 'anthropological' and archaeological specimens; famously, the Venus of Willendorf is housed among the fossils and stuffed birds).

I'd like us to start thinking about what's at stake in this institutional separation of spheres–a separation which has clear ideological implications, not simply in terms of our own relationship, as humans, to the natural world, but, as the last example suggests, the relationship of modern European humans, to non-European humanity? Curiously, the very need to distinguish something like nature and something like history at a museological level arises at the very moment when 'nature' in fact is beginning to reveal a certain temporality or historicity, while ideologies of history are starting to naturalise the latter on quasi-organic lines.

How are we to start thinking about the animals roaming about in your museums? Unabashedly stuffed, they seem to evoke the taxidermic specimens of the natural history diorama, while, wandering around freely within the museum, they escape the picture frame and displace the exhibition space that nonetheless defines them. What is their status in the space of exhibition and how do they alter this space? In this fantastic space that is opened up, is there a hint of a freedom–even if this freedom is absolutely non-idealised (the animals remain dead, stuffed, bear all the stigmata of their mortified condition)–an anarchic moment within the nonetheless frozen interior of the museum? Do we have a kind of return to the category of the marvellous that informed the cabinet of curiosities before the Enlightenment bifurcation of naturabilia and artificialia?

Karen Knorr: Taxidermy represents animals as idealised representations of the live referent (a bird in flight, a wolverine walking, a monkey climbing). There is something here akin to an idealised portrait of a human which succeeds if it looks lifelike. Taxidermy preserves the skin of an animal which it artfully mounts in a lifelike pose. Eyes are important: when they become dusty with age they no longer look lifelike. So there is a sense of a simulacrum of 'life' using what in fact is a cadaver of an animal. Yet these taxidermised specimens create a suspension of disbelief when photographed and people always ask: "Are they alive?"

I liked the idea of etymologically linking the wolf in the royal palace library in Turin (*The Peripatetic Philosopher*) to the Lyceum (Aristotle's school). Lycaon was in classical mythology a king transformed into a wolf to test the divinity of Zeus. Lyceum is the place of the wolves and the Apollo of Belvedere, the idealised body so cherished by Winkelmann. In *Lyceum*–the installation I exhibited with my video works *Being for Another* and *Movement of the Soul*–I used three wolf specimens from the collection of the Muséum de l'Histoire Naturelle in Paris. They are mounted on a base with their latin taxonomic titles of the nineteenth century. On the wall is a text from Xenophon's *Memorabilia* which refers to a conversation between Socrates and Cleiton, a sculptor, about how to render lifelike representations and the role of imitation. So the animals play with the founding mythology of origins in the academy linking it to the museum through the library which after all was the core of the museum.

Yes, there is an anarchic transgressive element with these animals roaming freely–a bit like women being able to roam in such rigidly demarcated institutions such as the Gentlemen's Club and the Royal Academy. I had a fantasy of bringing in a live wolf and letting it do its business among all the idealised canons of sculptor in the Royal Academy of Sweden in Stockholm, and I am now working on a film project at the Wallace Collection, where the camera position mimics the wolves foraging through the collection.

How, specifically, does photography respond to this question of natural history? Its ambiguous temporality seems on the one hand to repeat the frozen condition of taxidermy, on the other hand to evoke the transience associated with history. Does it point to a conjuncture of 'nature' and 'history' which the moderm museum at once represses and invites?

Yes, photography is part of the impulse to freeze temporality which can be found in nature petrified or preserved, whether through taxidermy or aspic. This frozen icelike or even glasslike objectness of the medium attracts and repels me simultaneously. I think it lead me to the use of glass in my most recent work.

Nature is cultural in that it can only be understood by humans through the distortions of science and its taxonomies. Arcadia does not exist except in death (Poussin) and representation. So photography, which arose out of an impulse to preserve or freeze history, to stop time, decay and death, is at the same time a putting to death of the thing itself; yet its distribution through books and catalogues gives the nature or history a certain prolonged life. A living death. Photography evokes history in its double temporality: "it was" and yet when we look at a photograph it is. So the past is in the present just as in a sci-fi sense, maybe, the present is also in the past.

The crude animation of the videos at Quai d'Orsai–the apes remain stuffed, their jerky movements manifestly a product of manipulation–points to the impossibility of spiritualising the dead animals by bringing them to life; the moving image here thus underscores, in its very movement, the permanent reification of nature (and

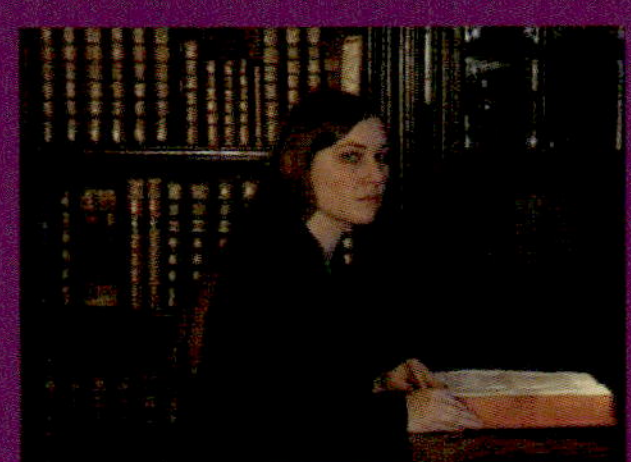
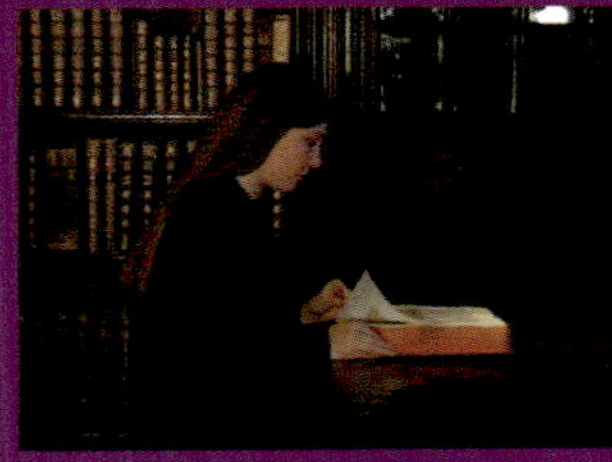
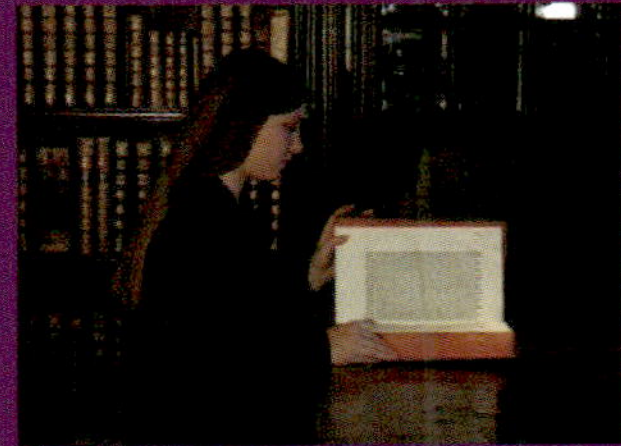
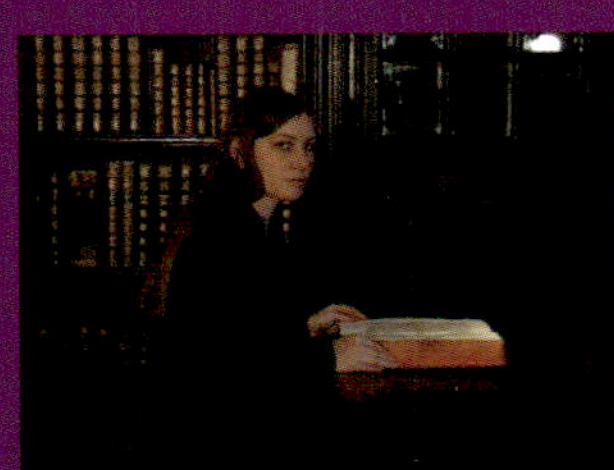
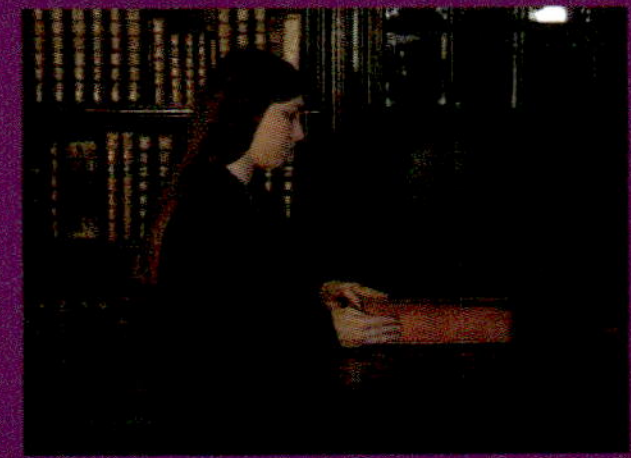

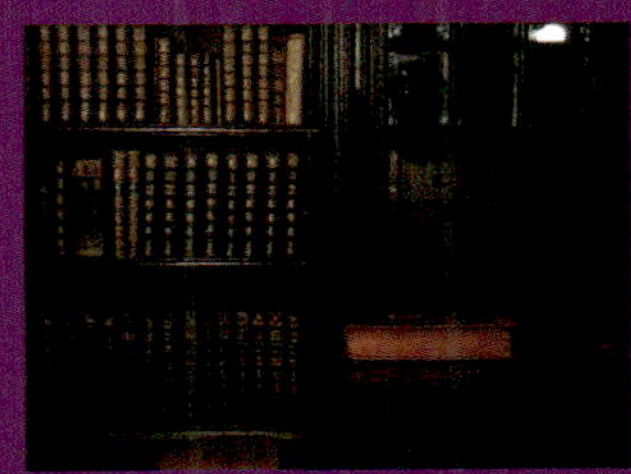

Portrait of an Artist
(video stills)

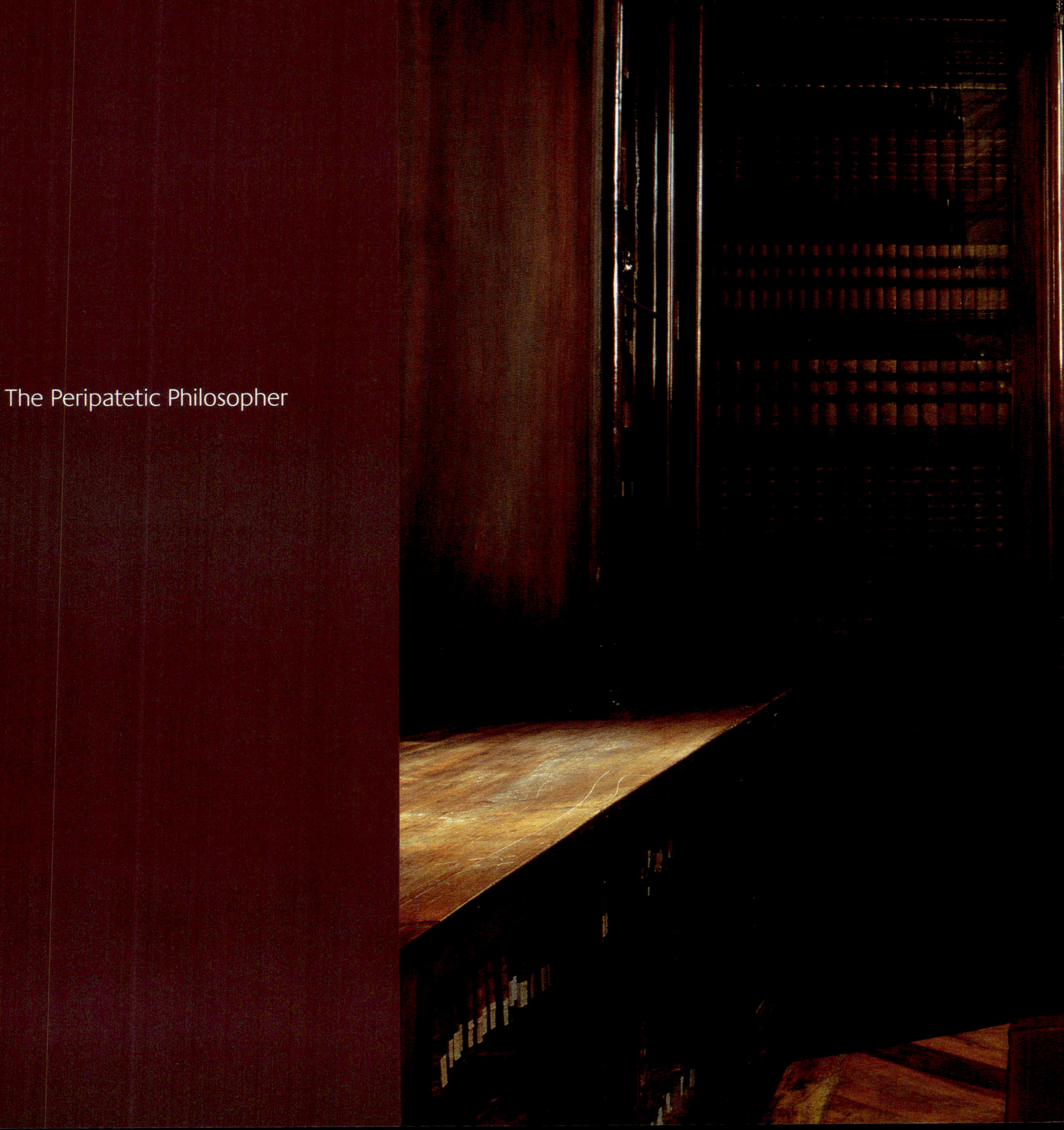

The Peripatetic Philosopher

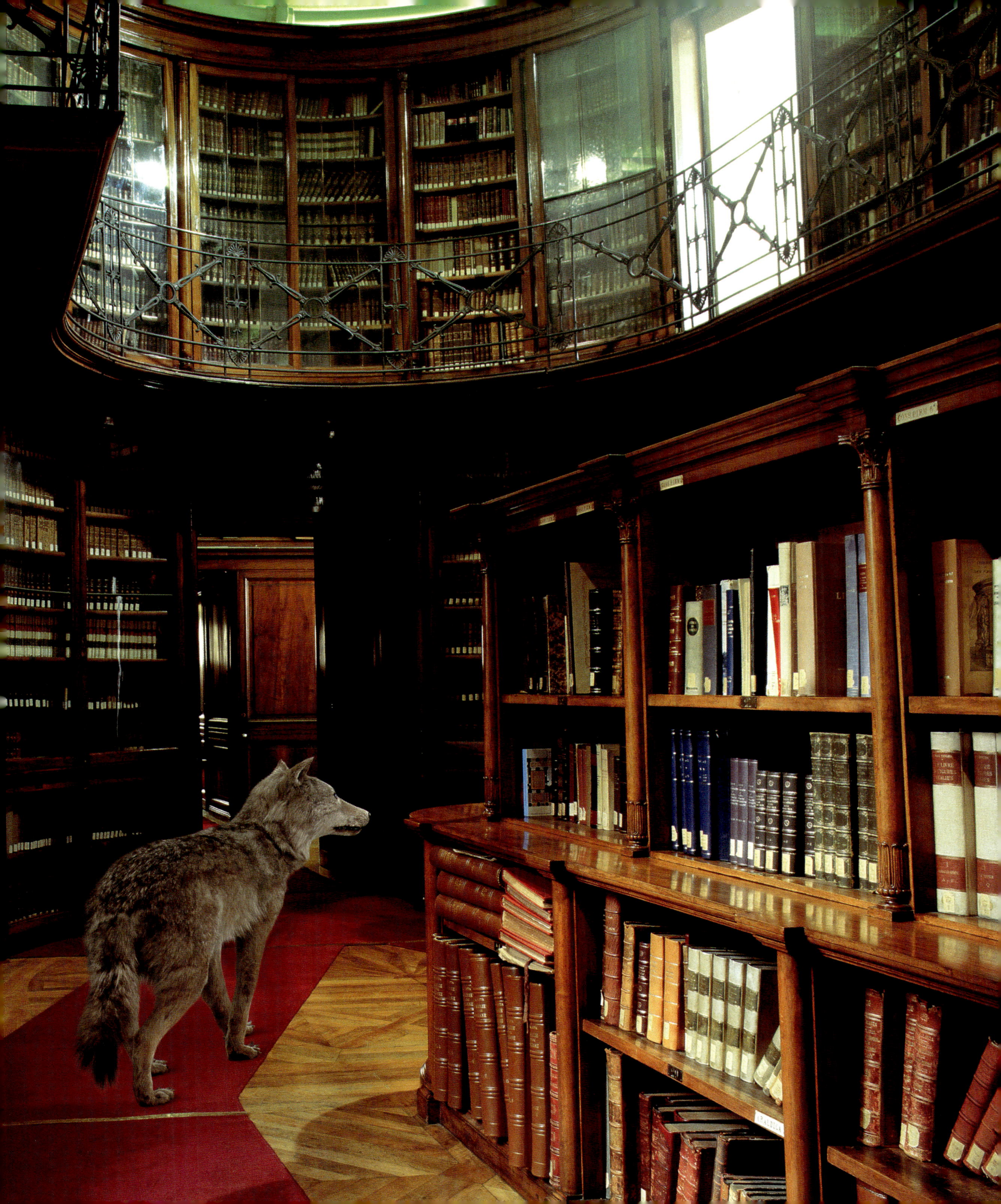

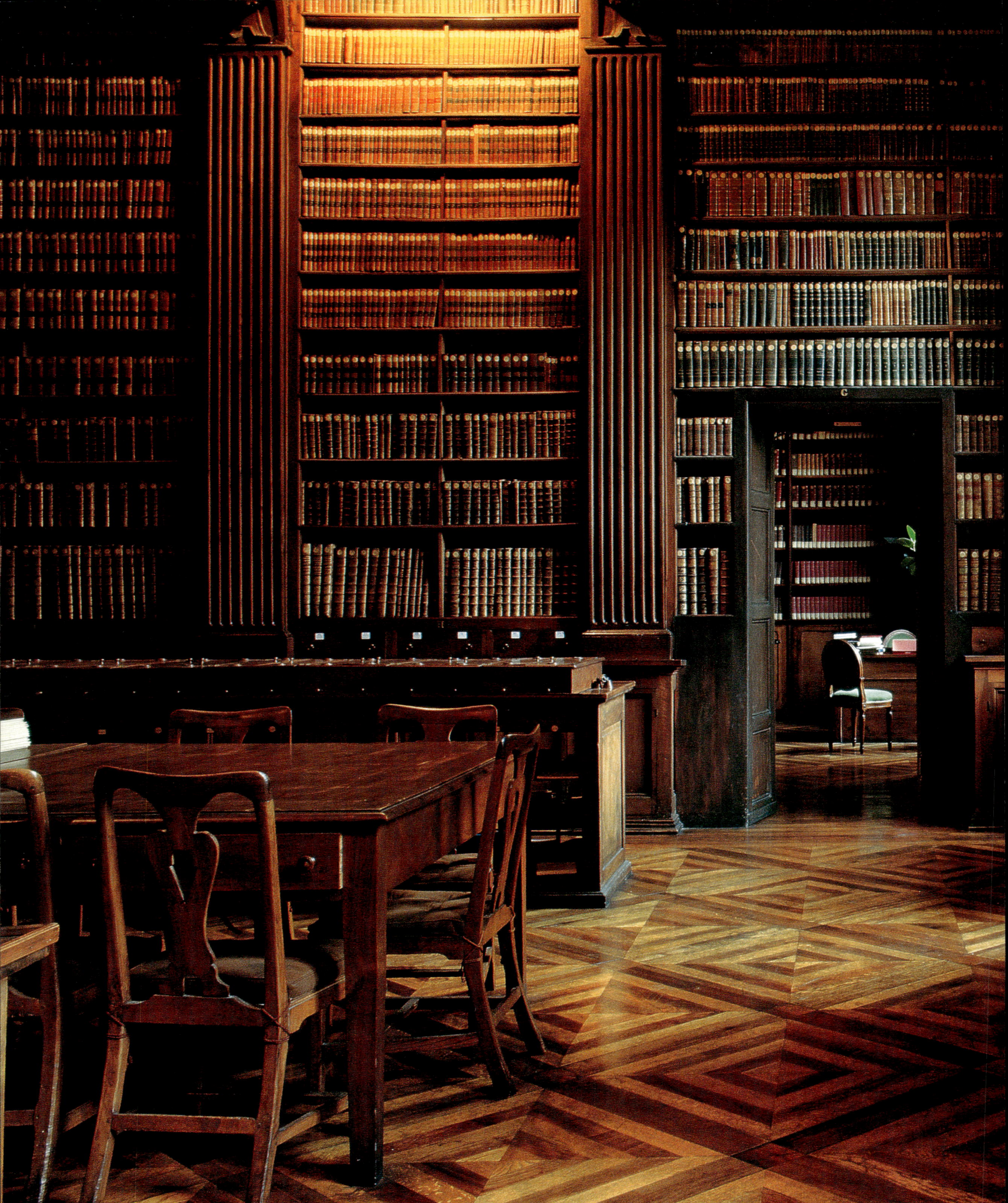

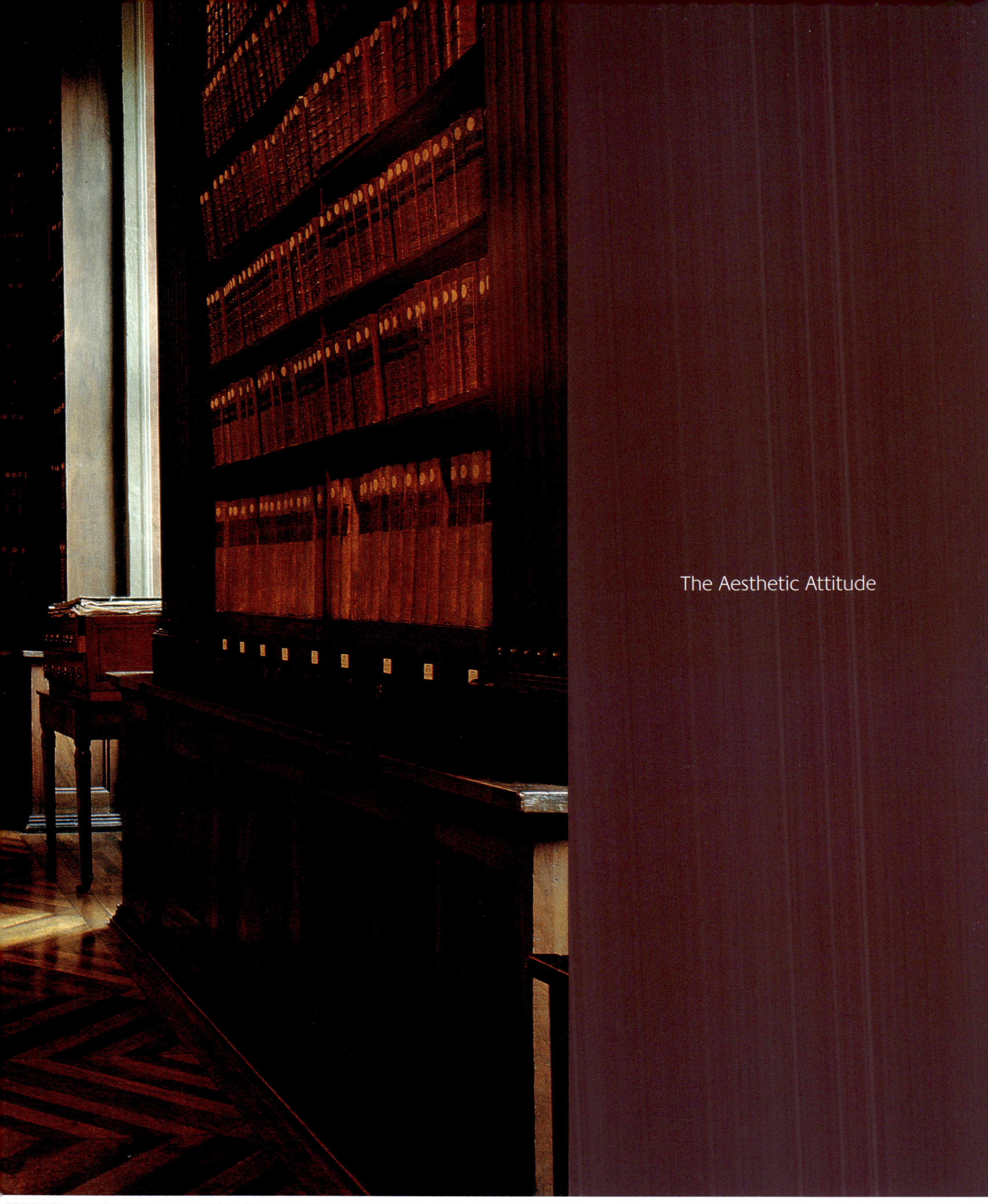

The Aesthetic Attitude

III

Capital

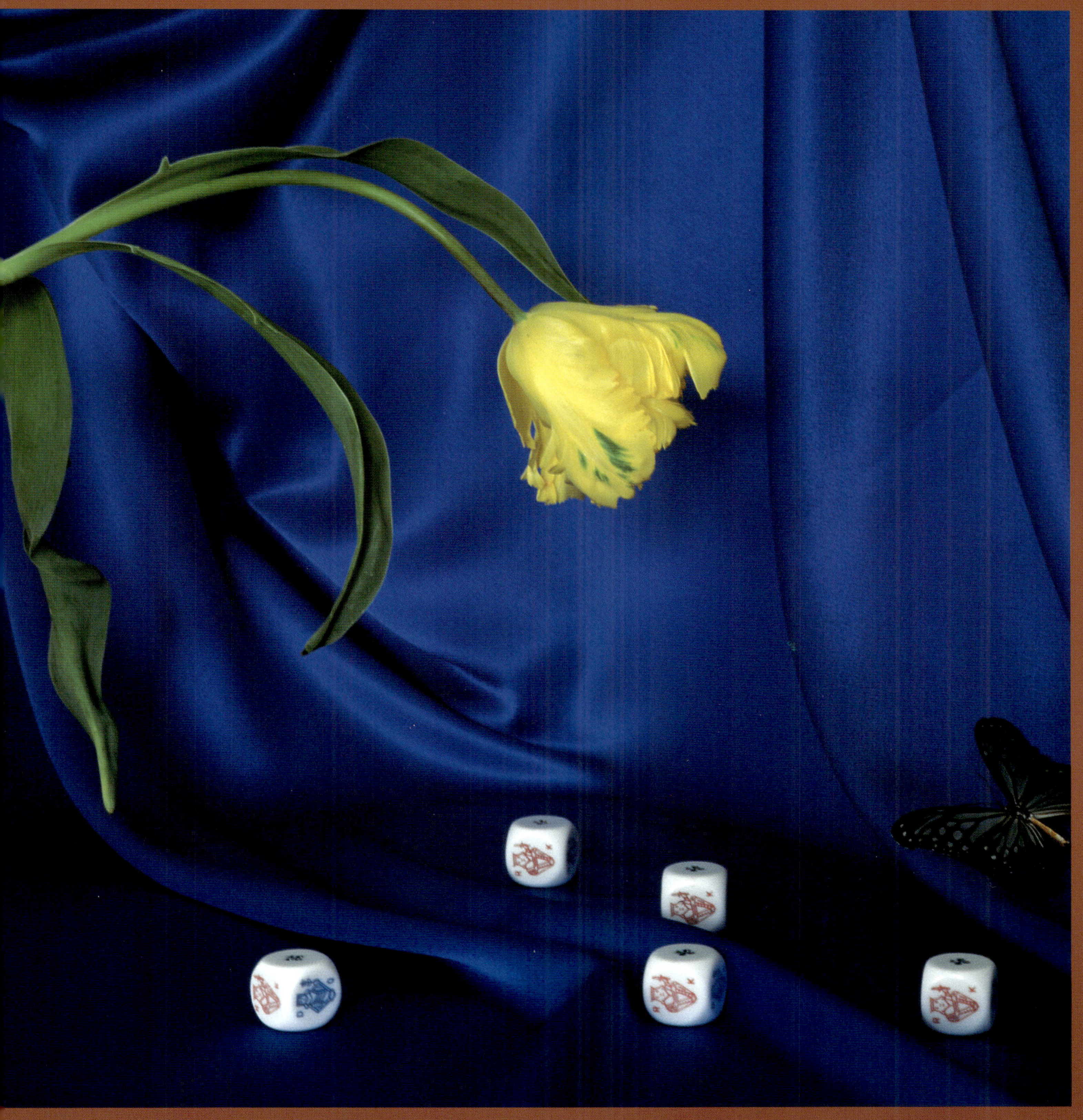

The Art of the Deal

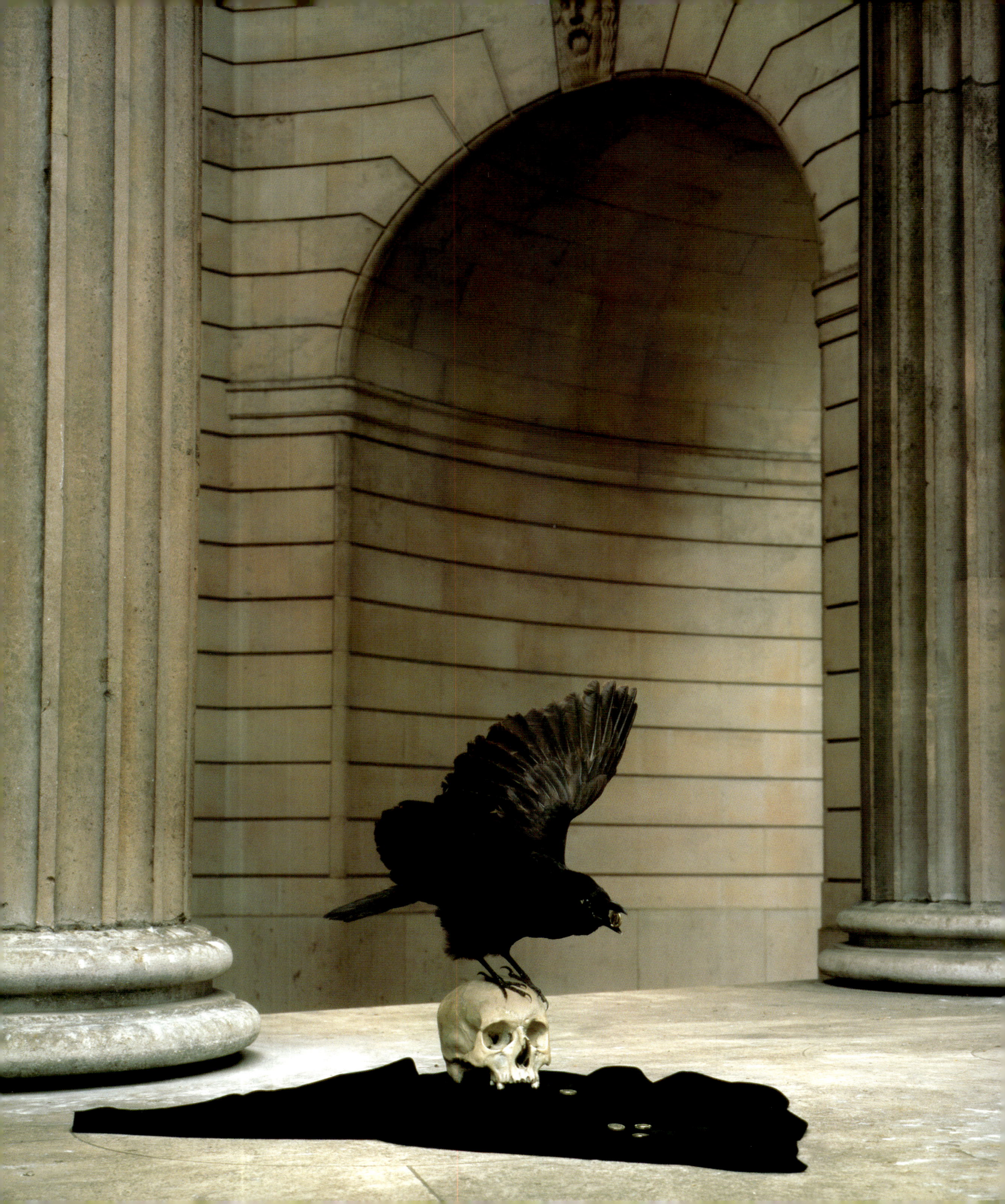

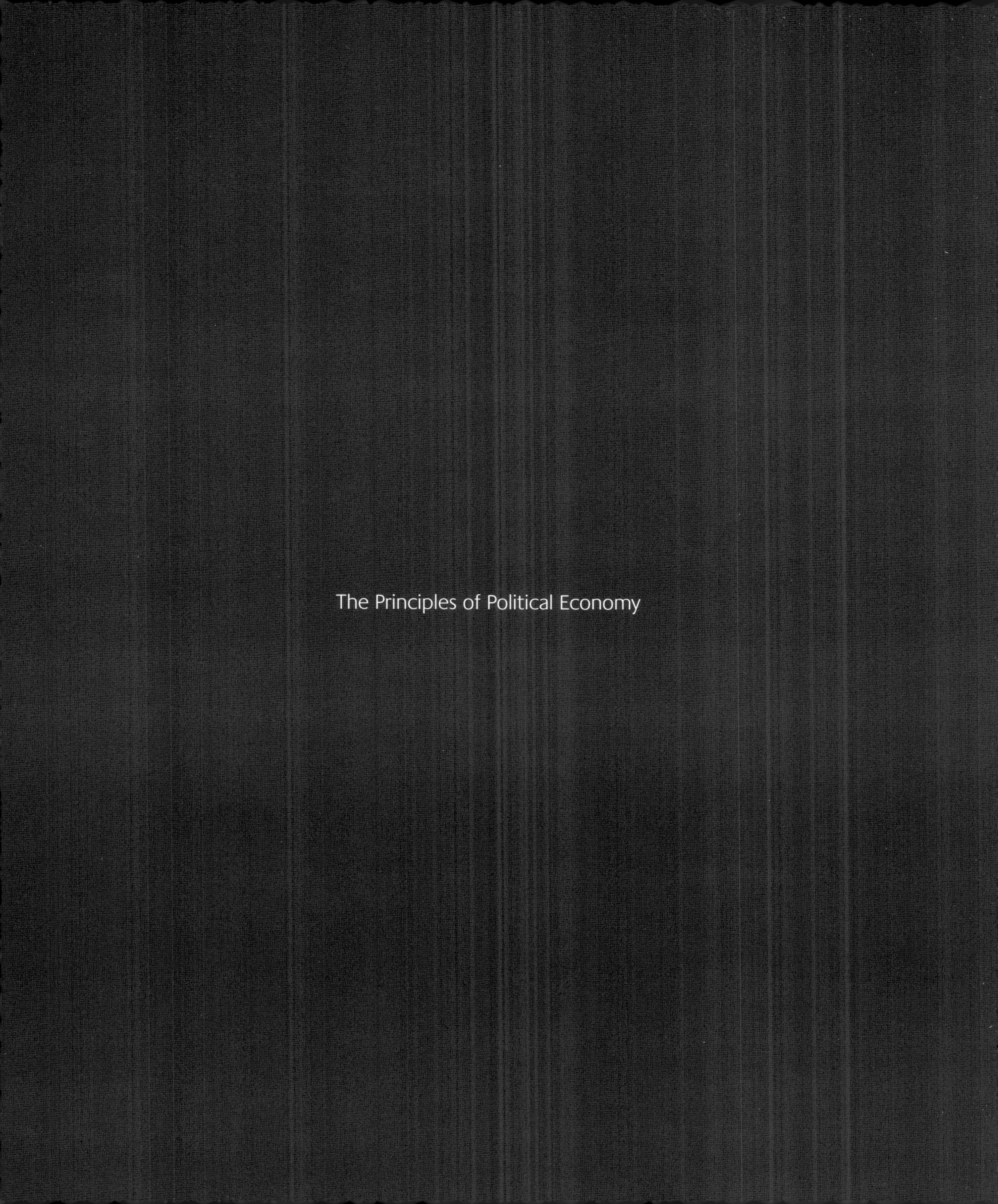
The Principles of Political Economy

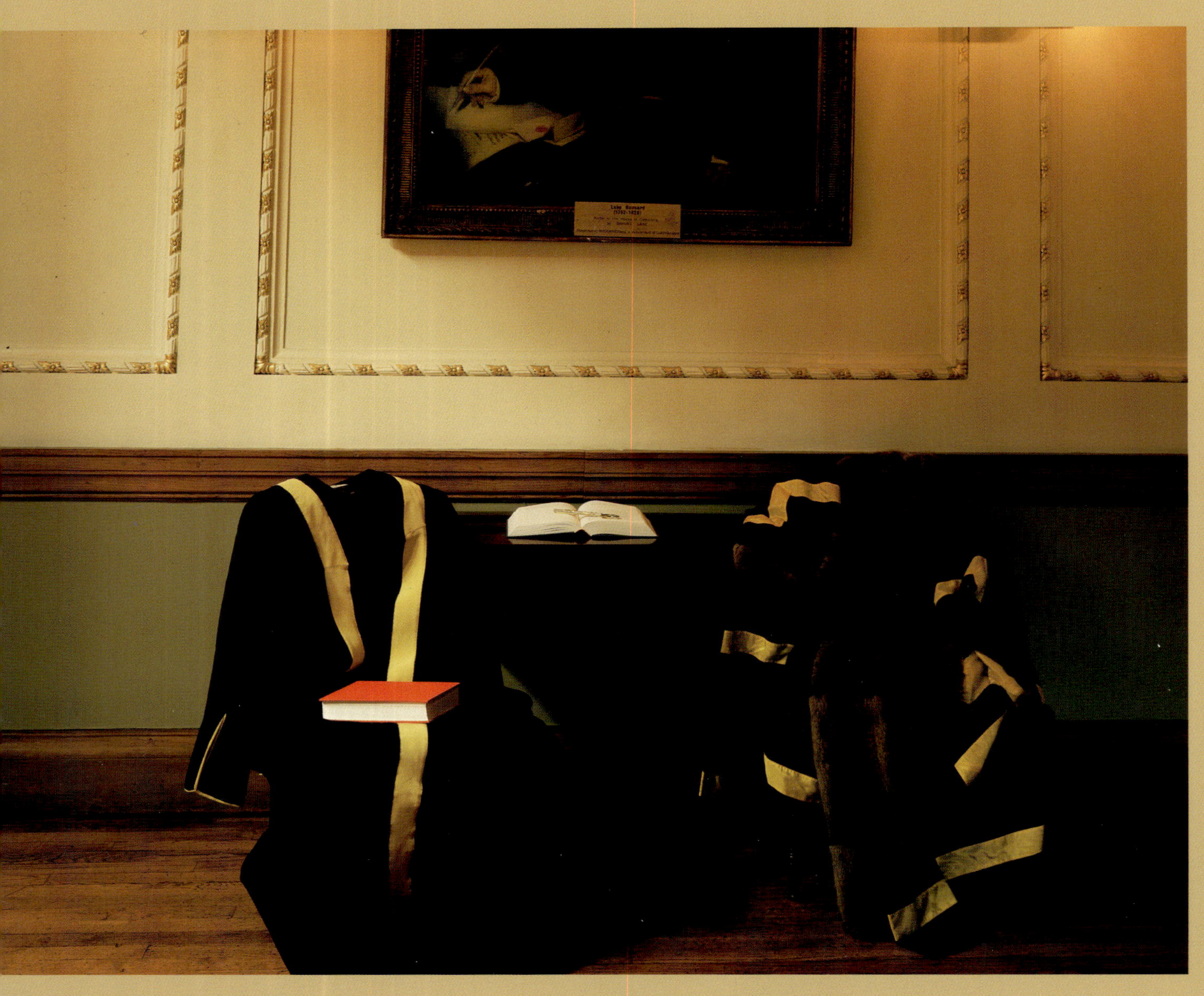

His Worshipful Company

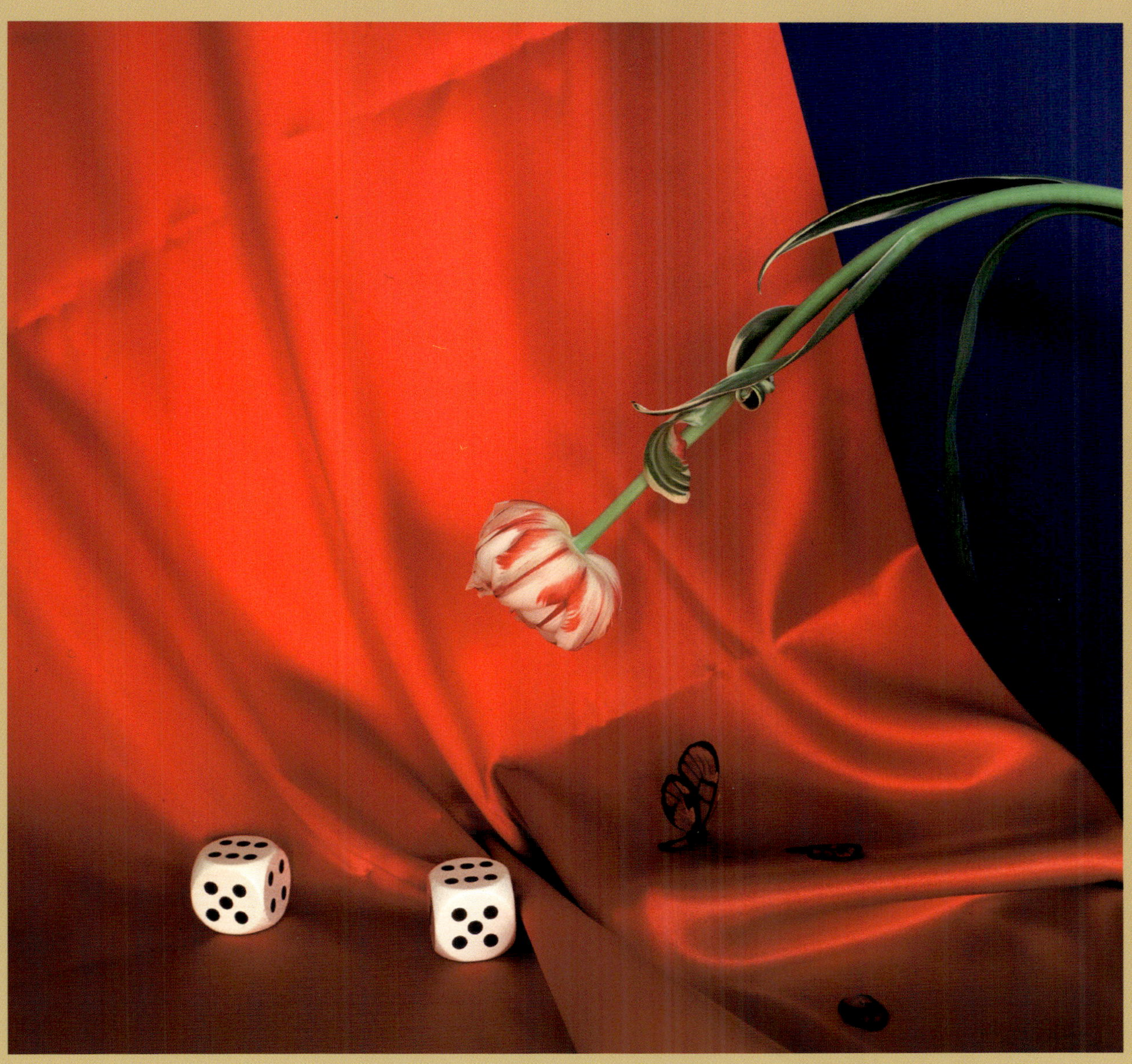

Hostage to Fortune

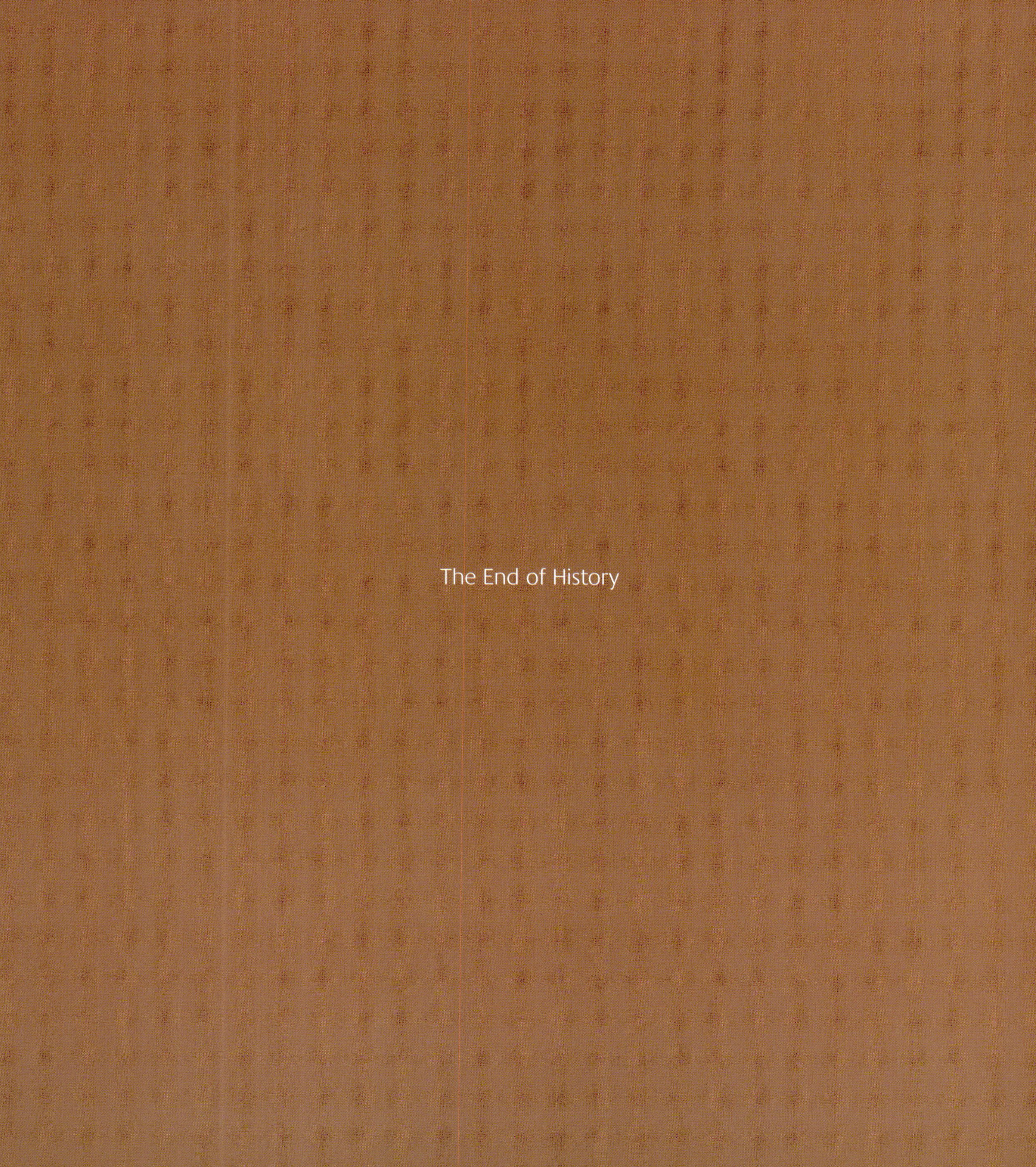

The End of History

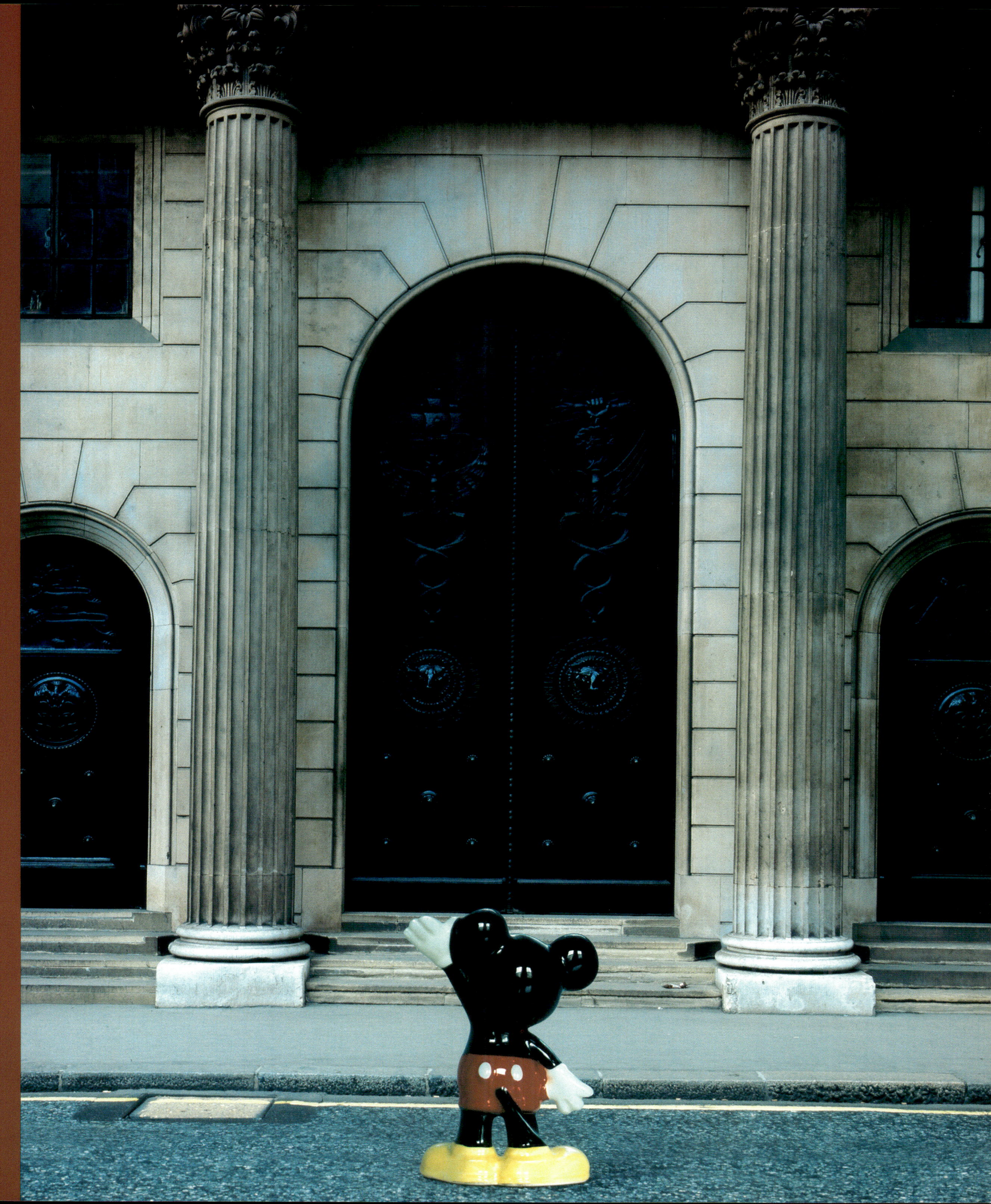

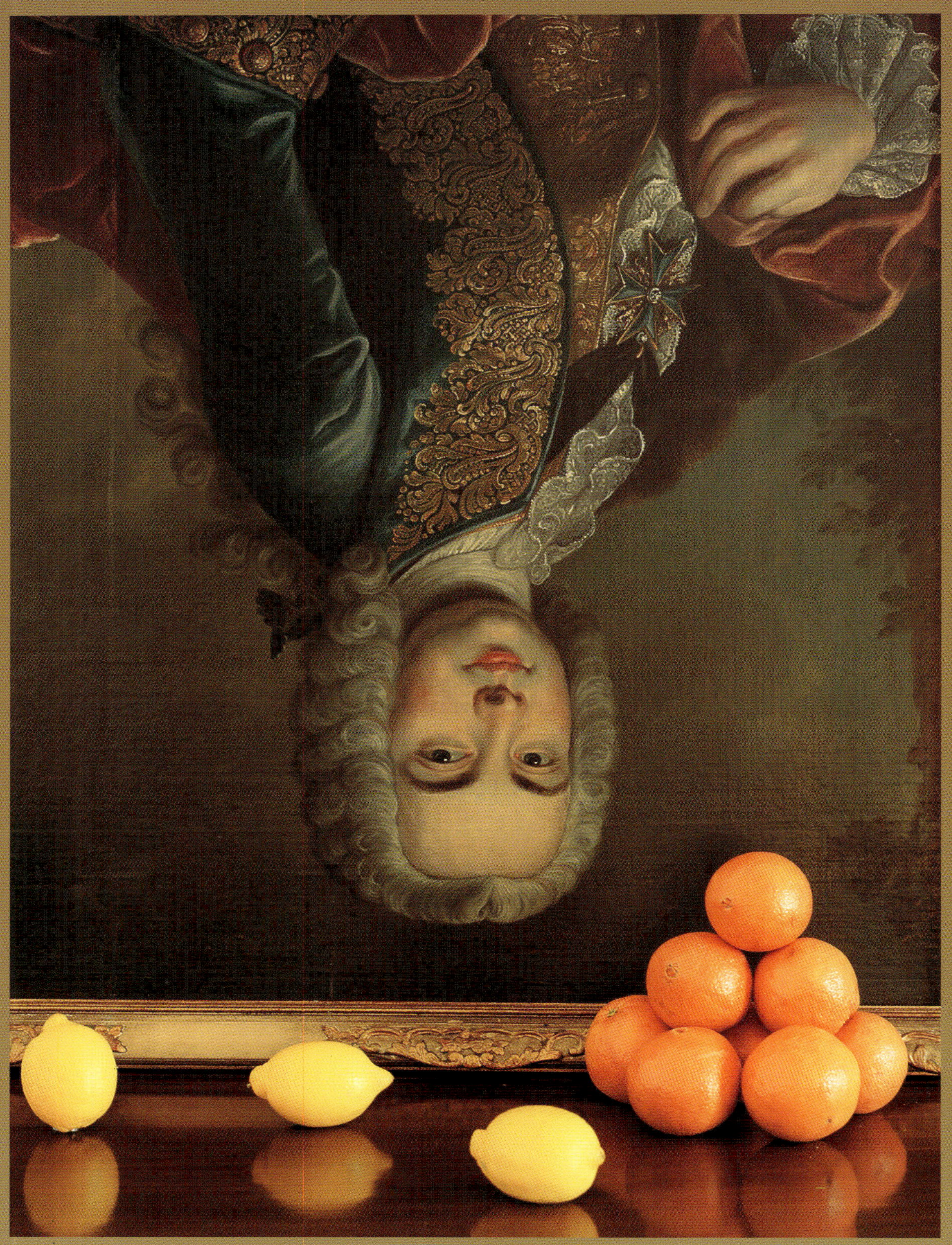

The Ingenu

IV

The Virtues and the Delights

O charming sex you will be free:
as do men, you will enjoy all the
pleasures of which nature makes a duty,
from not one will you be withheld.
Must the diviner half of mankind
be laden with irons by the other?
Ah break those irons nature wills it.

Alphonse Donatien de Sade
The Story of Juliette

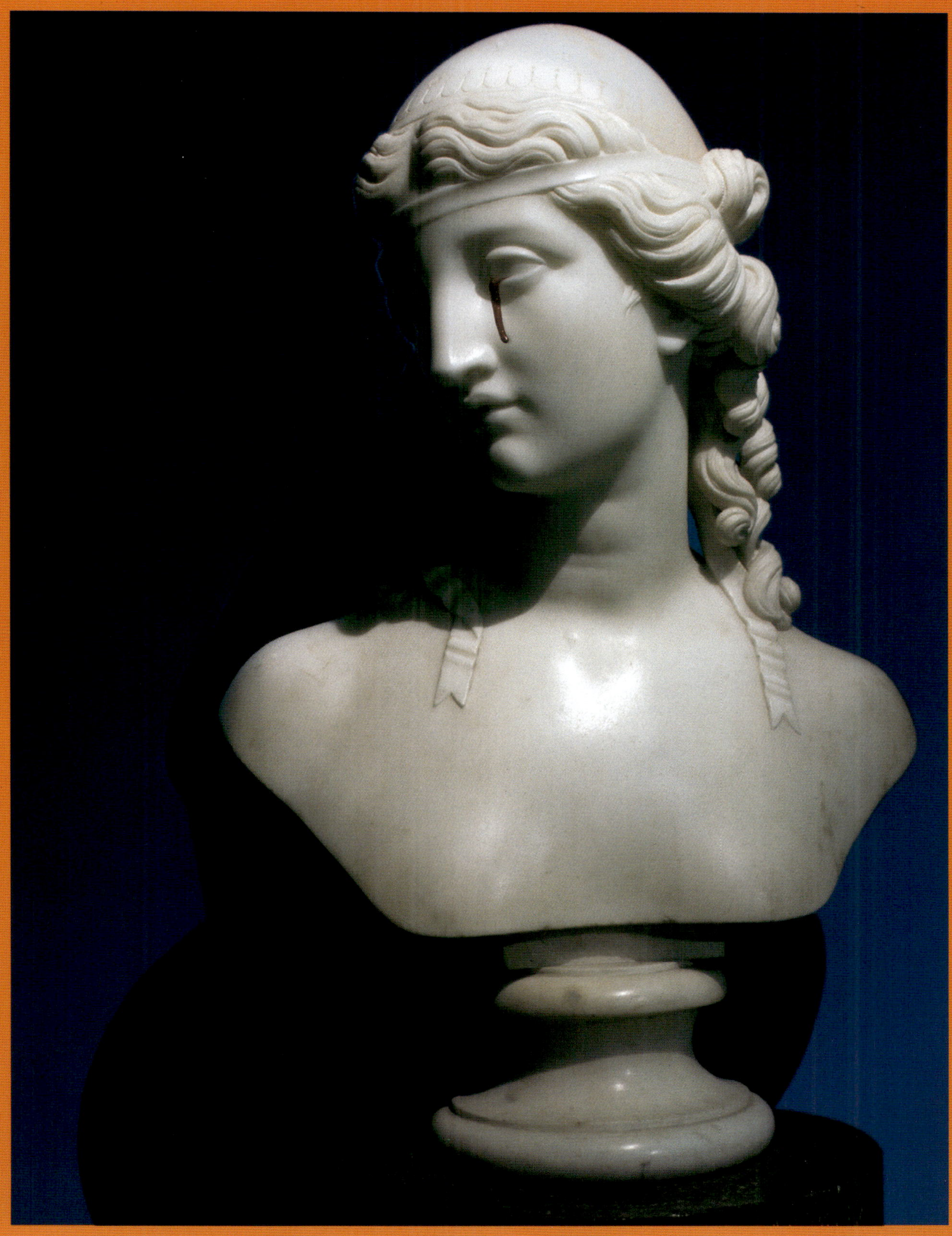

The New Justine

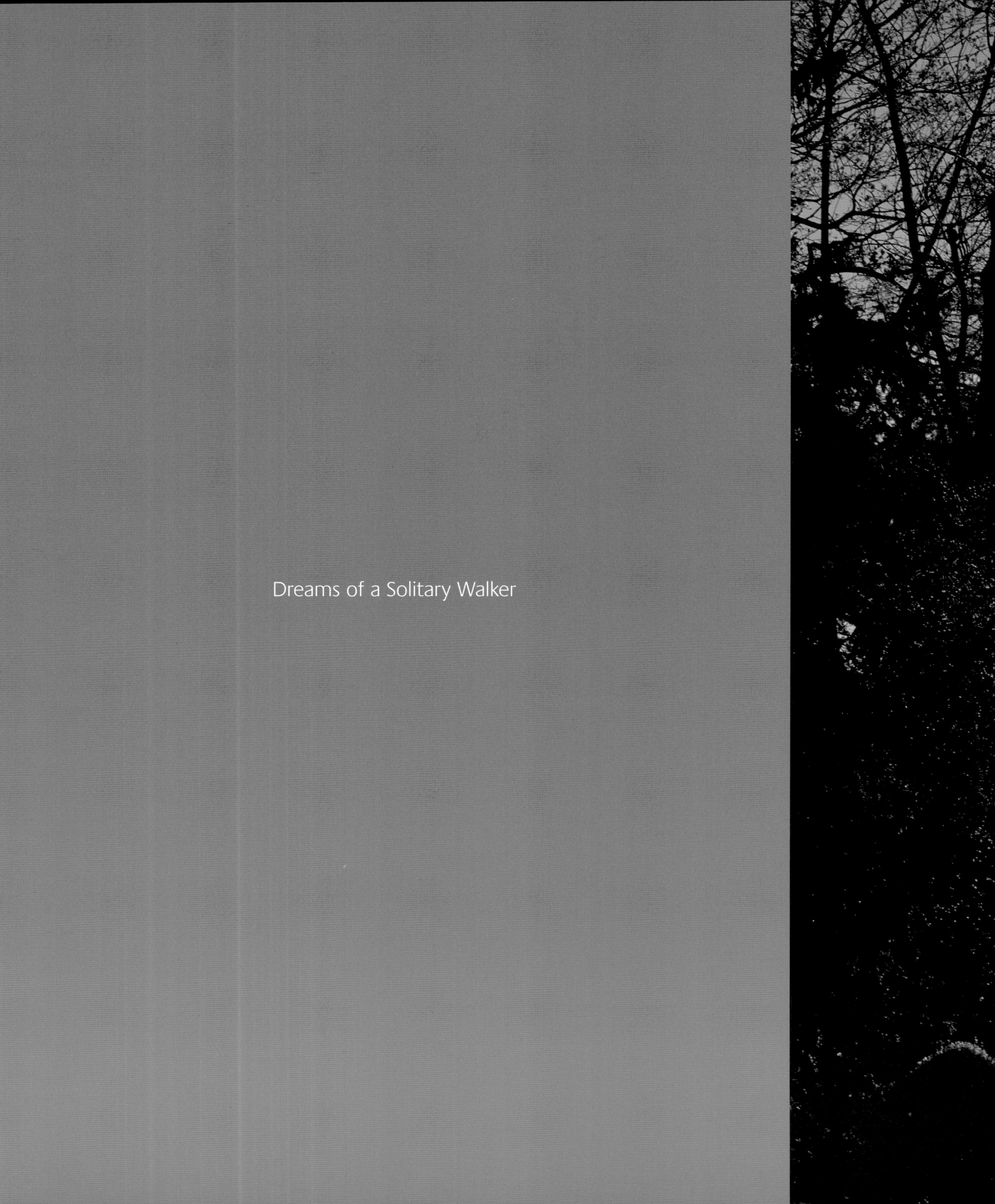
Dreams of a Solitary Walker

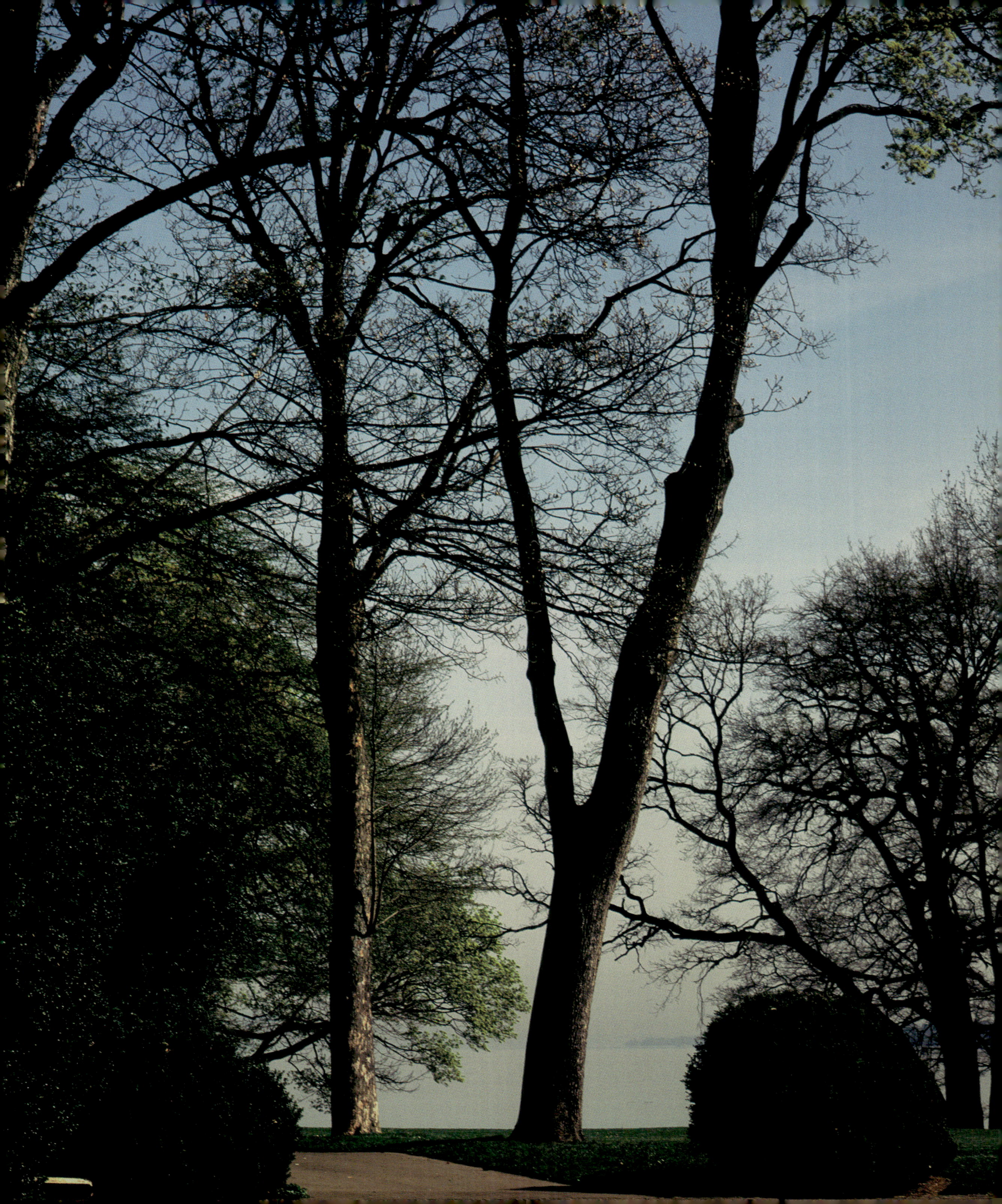

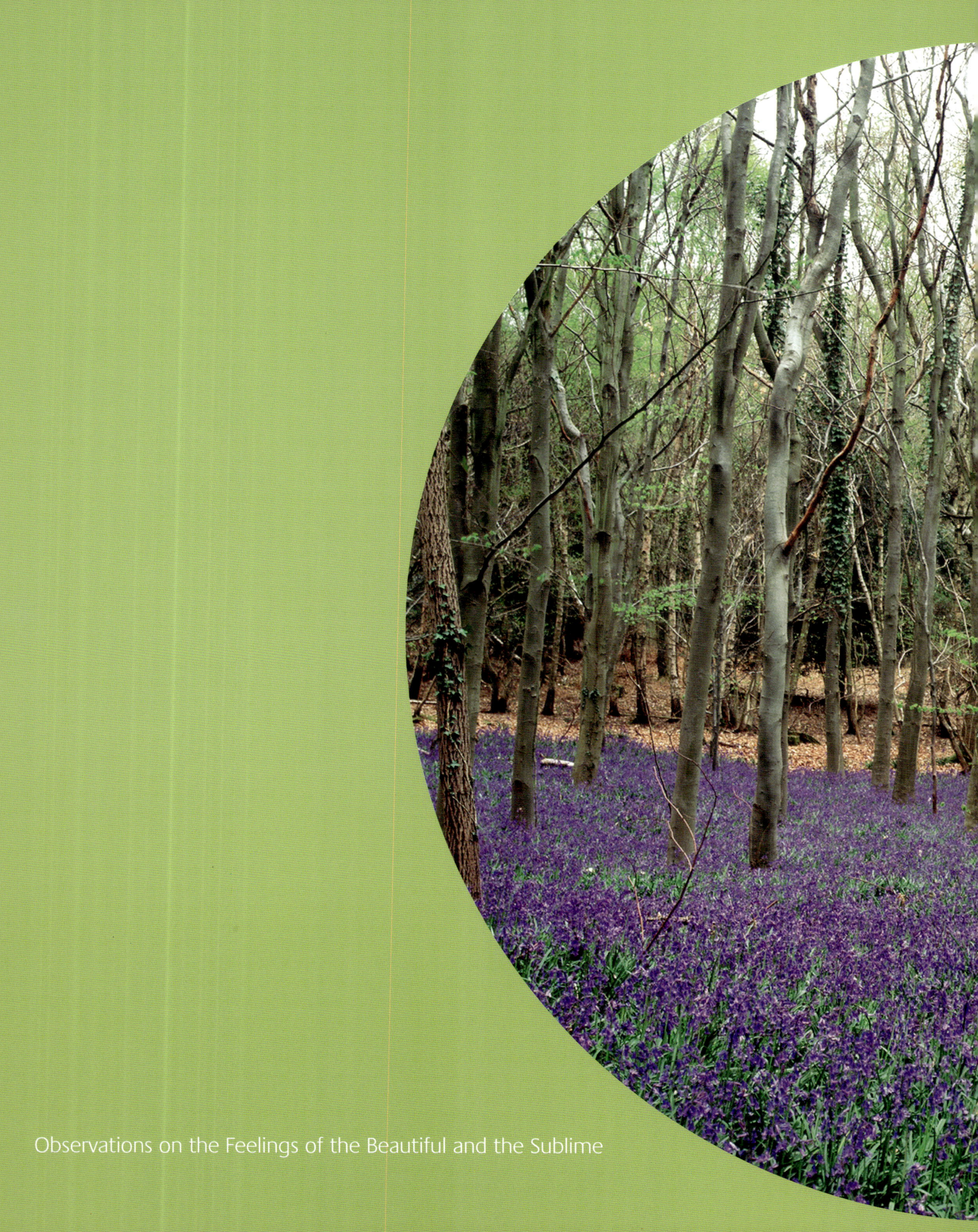
Observations on the Feelings of the Beautiful and the Sublime

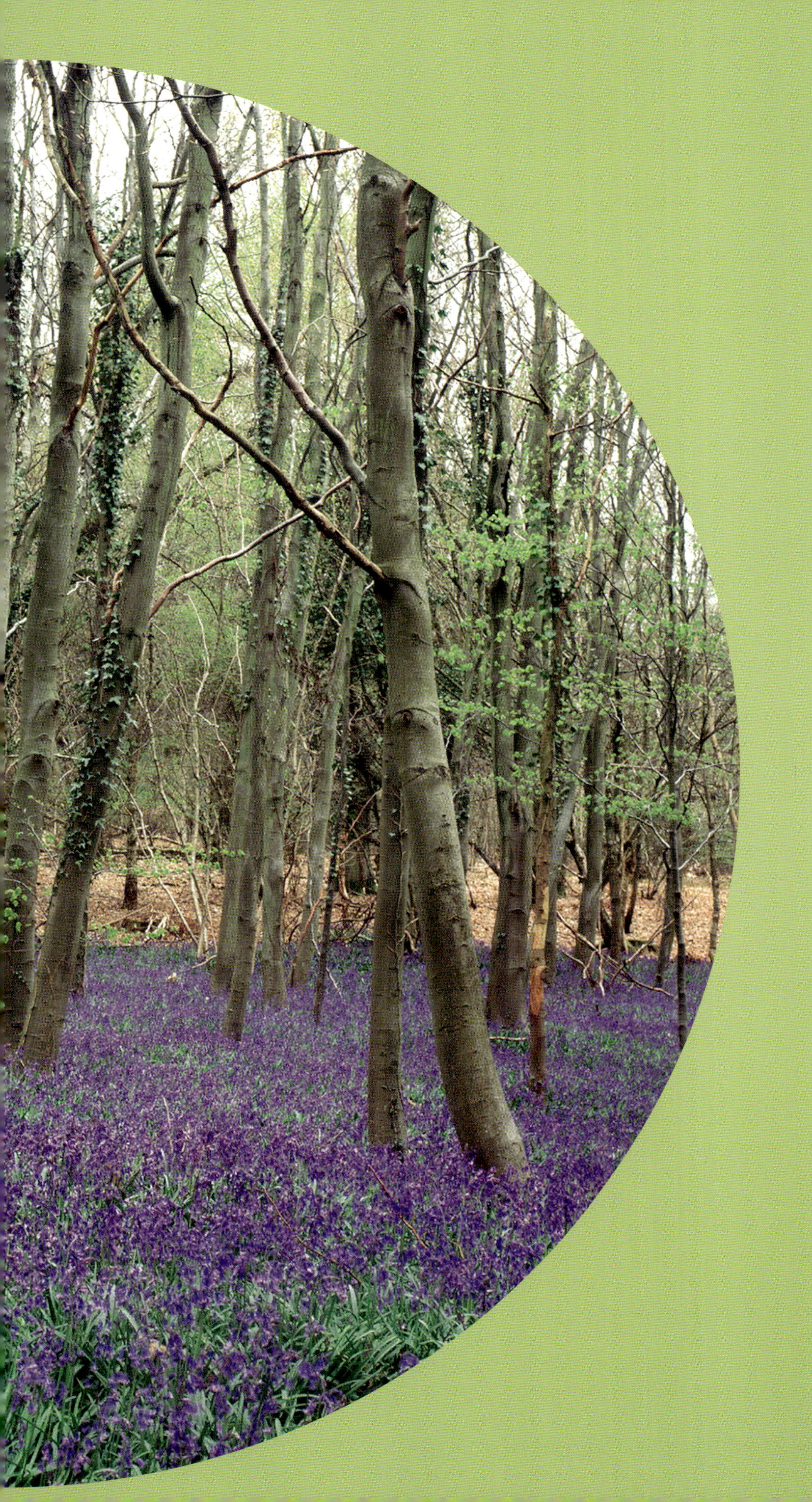

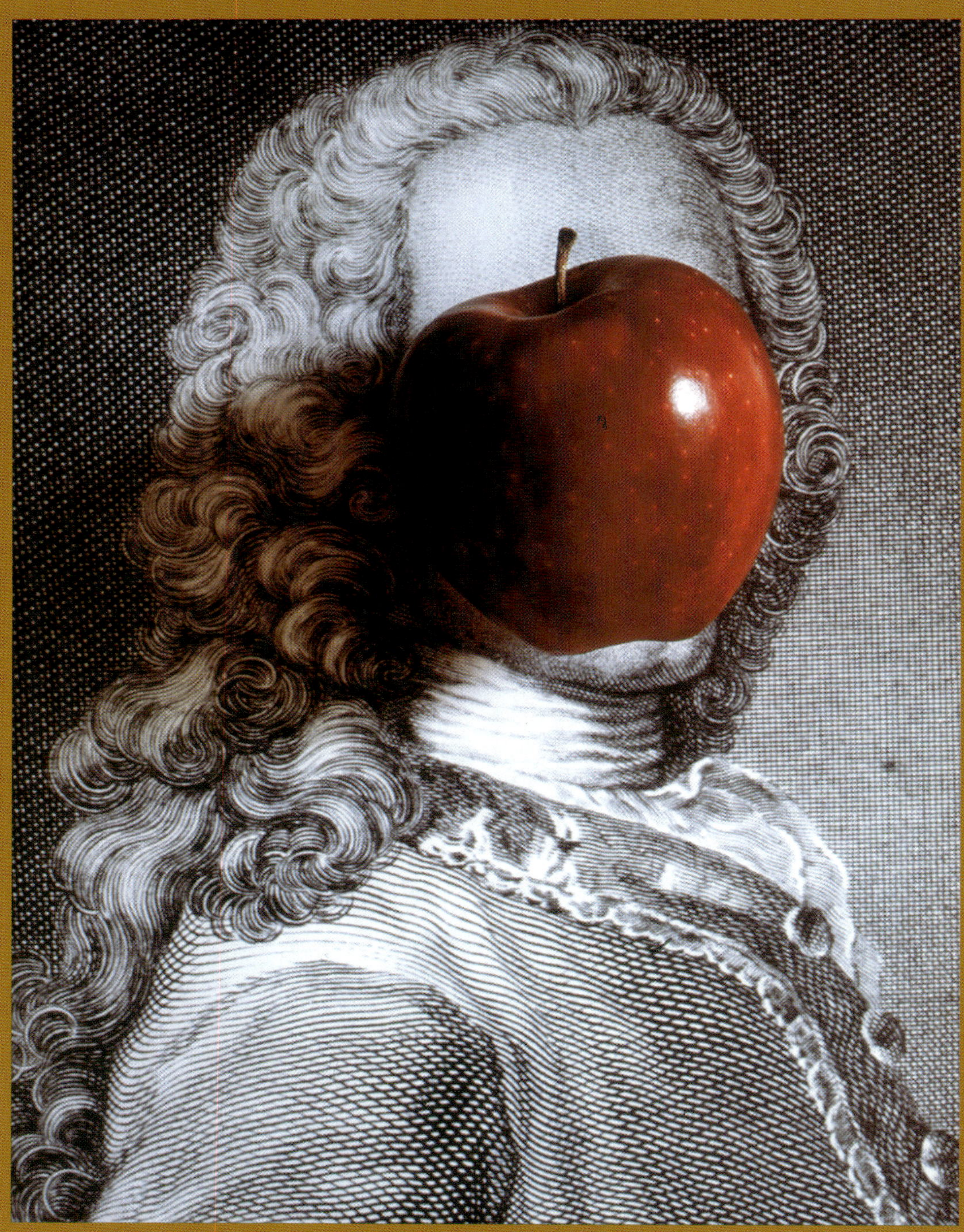

The Age of Reason

Now my dear pangloss tell me this:

when you have been hanged,

dissected and beaten unmercifully,

did you still think that everything

in this world is for the best?

Voltaire
Candide

Candide

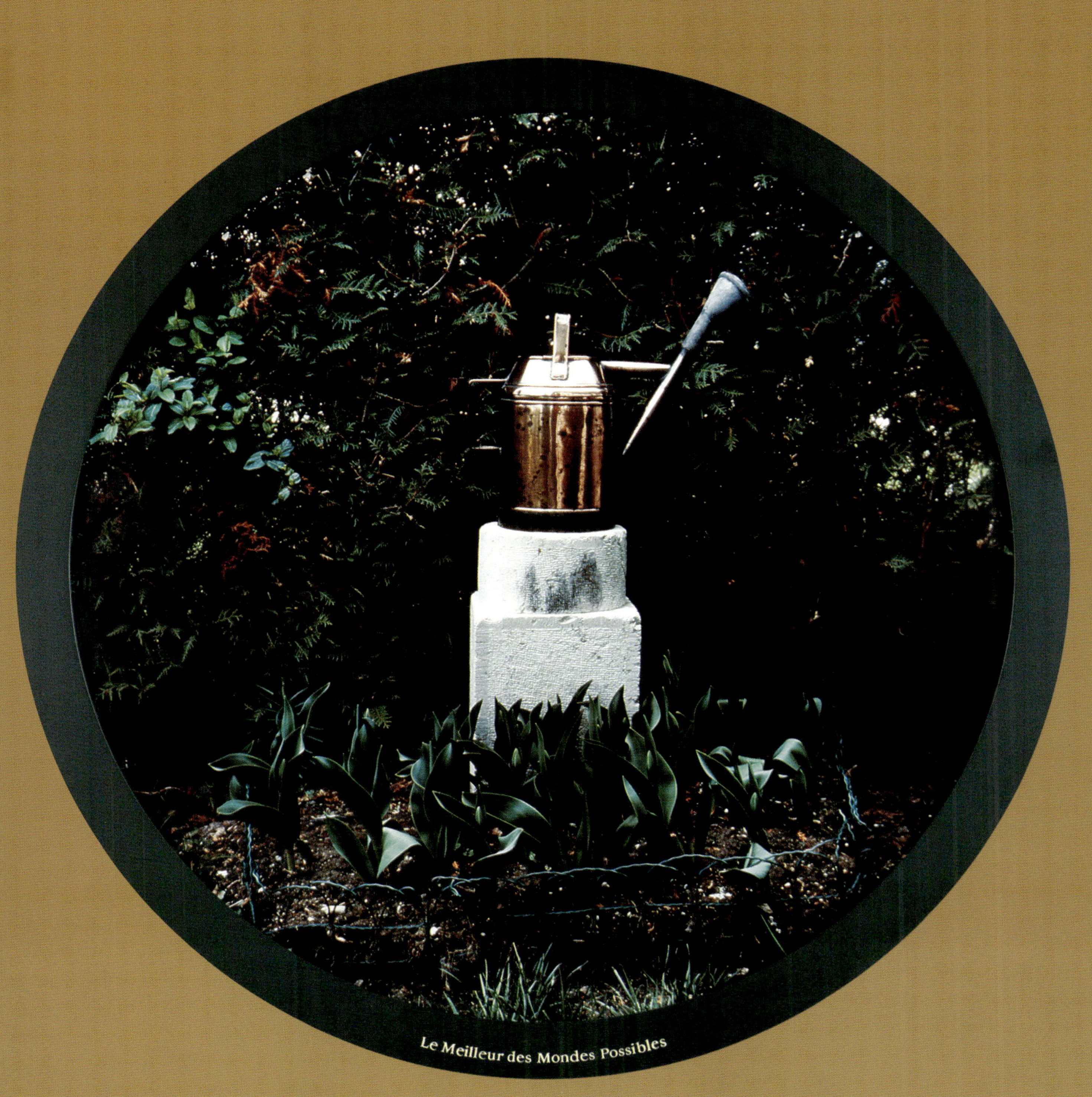

Le Meilleur des Mondes Possibles

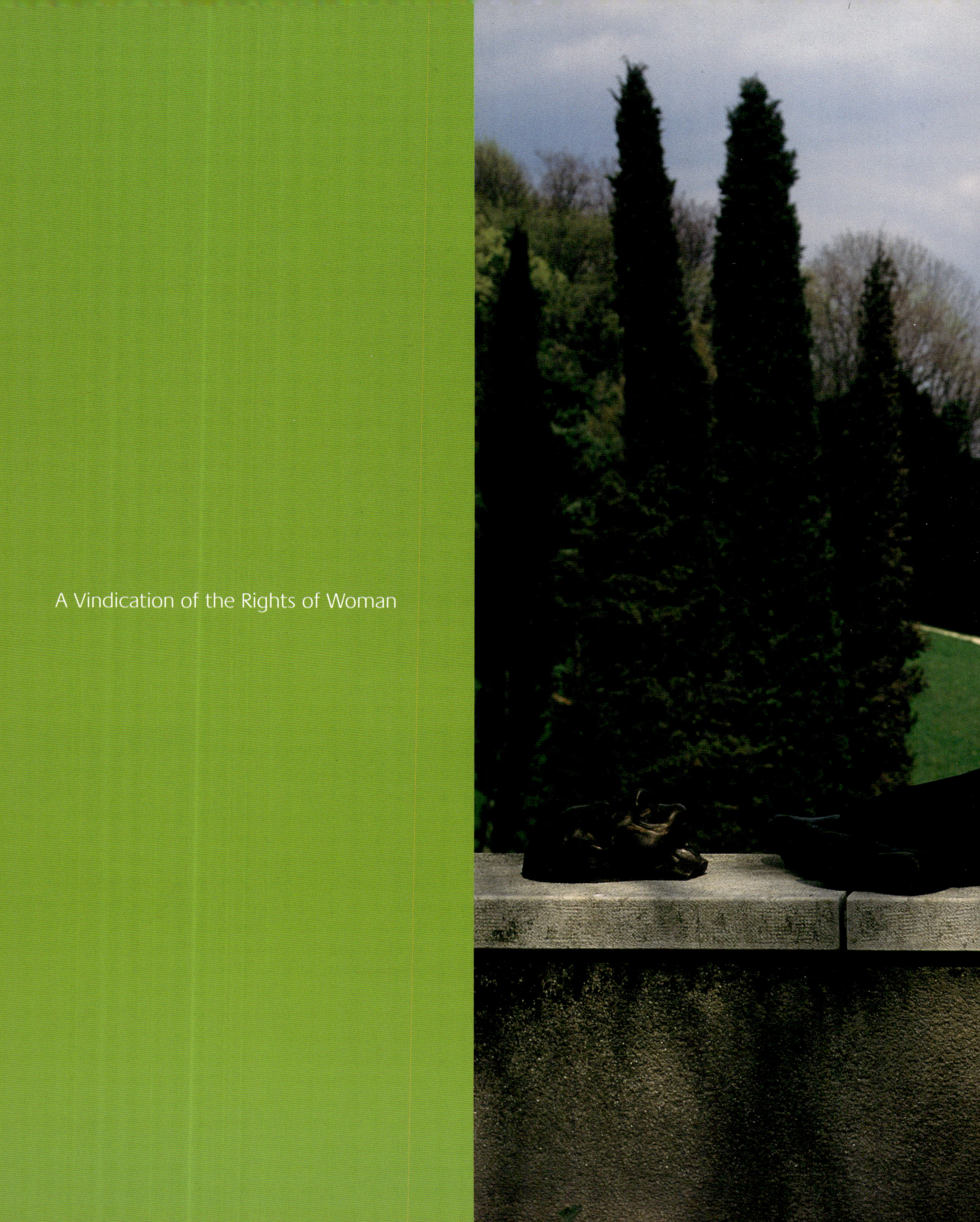

A Vindication of the Rights of Woman

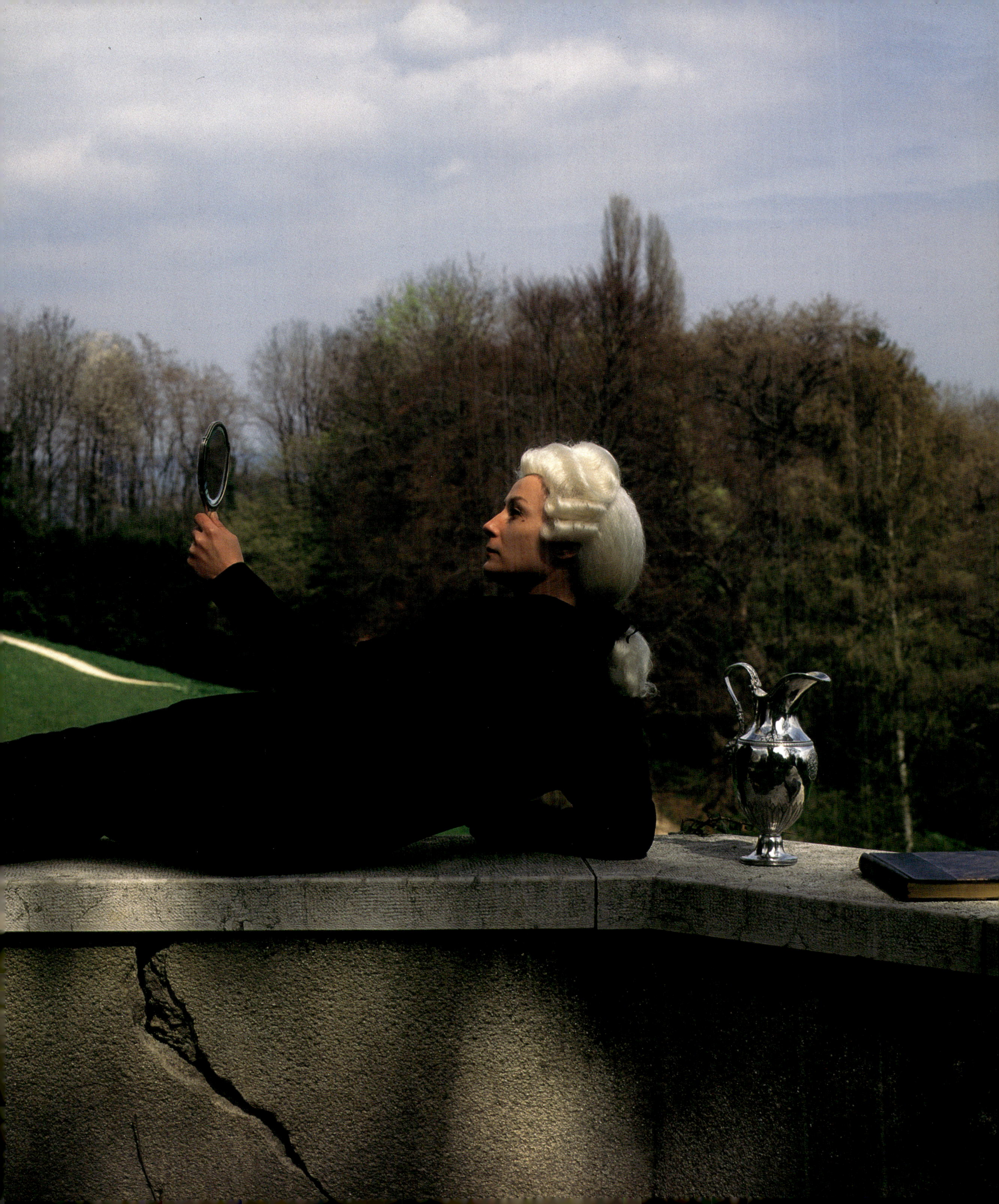

Sacred be the feelings of the heart!

Concentrated in a glowing flame,

they become the sun of life.

Without his invigorating impregnation,

reason would probably

lie in helpless inactivity,

and never bring forth her

only legitimate offspring- virtue.

Mary Wollstonescraft
A Vindication of the Rights of Men

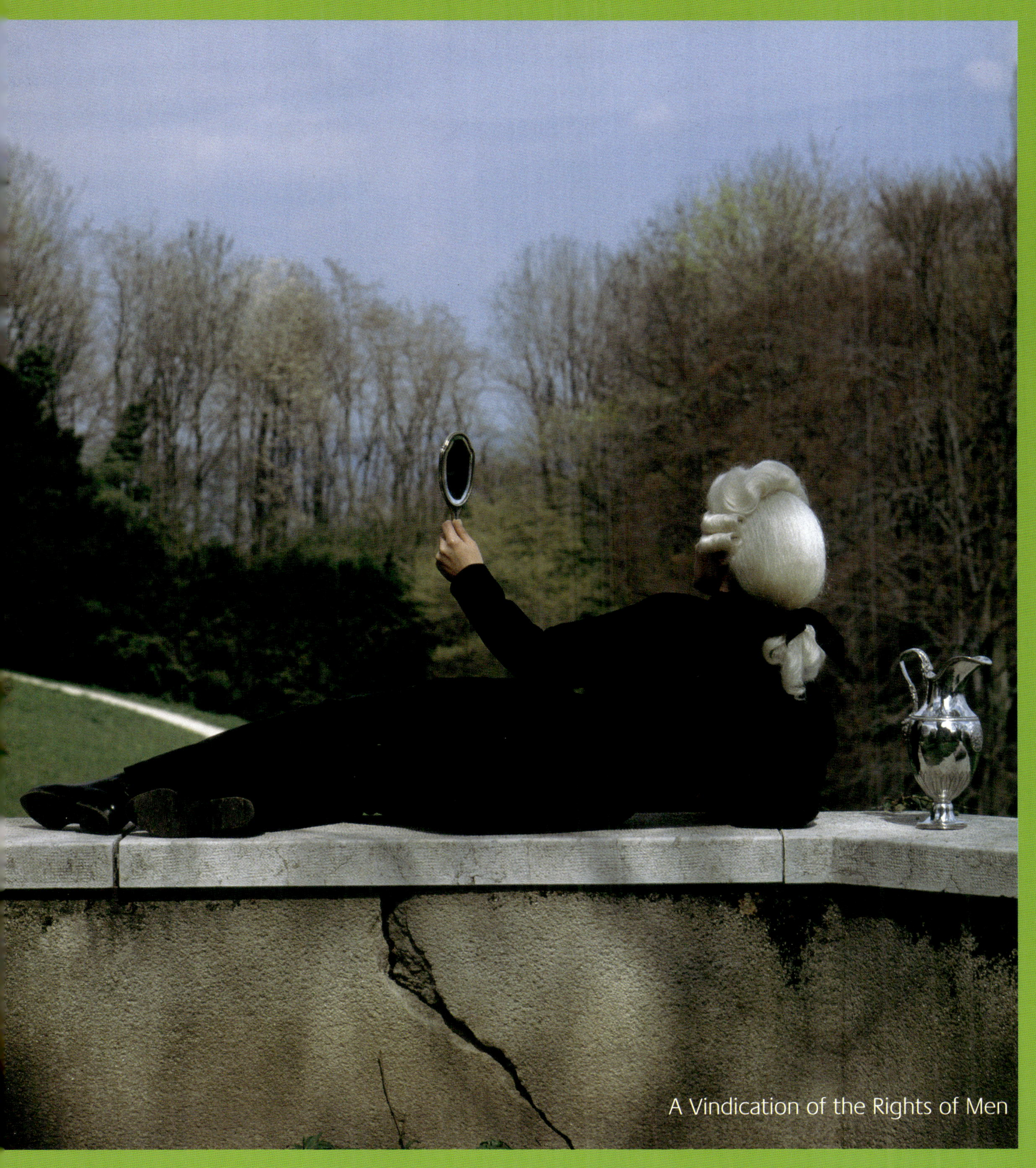

A Vindication of the Rights of Men

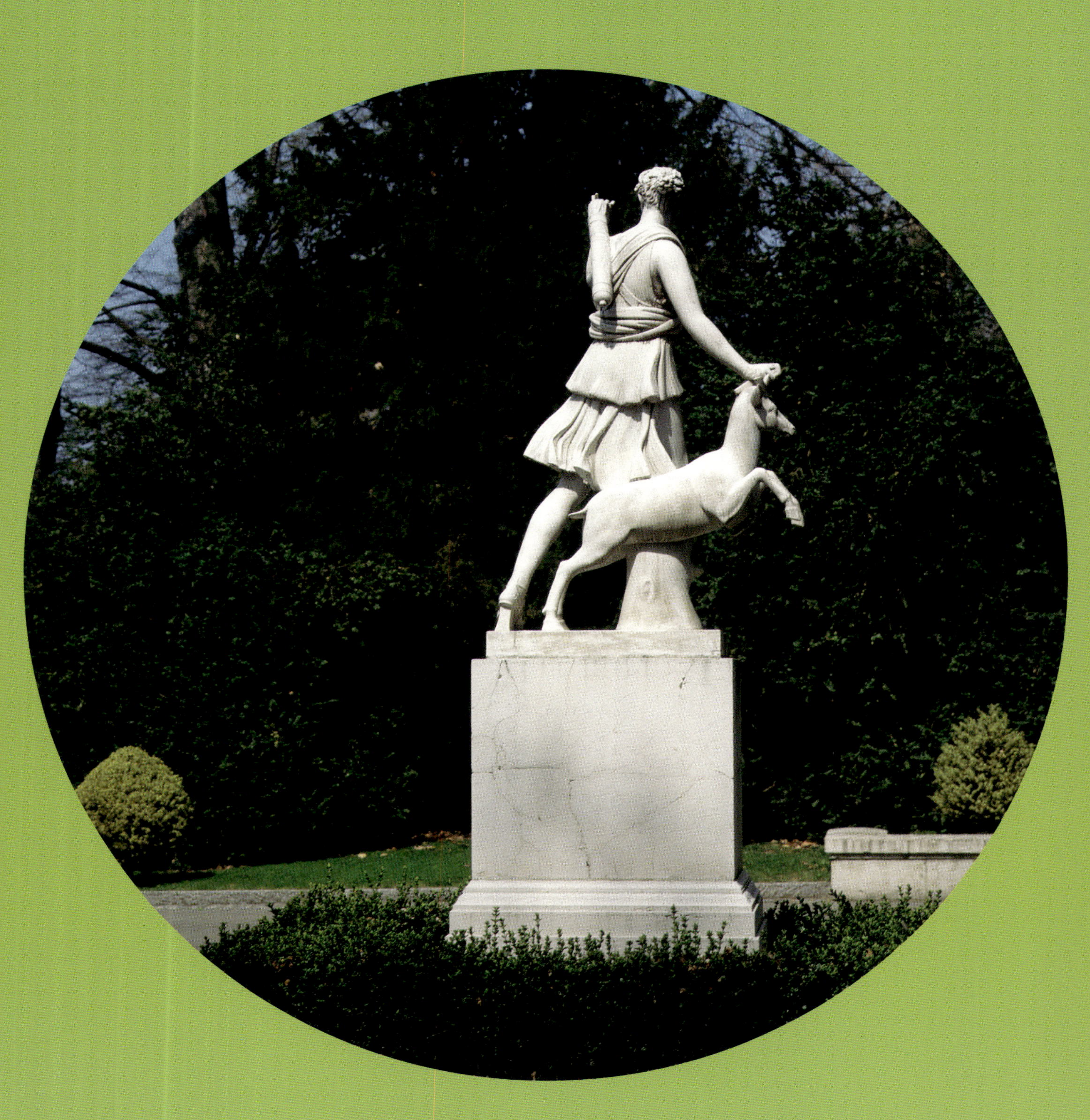

Discourse on Happiness

Friendship is a serious affection

the most sublime of all affections.

Because it is founded on principle

and cemented by time.

The very reverse can be said of love.

Mary Wollstonecraft
A Vindication of the Rights of Woman

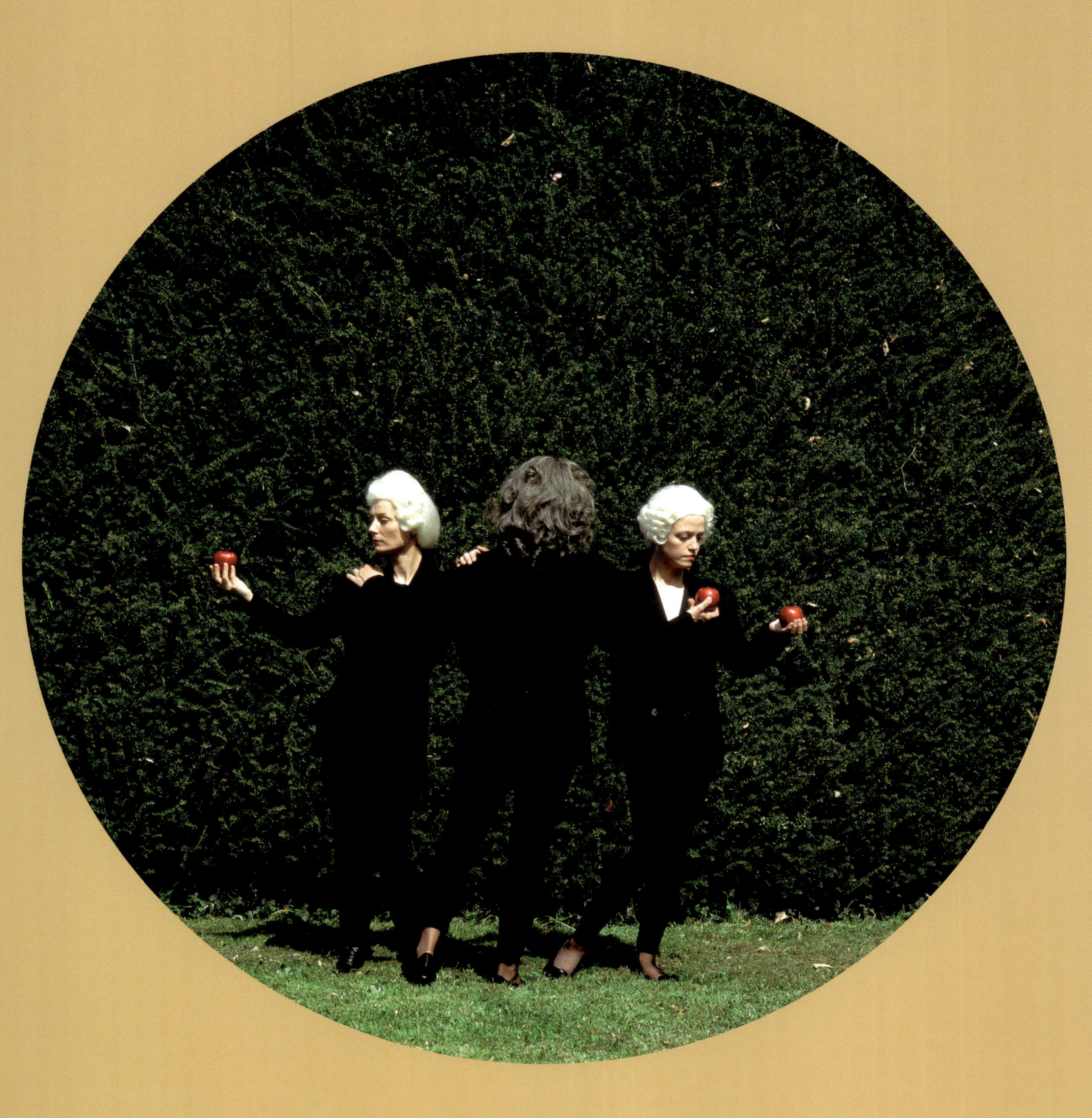

The Story of Juliette

V

Sanctuary

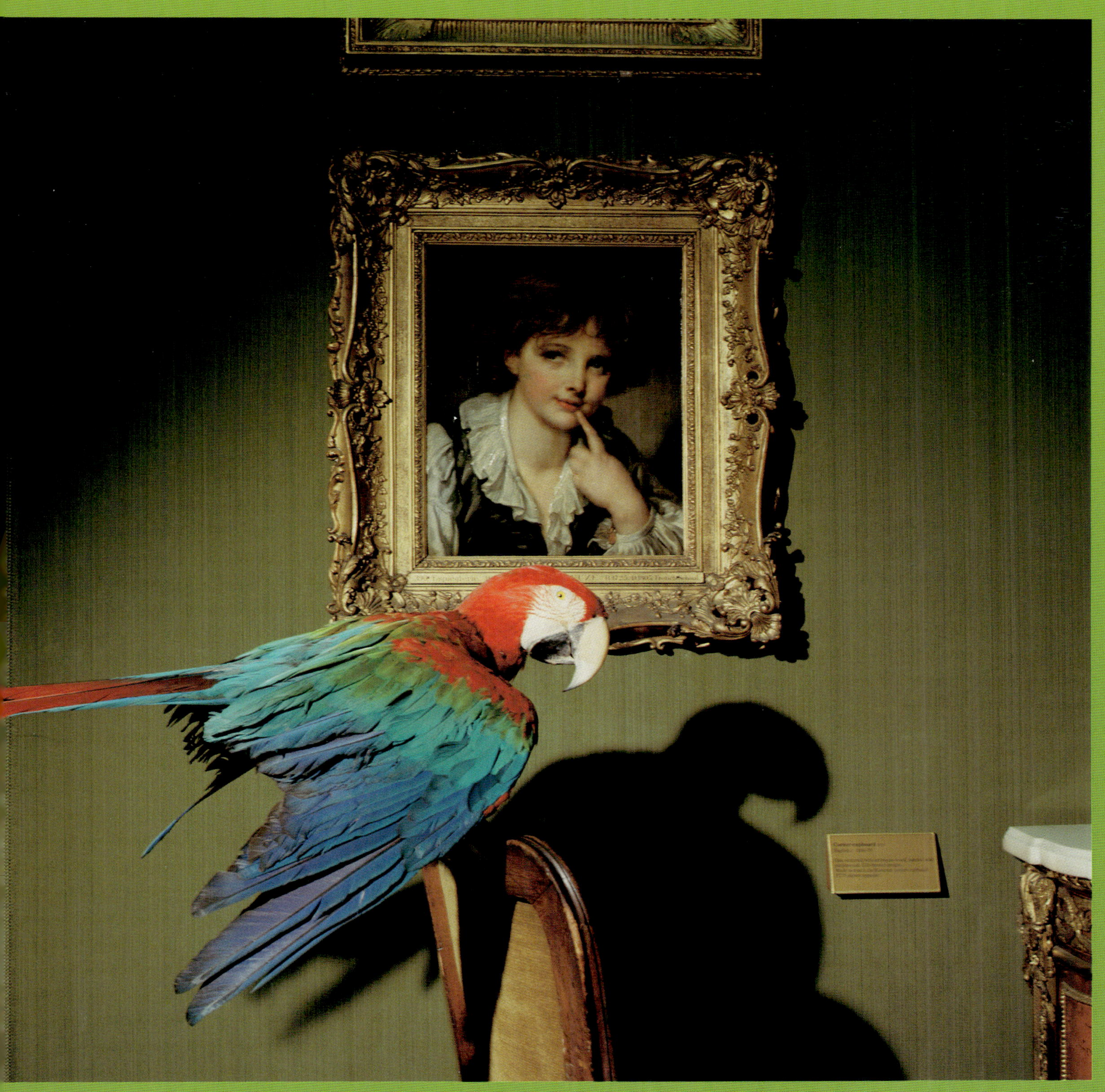

Flaubert's Parrot

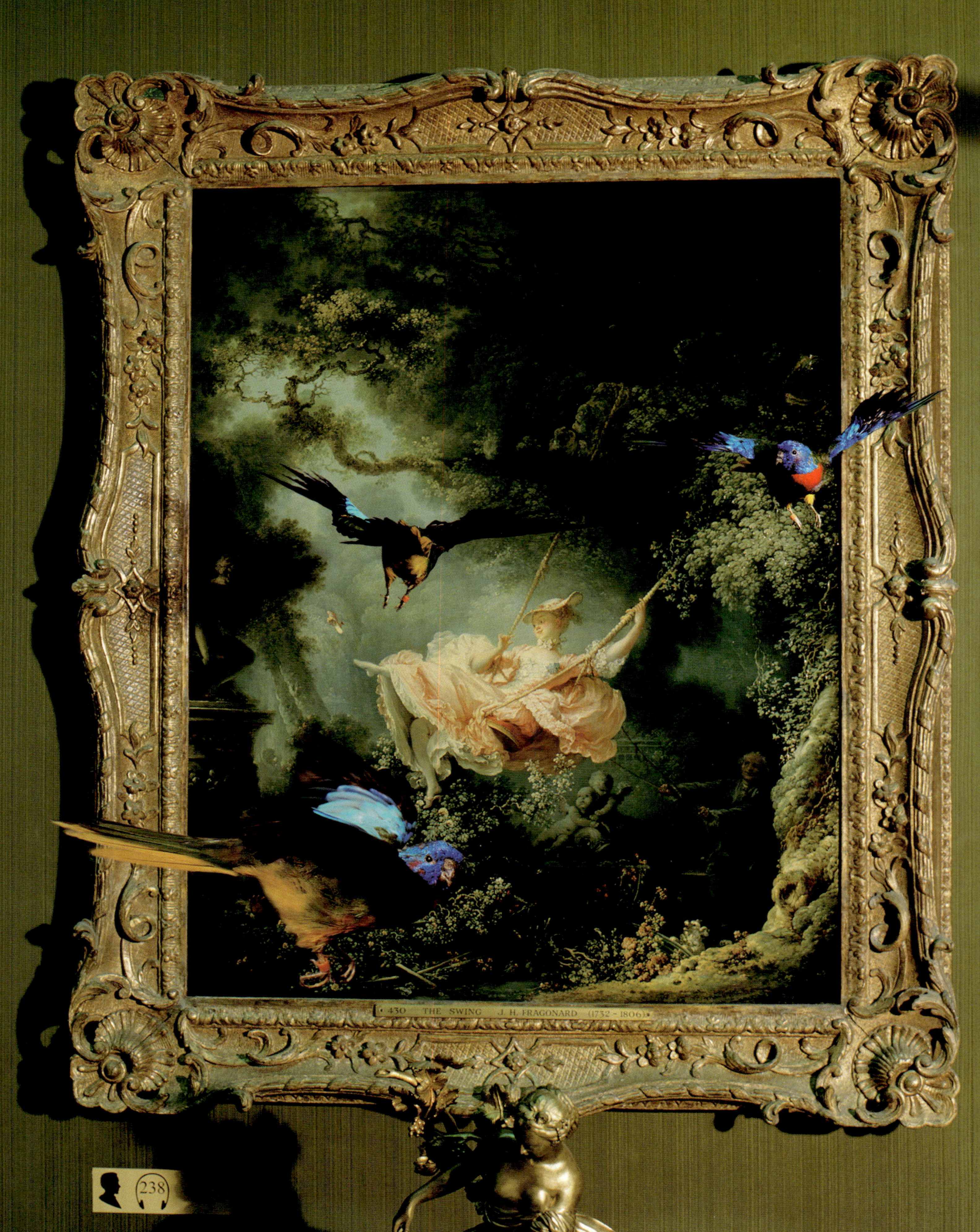
430 THE SWING J. H. FRAGONARD (1732 - 1806)
238

In the Green Room

Where have all the flowers gone? Long time passing.
Where have all the flowers gone? Long time ago.
Where have all the flowers gone?
Young girls picked them, ev'ry one.
When will they ever learn? When will they ever learn?

Where have all the young girls gone? Long time passing.
Where have all the young girls gone? Long time ago.
Where have all the young girls gone?
Gone to young men ev'ry one.
When will they ever learn? When will they ever learn?

Peter Seeger
Where Have All the Flowers Gone?

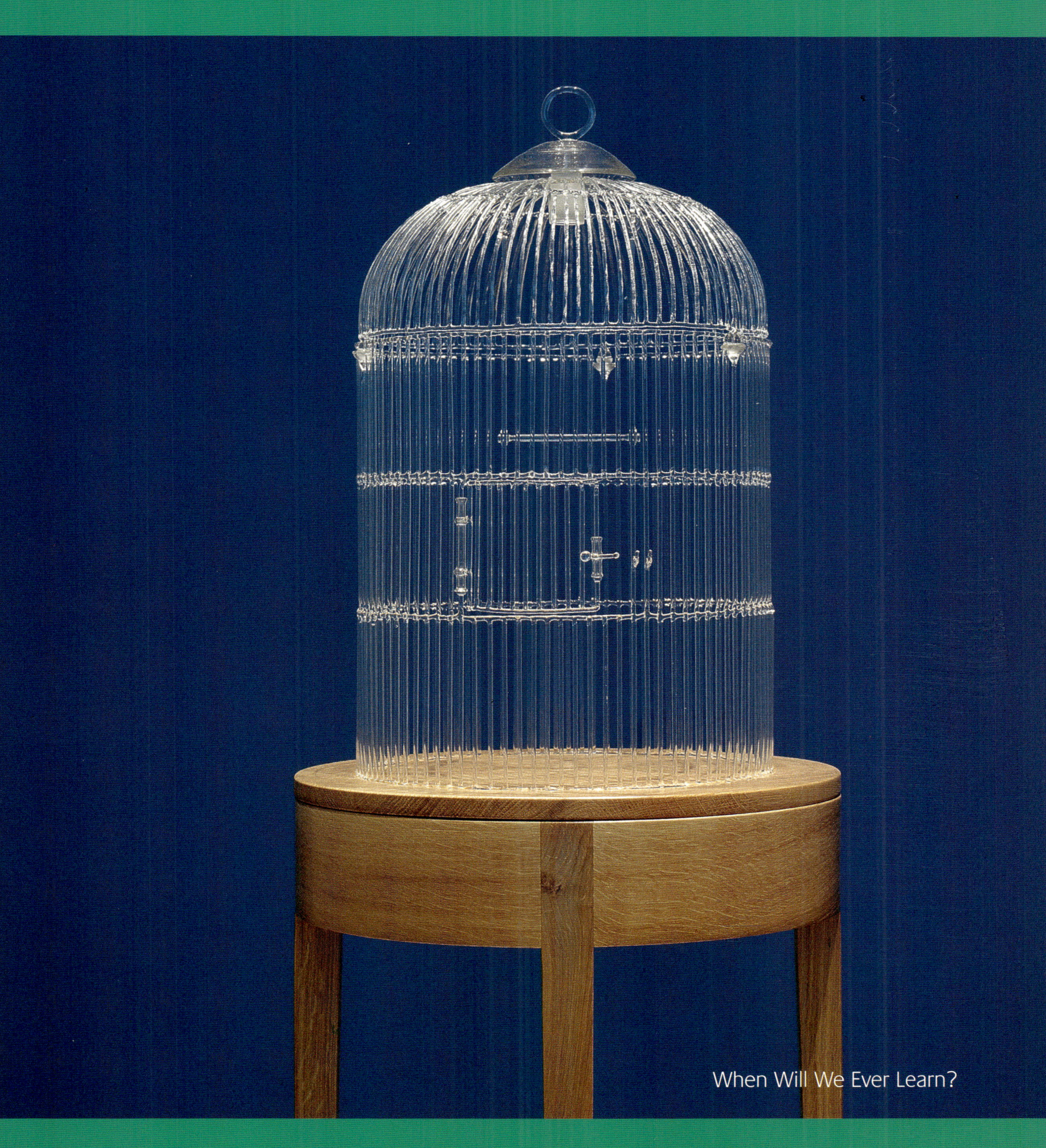

When Will We Ever Learn?

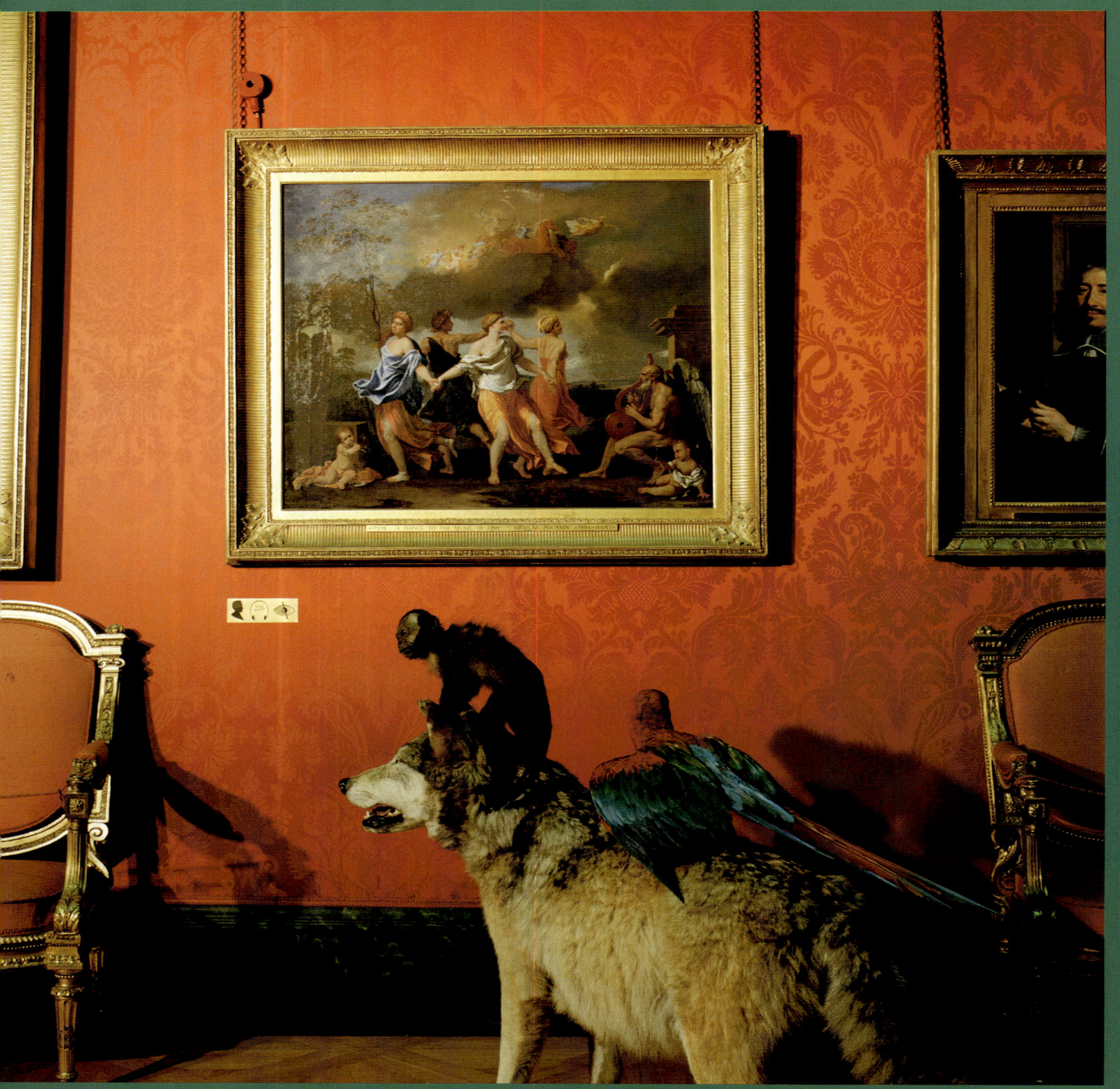

A Picture for Roland

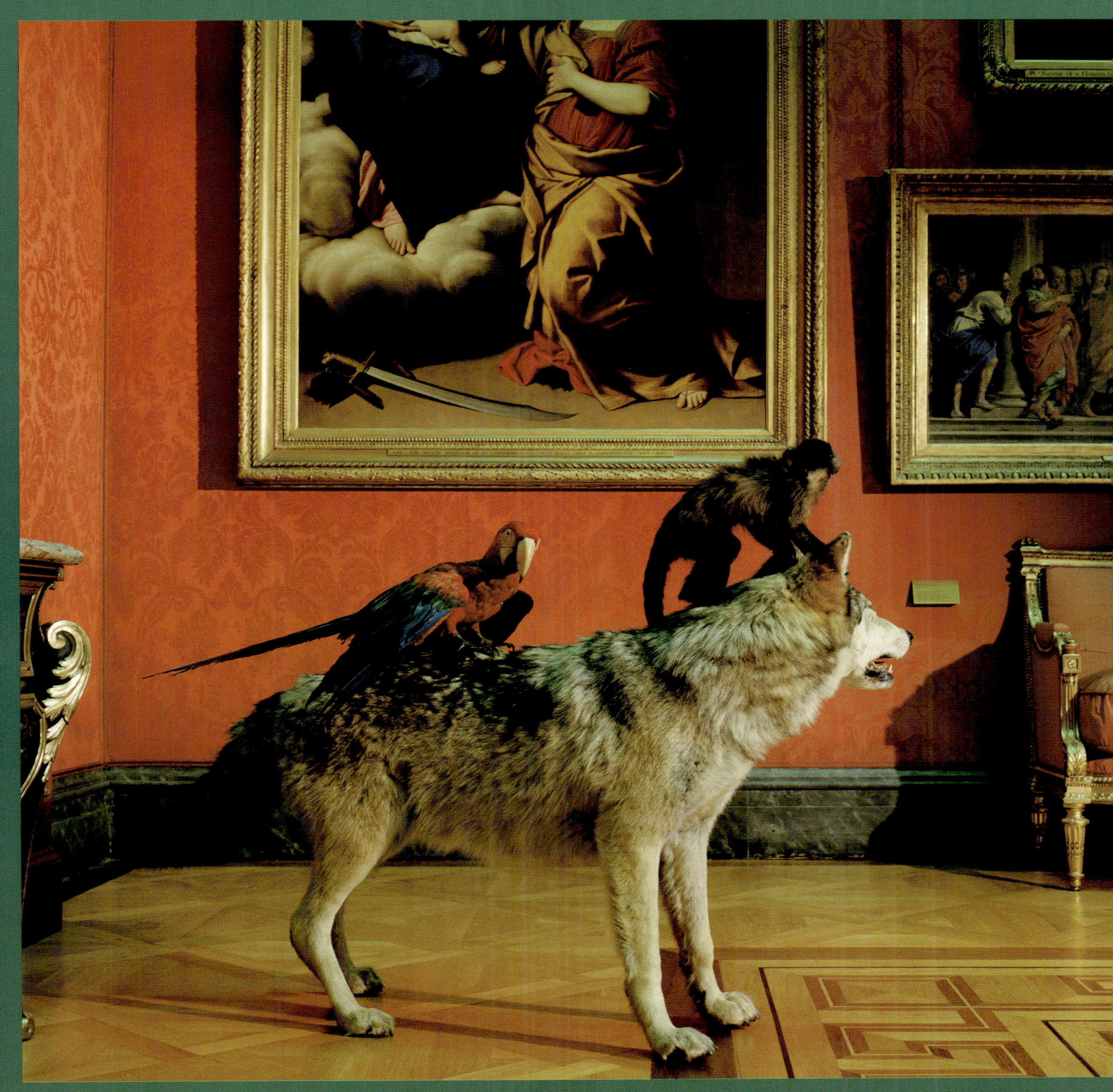

High Art Life After the Deluge

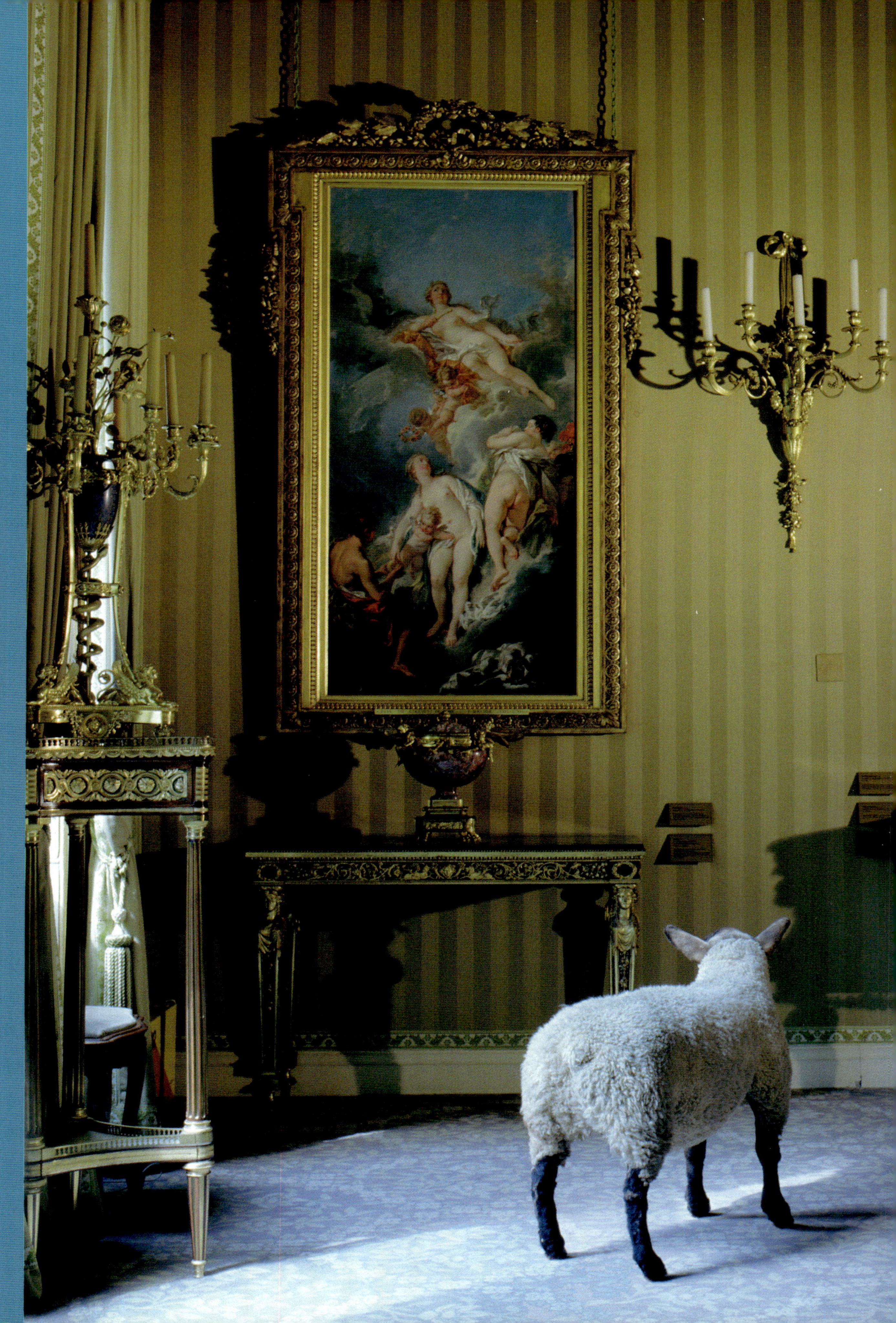

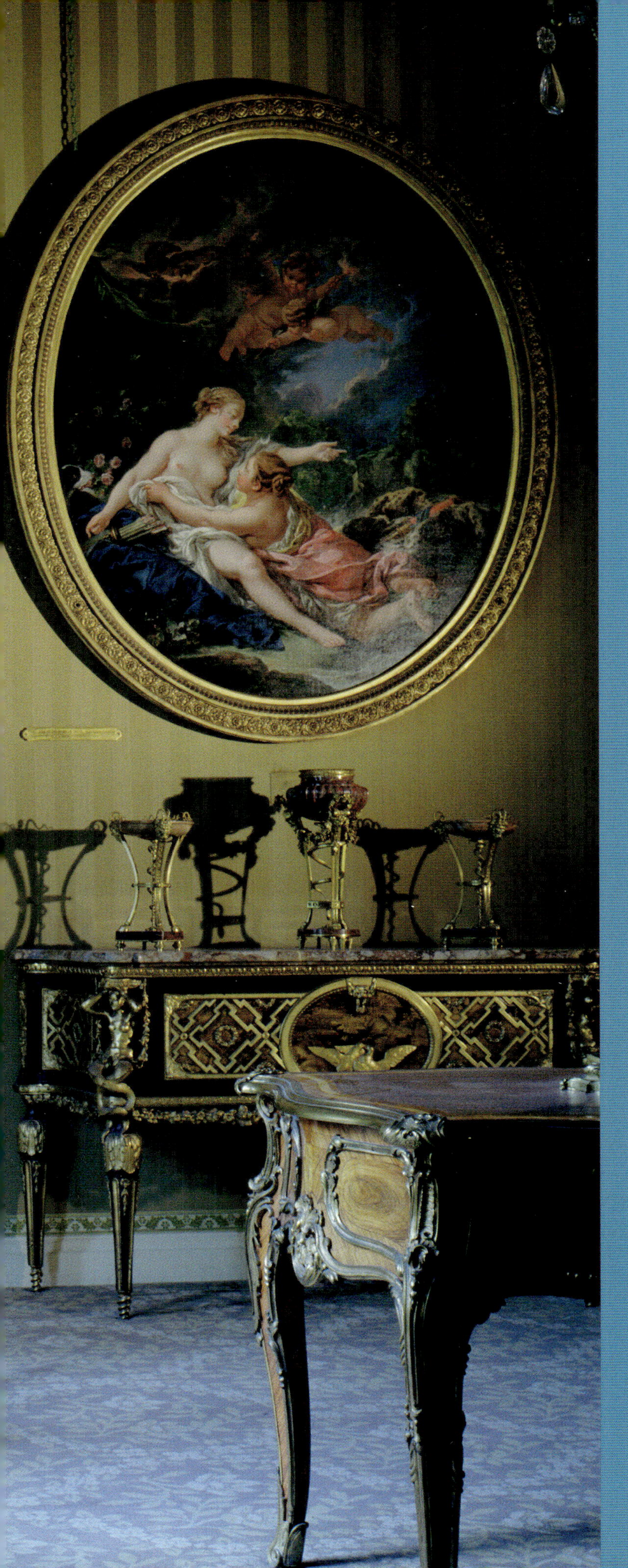

The Judgement of Paris

Lure
(video stills)

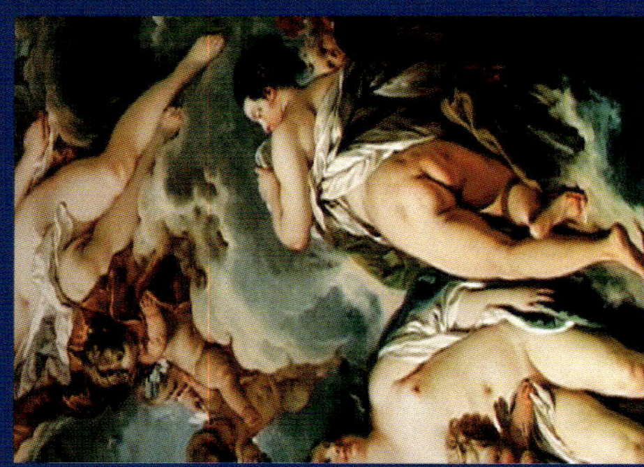
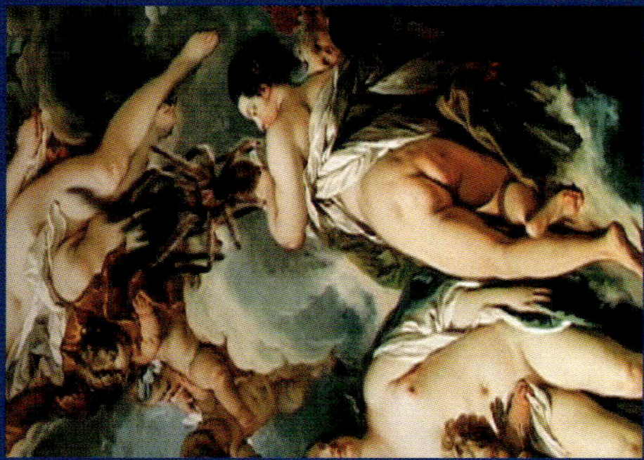
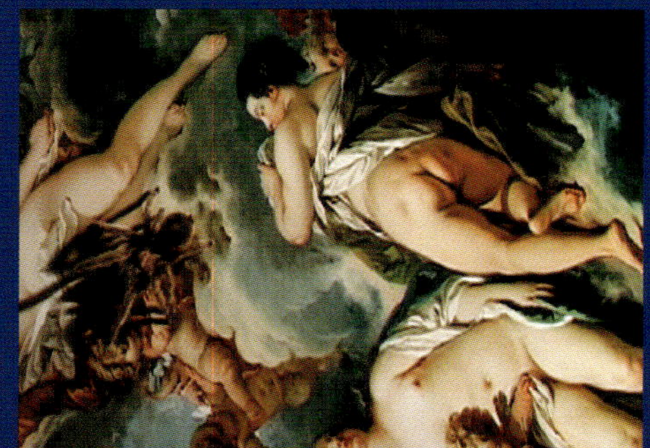
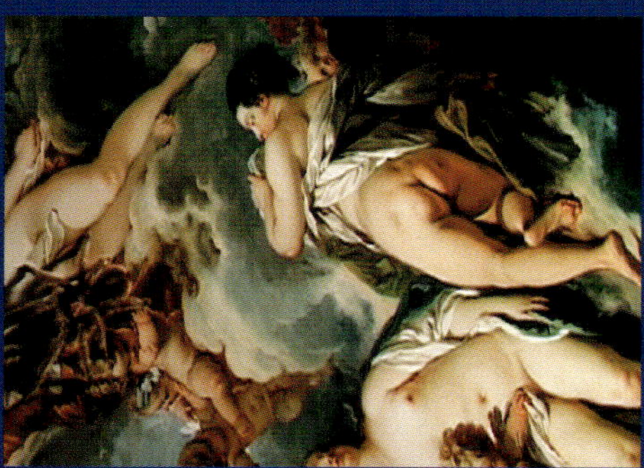

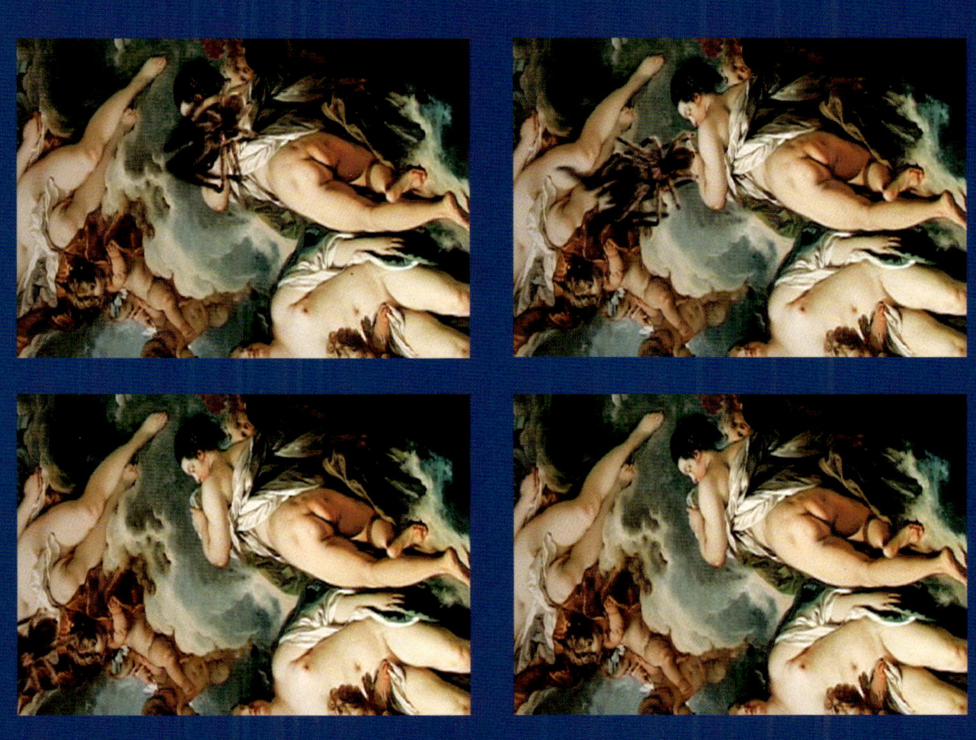

What is Human?

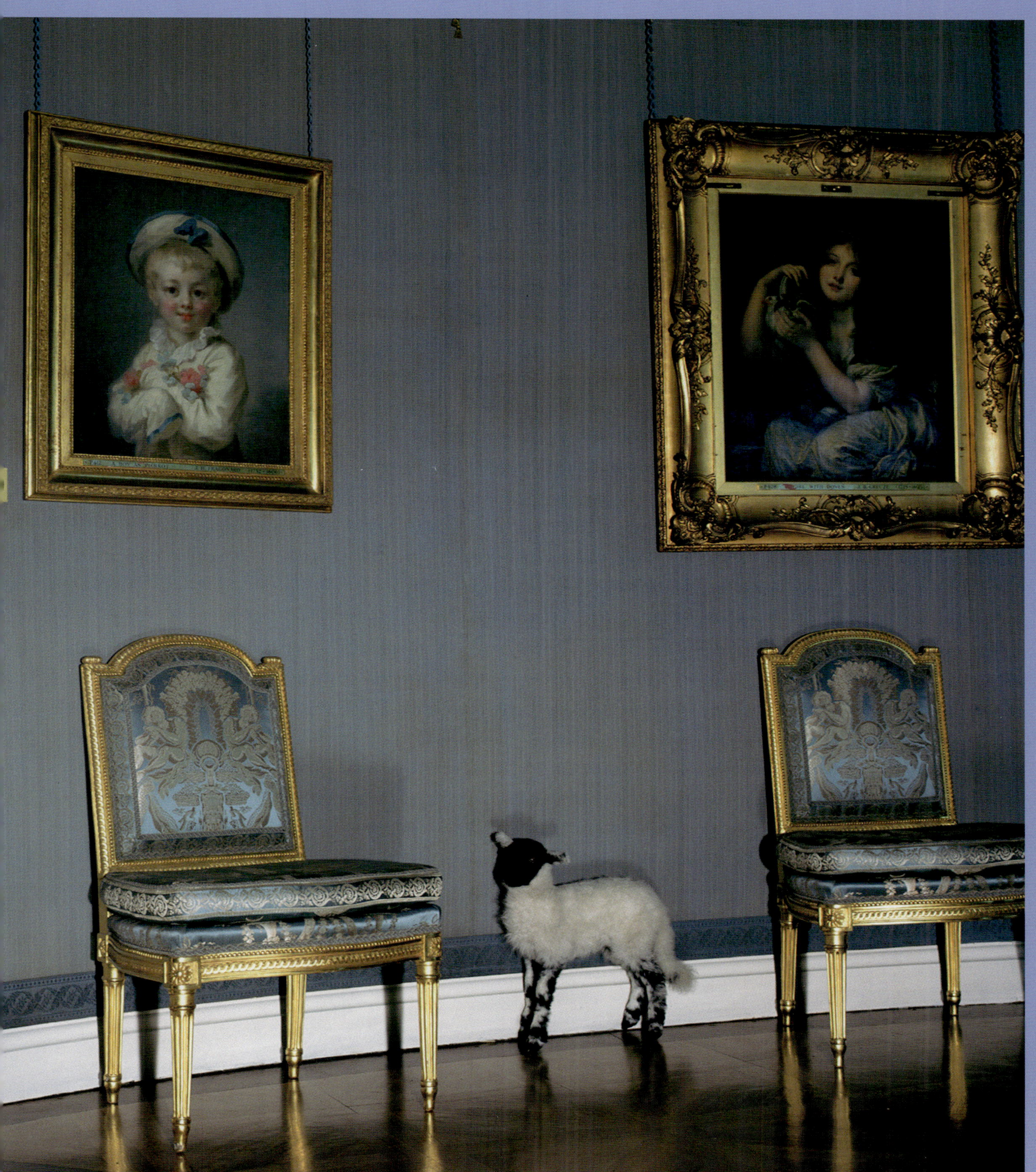

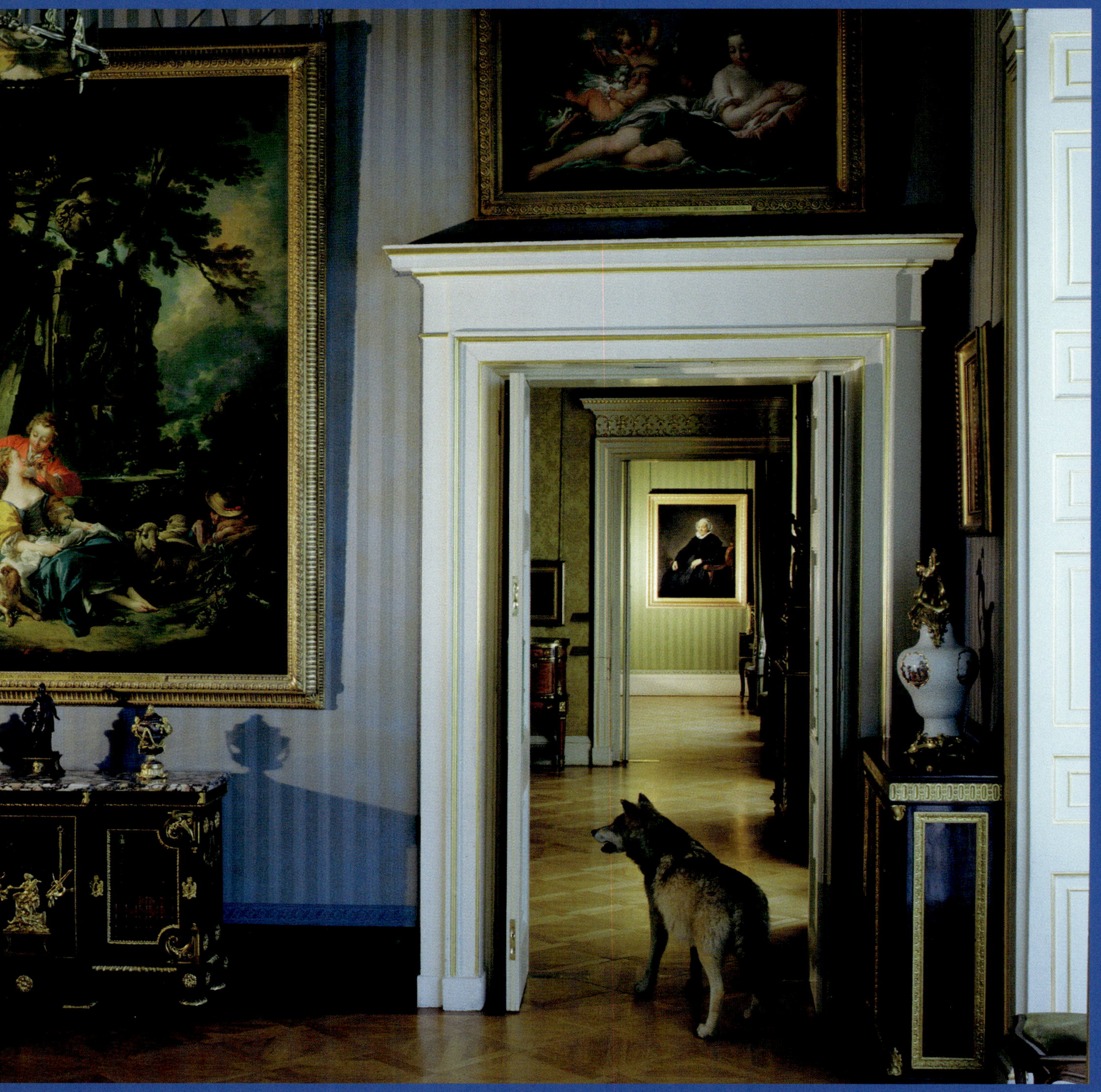

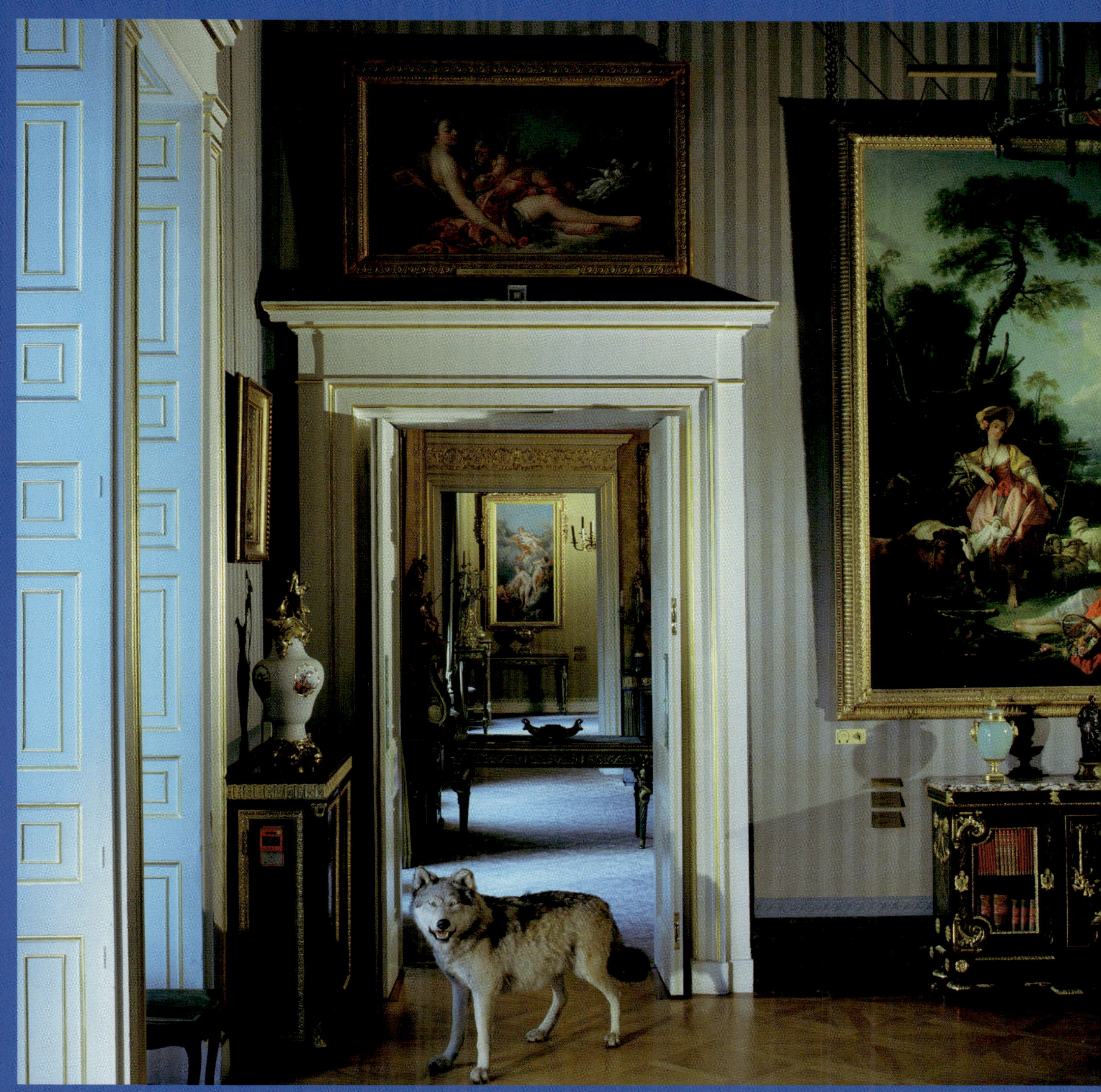

Where Have All the Sparrows Gone?

David Campany

Museum and Medium: The Time of Karen Knorr's Imagery

The encounter between two disciplines doesn't take place when one begins to reflect on another, but when one discipline realises that it has to resolve, for itself and by its own means, a problem similar to one confronted by the other.
Gilles Deleuze [1]

Like the mutilated classical statue, a photograph seems to result from the artwork's encounter with a scythe of real time, showing the bruise imprinted upon an artwork by a clash with a time not its own.
Denis Hollier [2]

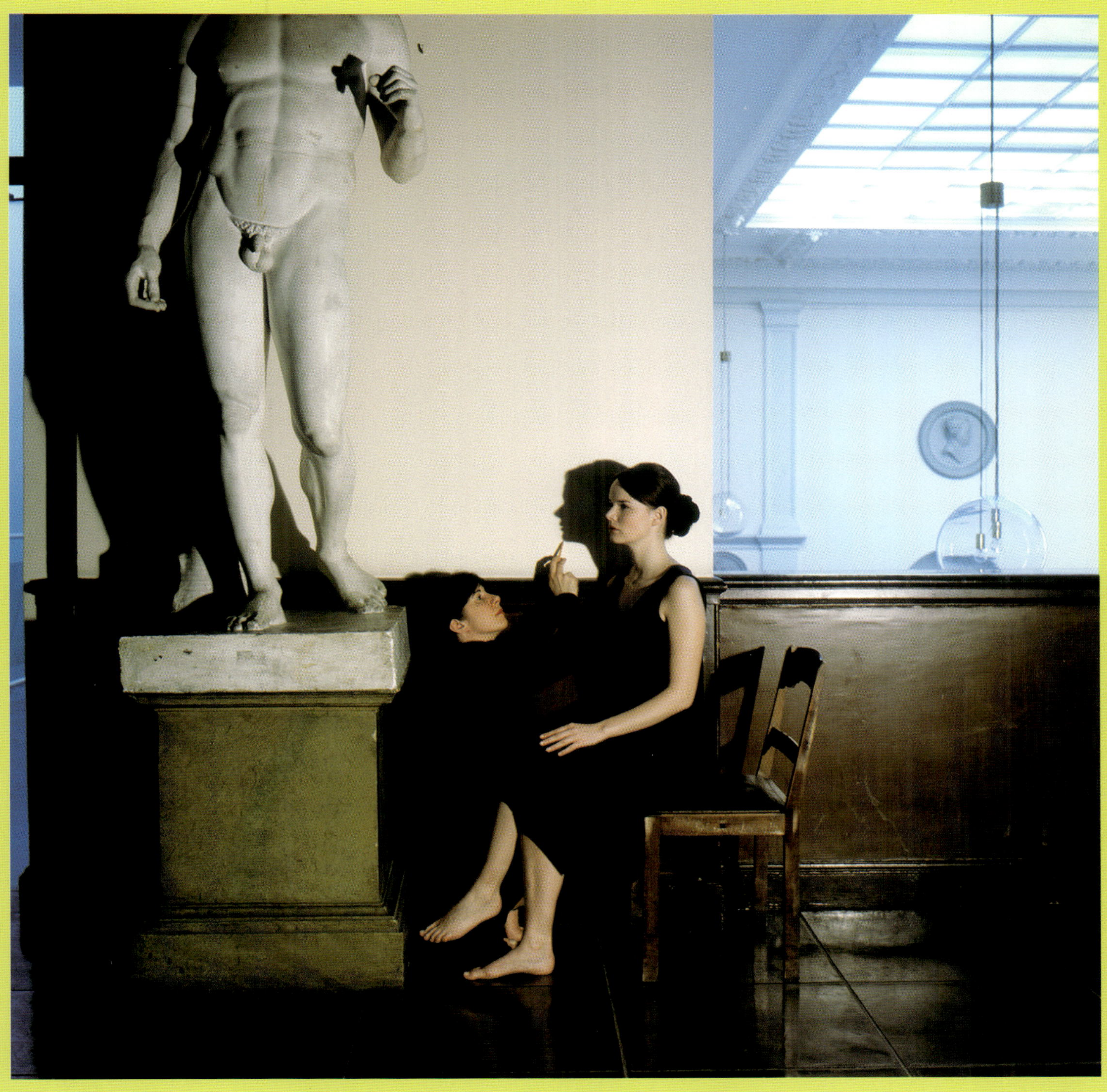

Butades' Daughter

Karen Knorr's photography isn't particularly easy to think about. It seems easier to think *with* it or *through* it. That is, with or through its subject matter. There is so much to think about within the images, that the images themselves become elusive. We cannot see the wood for the trees. Yet her images are in many ways particularly photographic. I think this reveals itself through their way with time. It wouldn't be quite right to say that the *meaning* of Knorr's images is a complex experience of time, but the layers of possibility within them are inextricably linked to their temporal character. So what I have to say here isn't so much a free-standing account of Knorr's photography as a speculation on the time structures that allow the images to mean whatever they mean.

I shall start with the past. Karen Knorr's work deals with cultural heritage. This has been her most continuous theme since the late 1970s. She deals with taste, power and histories older than photography. She looks at how the culture and ideology of conservatism seek definition. She looks at how they seek this in a past that sometimes never really was. This is why the museum, which constructs a representation of the past from the ideological needs of the present, recurs throughout her work as a theatre for making photographs. Within this theatre she photographs, among other things, works of art. This is a practice with its own long and complicated lineage. Indeed the photography of art has a pedigree as old as photography itself. Consider this short list:
A crumbling facade of Queen's College, Oxford; an elevated view of a Parisian boulevard; four shelves of China pottery; three shelves of glassware; a bust of Patroclus; an open door with a broom; a leaf of a plant; two shelves of books; a printed page of text; a haystack; a lithographic print; the bridge of Orleans;

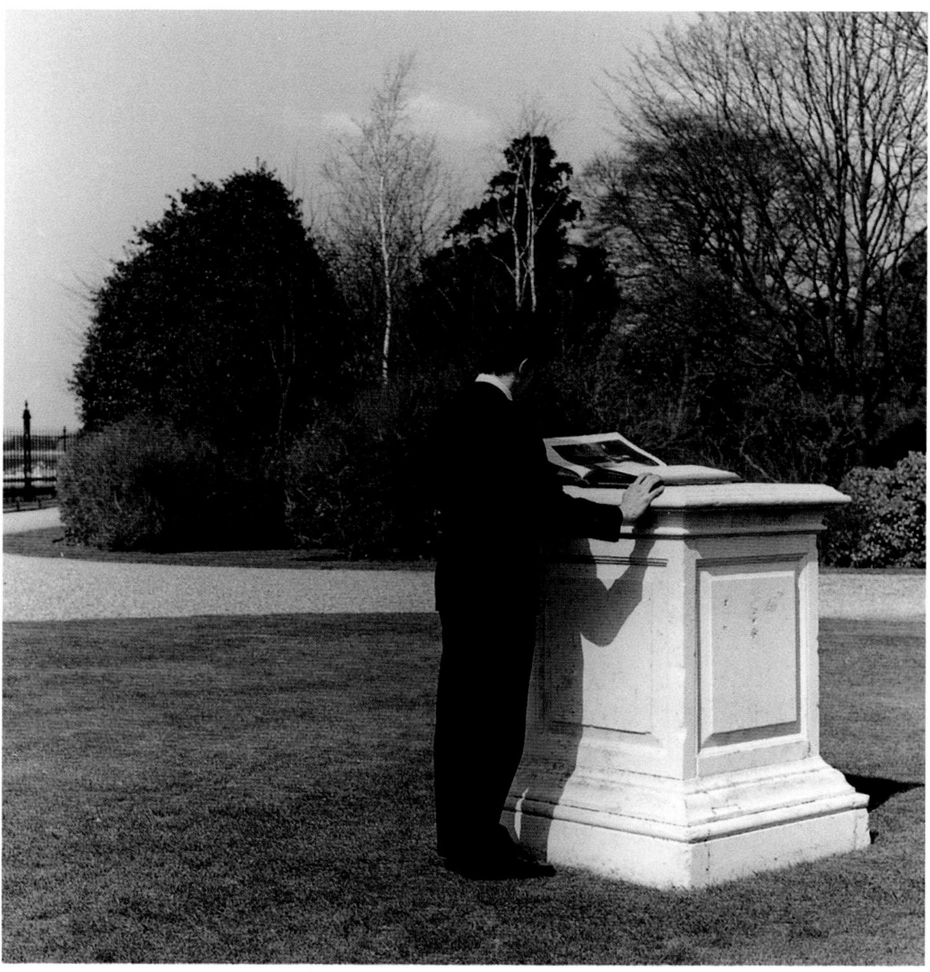

Analytical Inquiry into the Principles of Taste
1983

Queen's College Oxford again; three men and a ladder; Lacock Abbey; Lacock Abbey, again; the bust of Patroclus, again; Christchurch College, Oxford; Lacock Abbey again; some lace; The Martyr's Monument, Oxford; Westminster Abbey, a drawing of Hagar in the Desert; an arrangement of fruit.

This is an itinerary not too far removed from Knorr's own subject matter. No doubt the repetition of Lacock Abbey alerts the reader to the figure of William Henry Fox Talbot. In fact it is a list of the subjects that comprise his book *The Pencil of Nature* from the 1840s, a publication that aimed to outline possible uses for the medium. The list has a remarkable variety. In plotting out a range of potential applications of his technique, Fox Talbot anticipates so many of the ways in which the photographic was eventually exploited. Documentary, architecture, topography, tourism, modern publishing, advertising, taxonomy and modern art history are all 'pencilled' in here, in their nascent states. The abundance of artefacts and commodities before Fox Talbot's camera is in part a consequence of his class and social standing. As an educated man of means, he photographs what he owns, where he travels and what interests him. On top of this, such artefacts are inanimate and portable, which means they keep still and can be placed in the light (considerable advantages for early photography). But perhaps there is more at stake in the recurrence of art and artefacts in the list. Why might a photograph of an artwork be so well disposed to 'demonstrating' the medium?

A provisional answer might be that it allows two versions of time to clash–the time of the artefact and the time of the medium of photography. In clashing they emphasise each other's particular characteristics. The answer is provisional because the reality is more complicated. For example, it could be said that all photography clashes with a time not its own. It brings a moment into another moment. We might also say that any artefact clashes with a time not its own in so far as it is a representation. Moreover an artefact might be further wrapped in other times by the activities of collecting, exchange, display and so on. Still, there is some truth in the provisional response, for when media are made to clash they tend to suppress their own internal complexities in order to offer up the more obvious differences to each other. We tie ourselves up in knots attempting to define 'painting', or 'sculpture' or 'photography' in isolation, and opt for the ease with which media appear to clarify themselves through comparison. Perhaps only much later are we able to grasp–or in Karen Knorr's case, *stage*–the problematics within and between media at the same time. But let me keep things simple for a while longer.

Very early on art photography had a spell of a few decades in which it took up artworks as subject matter. These were decades before the understanding of all art came to be percolated through mass reproduction. In the 1850s and 1860s the photography of artworks was a recognised genre of art photography. Interpretive expression of the essence or spirit of the artwork was the aim.[3] Artistic photography and the photography of art were not mutually exclusive. It was a rich, strange and frustratingly brief period, cut short when art history was rationalised and expanded by the more utilitarian and artless deployment of photography as publicity. The photography of art soon became so ubiquitous that it began to mask rather than reveal the character of both artwork and photograph. Modern art history established itself by using photography mechanistically. It exploited the photograph's powers of description and reproduction to give us the slide lecture, the catalogue, the journal, the monograph, the popular print and the portable history. It isn't a coincidence that the great and false battle over the 'soul' of art photography, the battle between the painterly and the 'straight' image that replaced that earlier hybrid moment, took place against the becoming mass, the becoming popular through reproduction of the art of the past. All that uncertainty

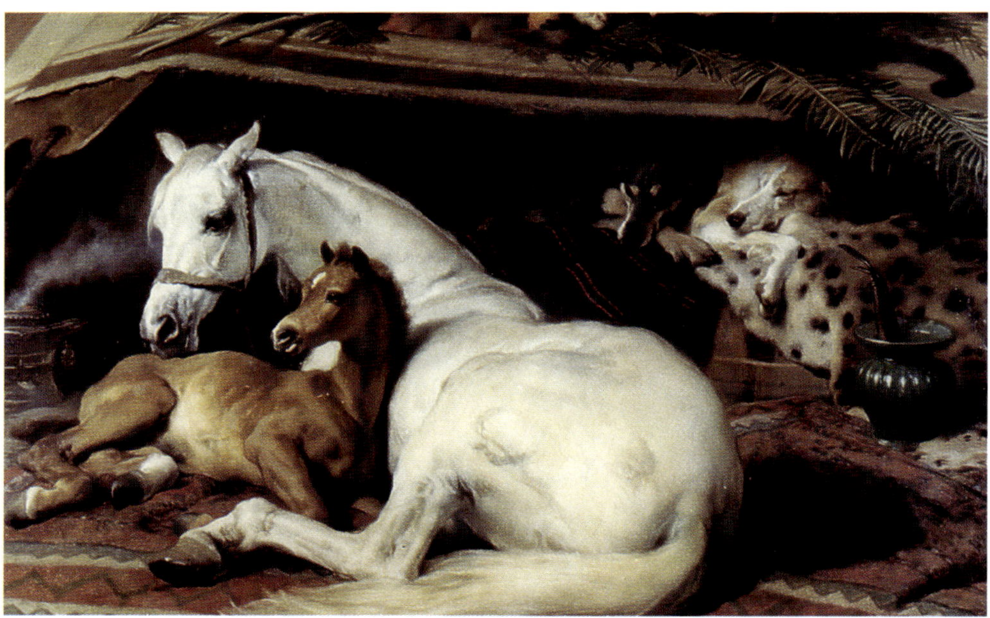

Edwin Landseer
The Arab Tent
1866

as to whether art photography should mimic painting's crafted singularity or Modernity's multiplicity was in effect a consequence of the fundamental shift in understanding of the very category of 'art' itself that was wrought by mass reproduction. Photography became art firstly as homage, then as imitation of the painterly and eventually became modern only within this new concept of art that was tacitly organised and regulated by reproduction. Since then photography has had two roles in modern art history: as an art itself, and as a mute, nameless mediator of all art. This of course puts it schematically. These aren't so much roles as *poles* of the general tension between the photograph's objectivity and its subjectivity. On the one hand art photography has always negotiated with the utilitarian aspects of the medium, and on the other the photography of art regularly has its utility undermined by accusations of partiality. The ambiguities of Knorr's photographs derive from this polarity. Somehow we expect a photograph of an artwork to function as a record of it. We expect it to be trustworthy and silent, and there certainly is this aspect to her photographs–they do tell us what artworks look like and what particular museum installations looked like.Yet at the same time–but with a different *relation* to time–the images are not just objective but critical. This is because they are themselves artworks. They are put back into the spaces and discourses of art.

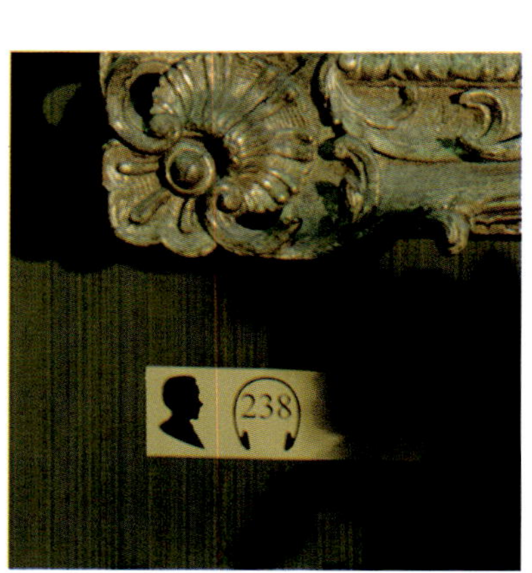

In the Green Room
2001
(detail)

Knorr's photography stages the clashing of times in very specific ways, although to my mind the results are far from specific. In general, the art of the twentieth century is not present 'in' her work. With rare exceptions the artworks described or contained in her ouevre predate photography. This has three consequences. It gives both the photography and the subject matter space to breath before they come to 'clash' with each other. It gives the images a deceptively simple entry point (on some level photographs are always easy to look at). It also means Knorr neatly leapfrogs all those bad infinities and arguments about copies of copies that so preoccupy more excitable speculations about reproduction.

Much art of the twentieth century, concerned as it was with the 'nature' of art and conceived wholly within the time and the aegis of the modern art museum, was either aspiring to unattainable timelessness (for example, abstract expressionist painting) or bouncing around with ecstasy or horror (usually both) in the excesses of industrial image multiplication (for example, Pop Art). Knorr's work loops back to set up a dialogue far more complex than such rejection or repetition of the time of the museum. But it is not simply a dialogue 'with' the artworks she depicts. It is a dialogue with what the modern museum did with them for us, good or bad. It is a dialogue with the layers of time that build up on these works as surely as the dust is removed from them.

All of this begs some difficult questions. Can an artwork carry 'its time' with it like some kind of melancholic passport through all the trauma of displacement and historical change? The ideology of the museum encourages us to accept, or *expect* that a painting or a sculpture might be able to cling to a sense of time and place that is 'true' to it. As if we see it *in* the museum but not belonging *to* the museum. Can photography do this too? Or do we expect that photography, by taking on, by *assuming* the character of other times and places, keeps nothing for itself? Does it *have* a self to keep? Perhaps like the filmmaker Woody Allen's allegorical figure Zelig, it clings to nothing but the circumstance in which it finds itself. What happens then when photography clings to painting or sculpture? Onto what layer of time can it hold?

We can see now that a simple notion of 'clashing' is not really going to account for the complex registers of time in Karen Knorr's photographs. These images are temporal puzzles. Perhaps the allegories they speak, and speak of, are in the end only available to us through a more mute allegory of time. The late Roland Barthes once spoke of the *punctum*–a rare occurrence whereby a photographic detail or disposition might prick the viewer's consciousness and throw them out of the time of the image and into disjunction with their own unconscious, their own history. If I'm honest, I hadn't thought Knorr's photography would really allow for such inadvertencies of spectatorship. They appear so controlled. So conscious. Nevertheless standing before her image *In the Green Room* installed in the Wallace Collection in London, I was struck by a particular detail. Lurking below the frame of Fragonard's painting *The Swing* is a little sign, made up of two icons: a silhouette or shadow of a human profile, and a pair of headphones. It indicates that a spoken commentary on this painting is available. One may borrow a Walkman and be guided around the museum by a commentary in one's head. I hadn't paid much attention to these signs until I caught sight of this one in Knorr's photograph. In a rebus too dense to grasp fully, images and words raced through my mind: all those versions of 'The Origin of Painting' in which the cast shadow of a profile is traced on a wall... all those books in which photography is described as "the art of fixing a shadow"... all those reproductions of allegorical paintings in art history books accompanied by written elaboration of their half-defunct codes... memories of gallery visits watching people crane to read titles and descriptions... my own first use of such a headphone commentary which threw me into the time of the art but out of the social time of the museum. I was involuntarily fixed before *In the Green Room*. Not transfixed. The image didn't swallow me. It occupied my eyes while my mind went elsewhere momentarily. My vision and my knowledge were allegorised for me, by a detail that is not actually in Fragonard's painting (although it depends on it in some ways) but *is* in Knorr's photograph. At such moments one feels one's eyes both alive and dead at the same time. They are stimulated but not connected to a consciousness, like an automaton or a mannequin... or a stuffed bird.

We could see the presence of animals in some of Knorr's photographs as irruptions into the decorum of the museum. If they are, they are as much irruptions in time as space. For what is the time proper to an animal? They mock the distinction between ancient and modern. And their taxidermy mocks photography's ability to freeze things in time (a stuffed bird will look more alive in a photograph than anywhere else).

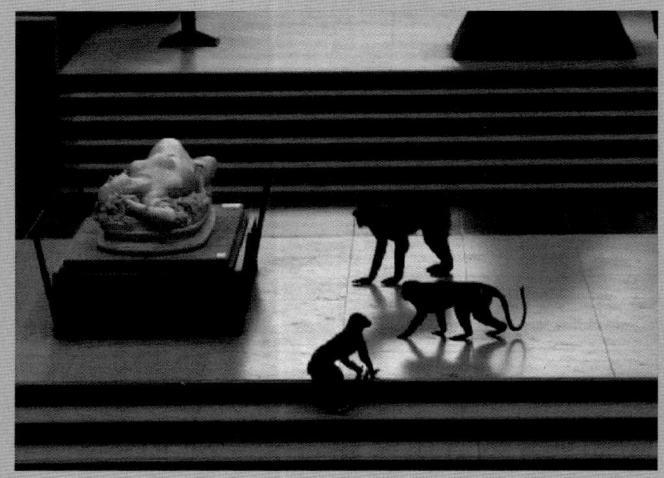
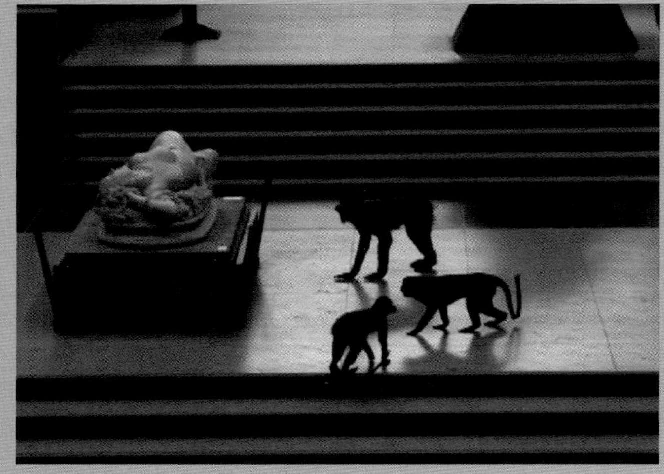
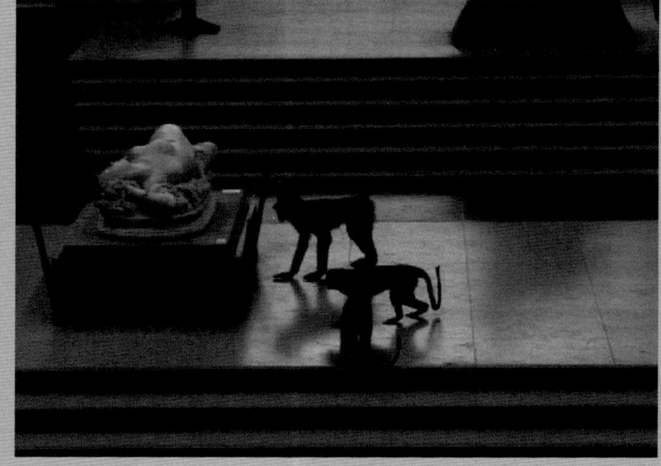
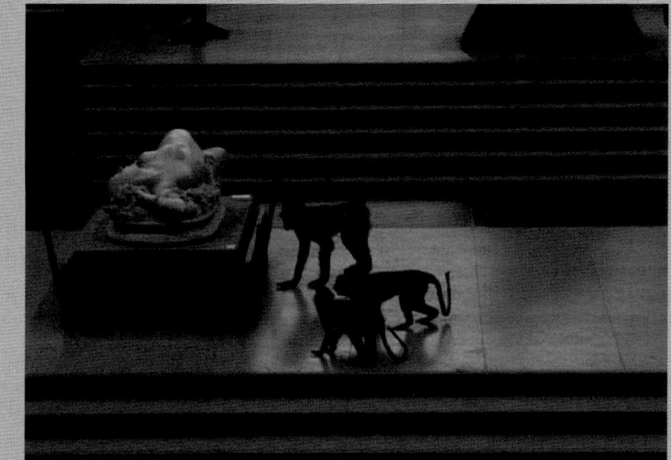

Visitors
(video stills)

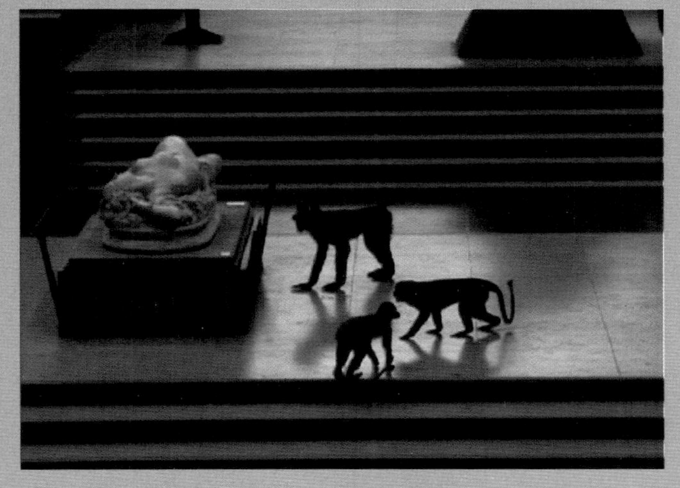
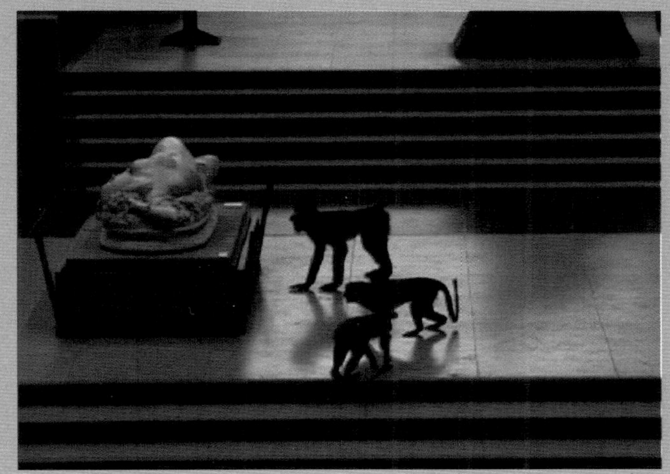
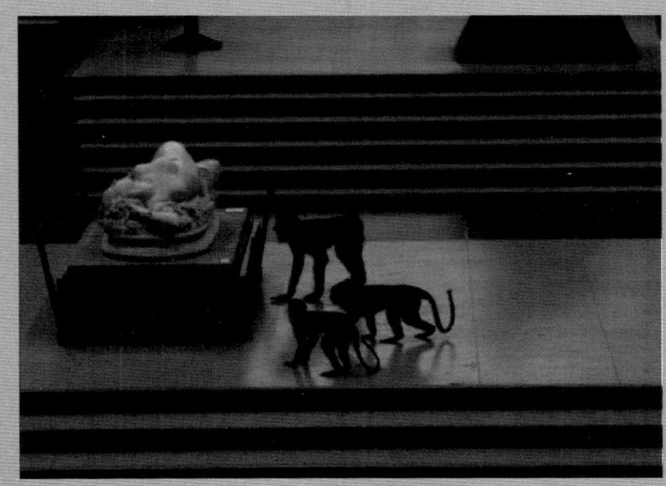
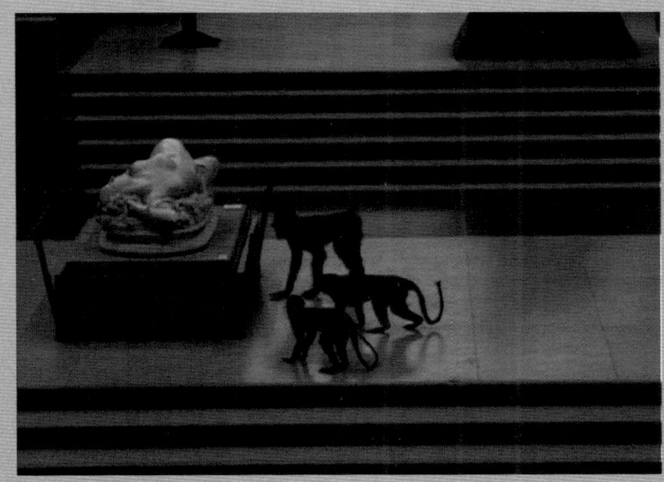

VI

Visitors

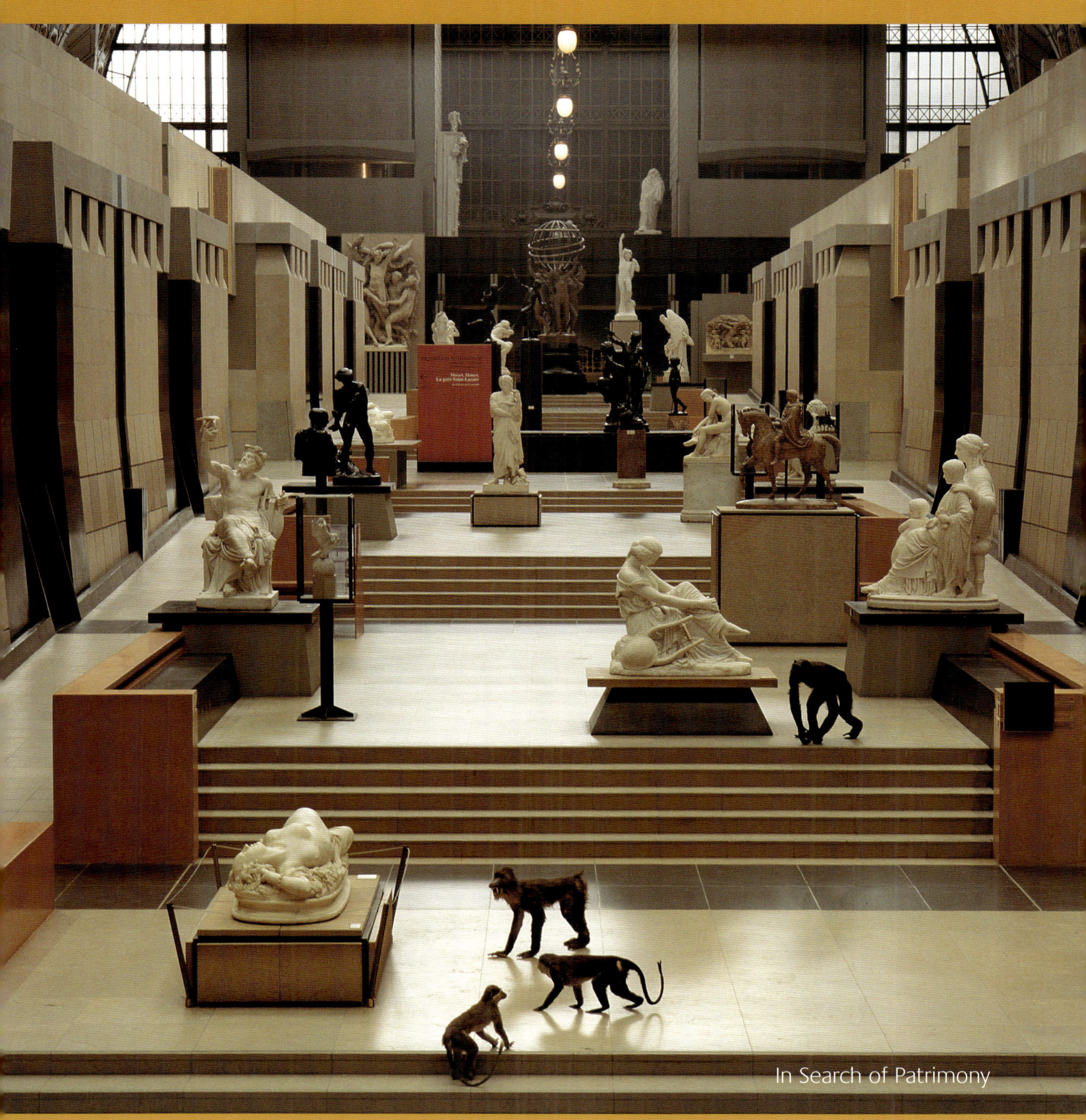

In Search of Patrimony

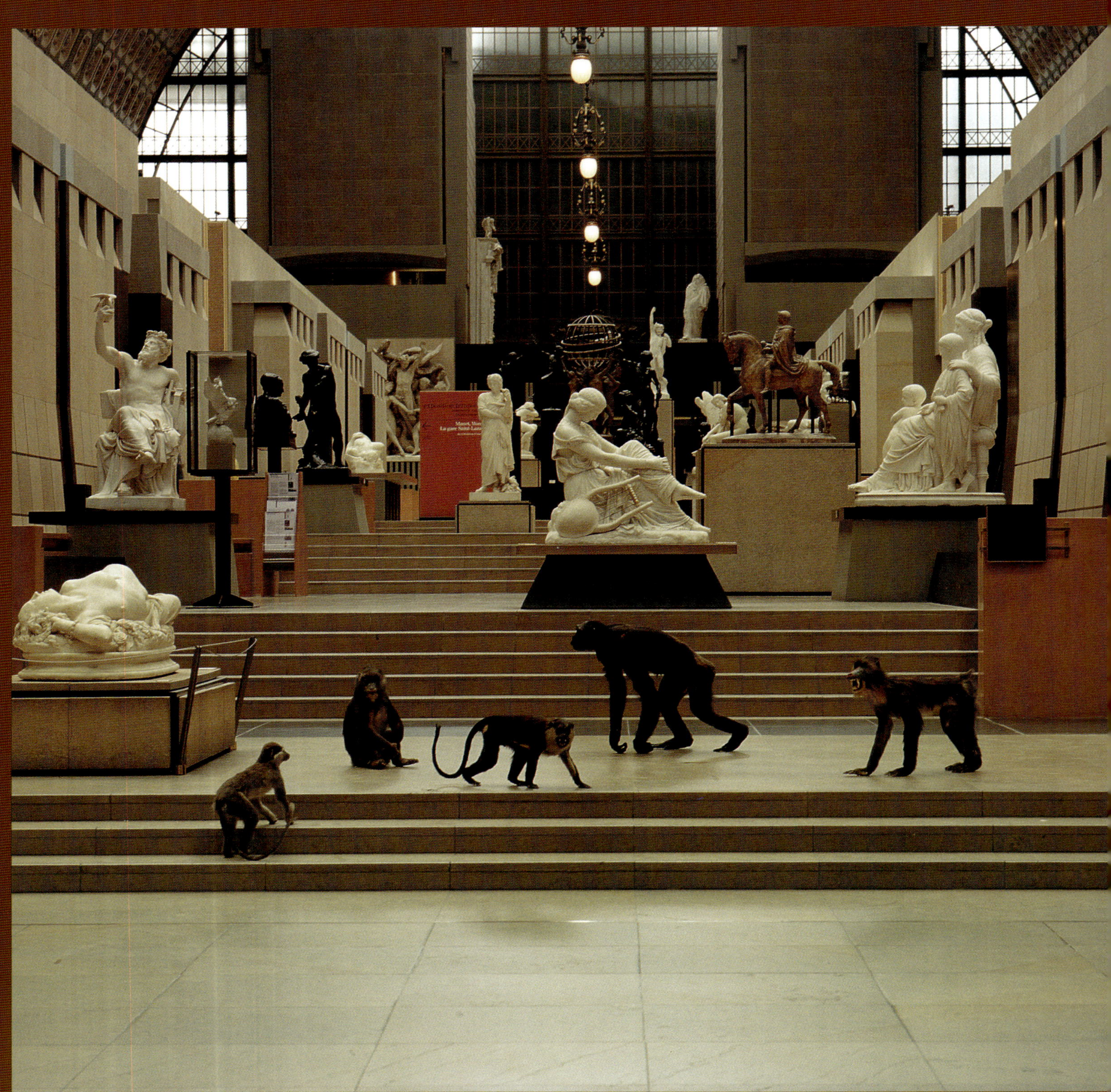

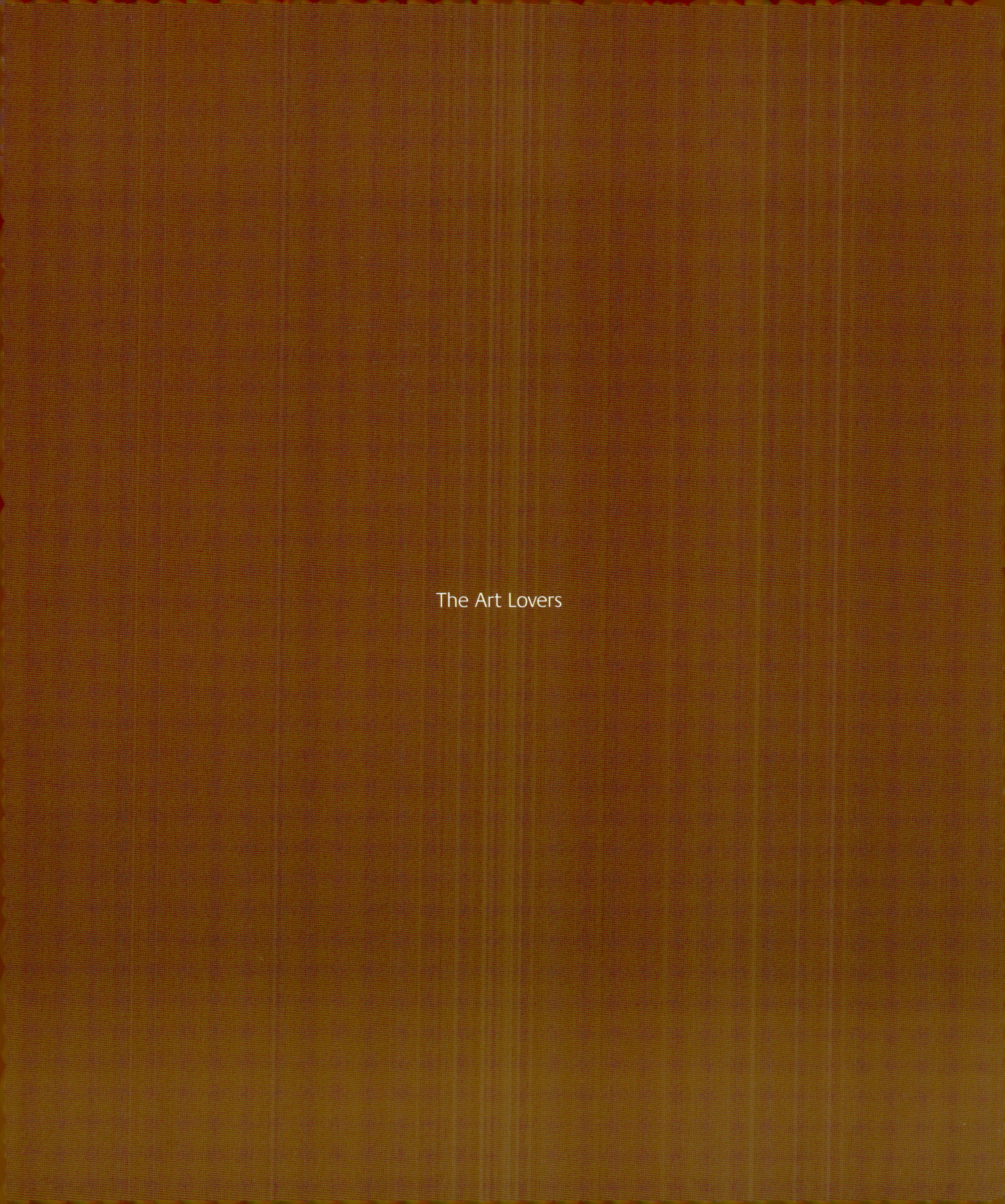

The Art Lovers

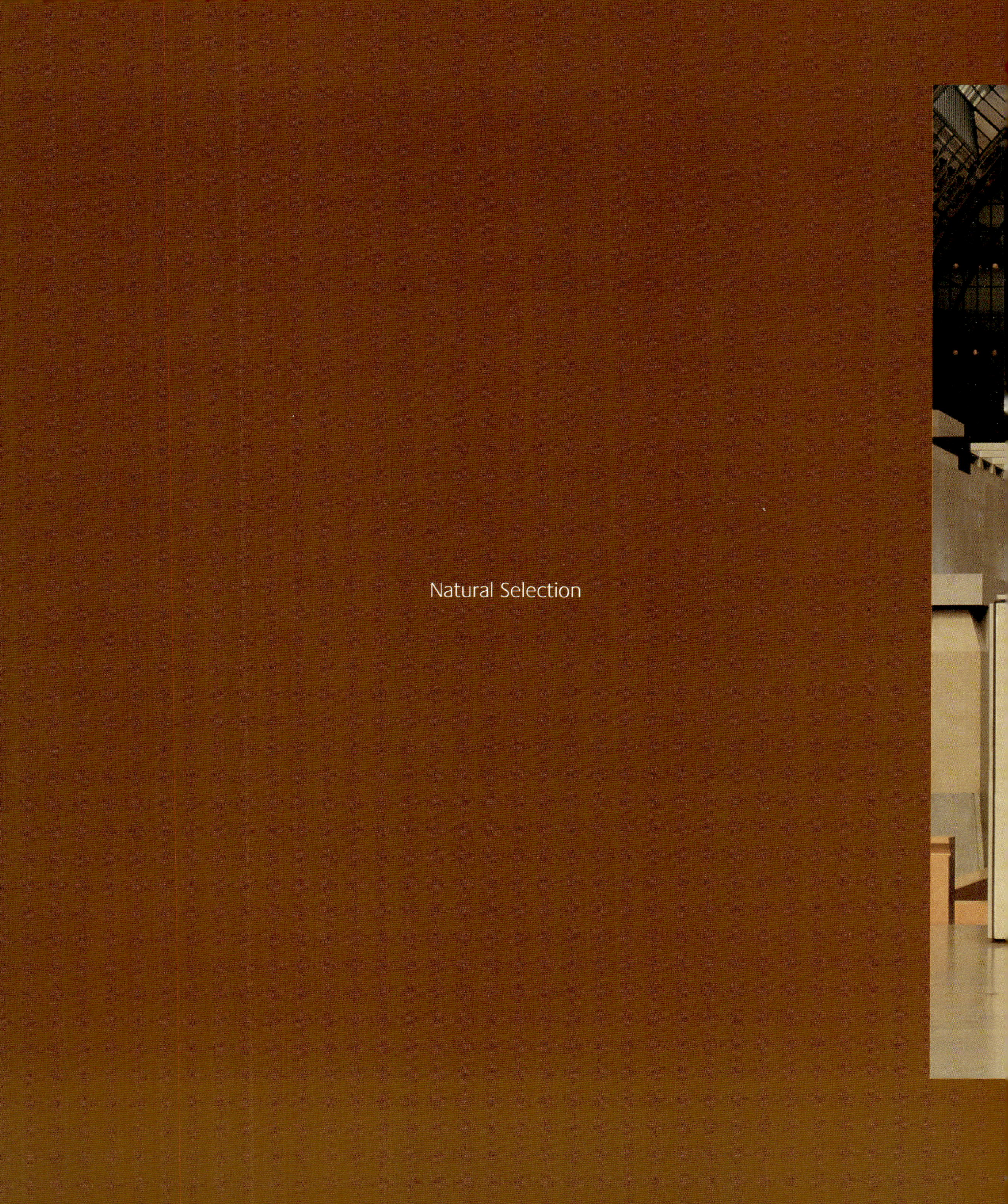
Natural Selection

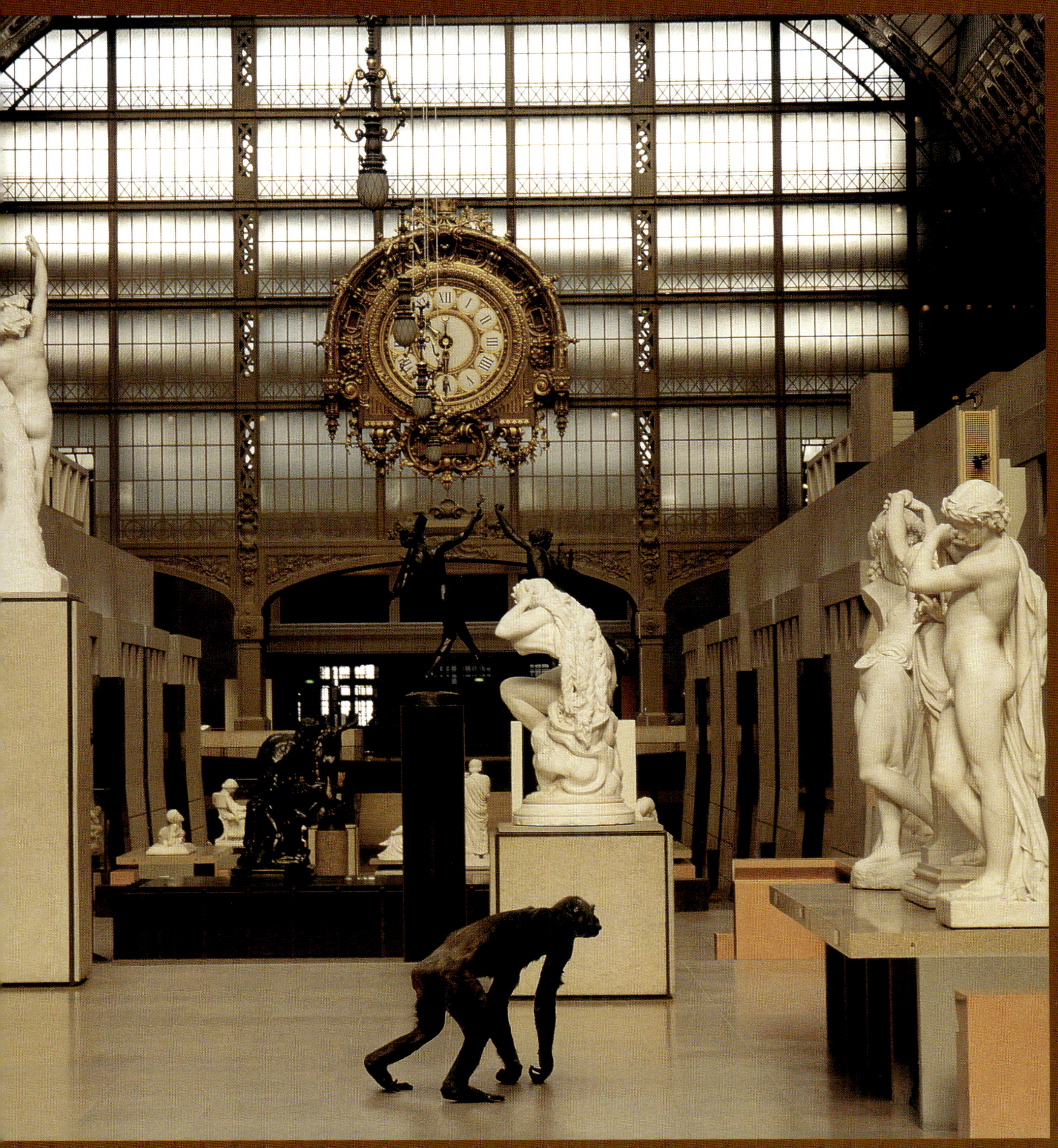

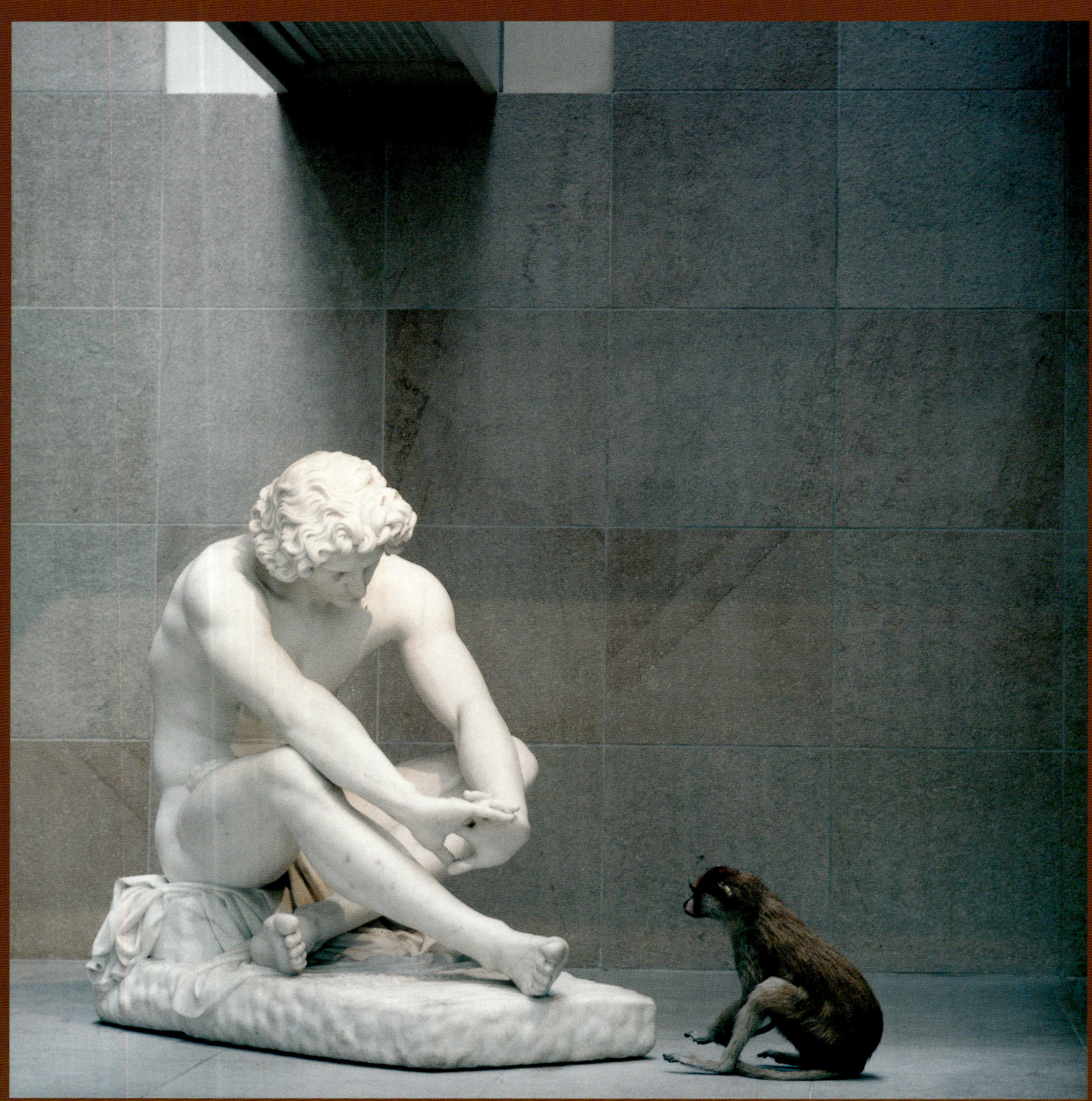

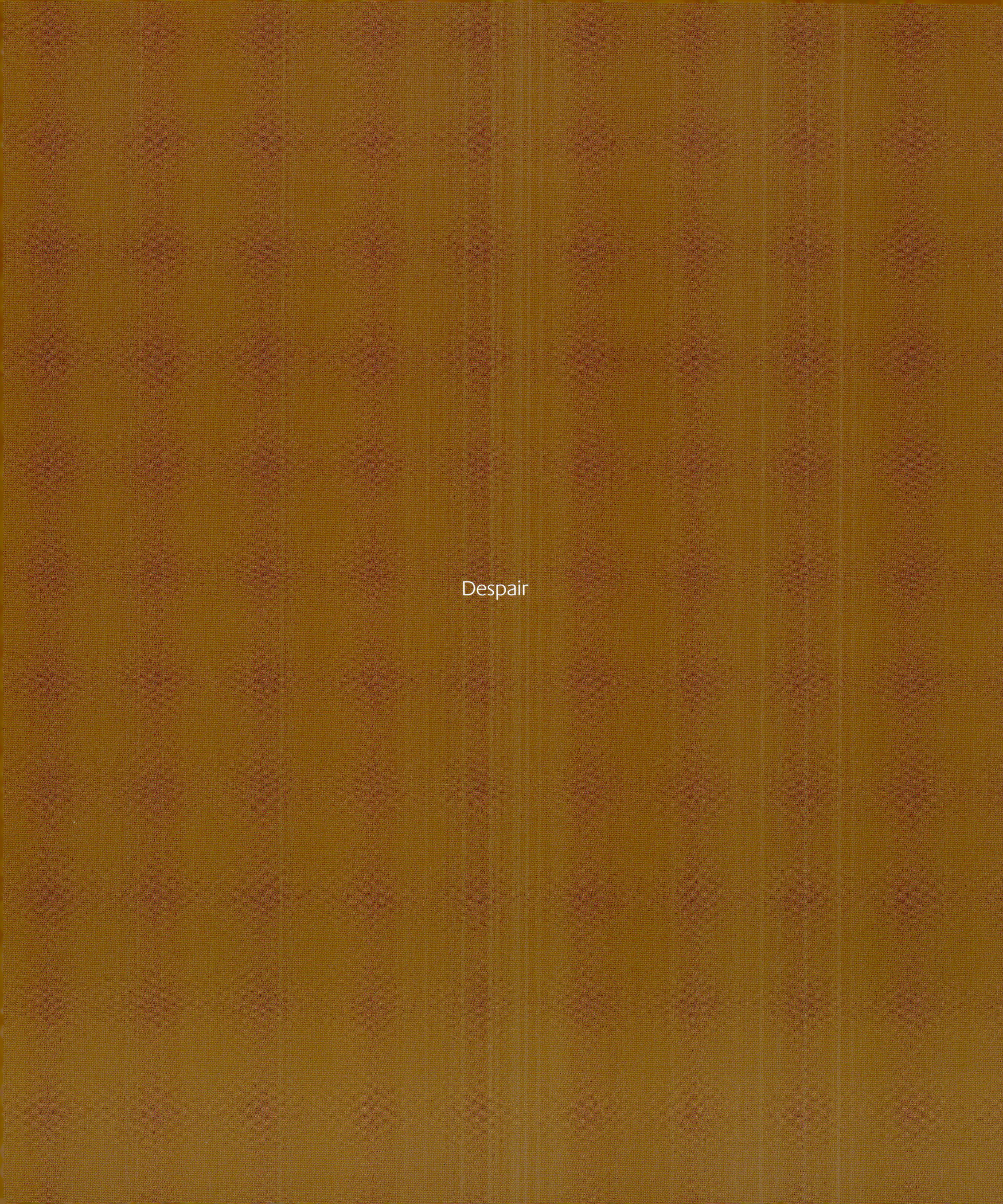

Despair

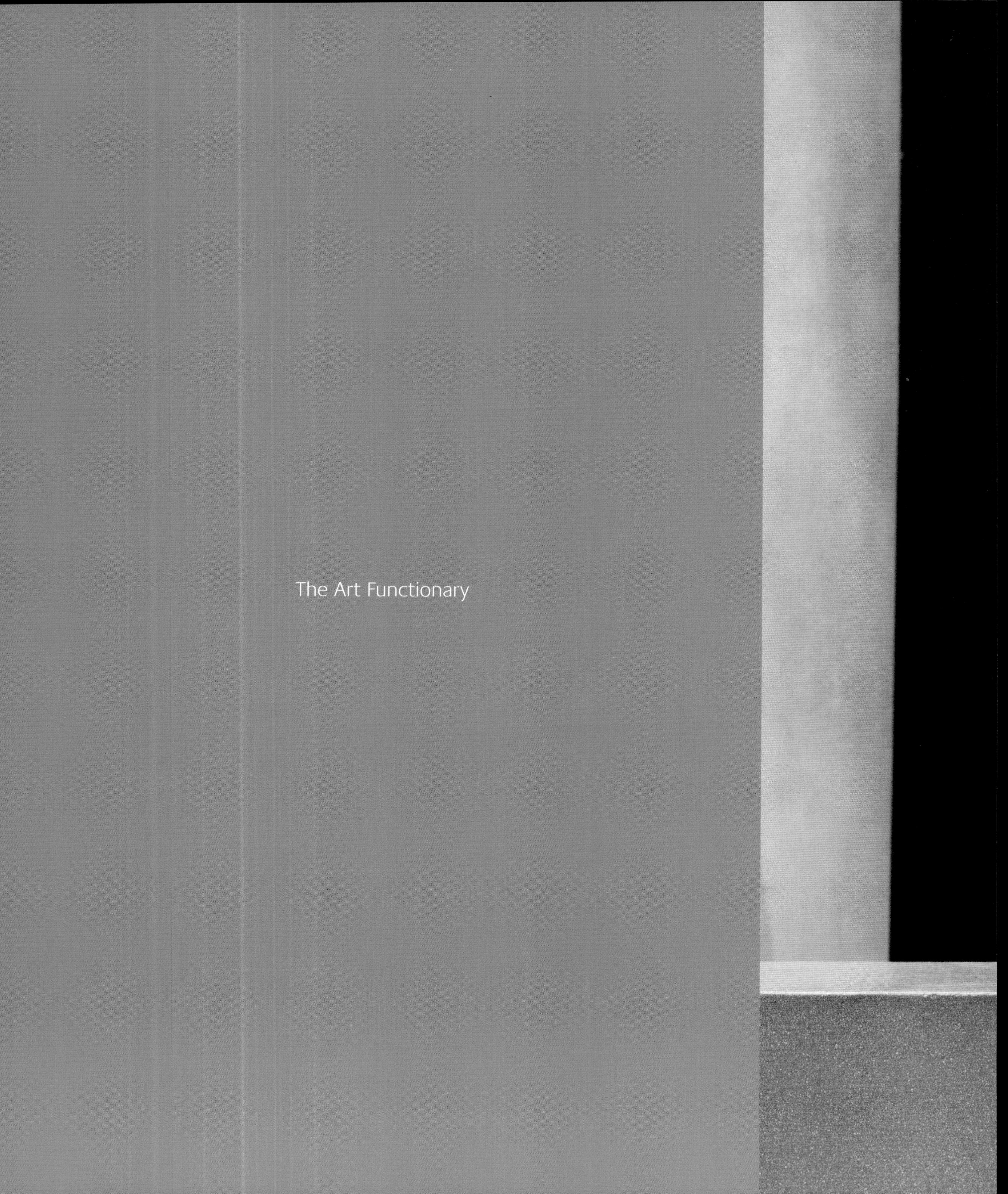
The Art Functionary

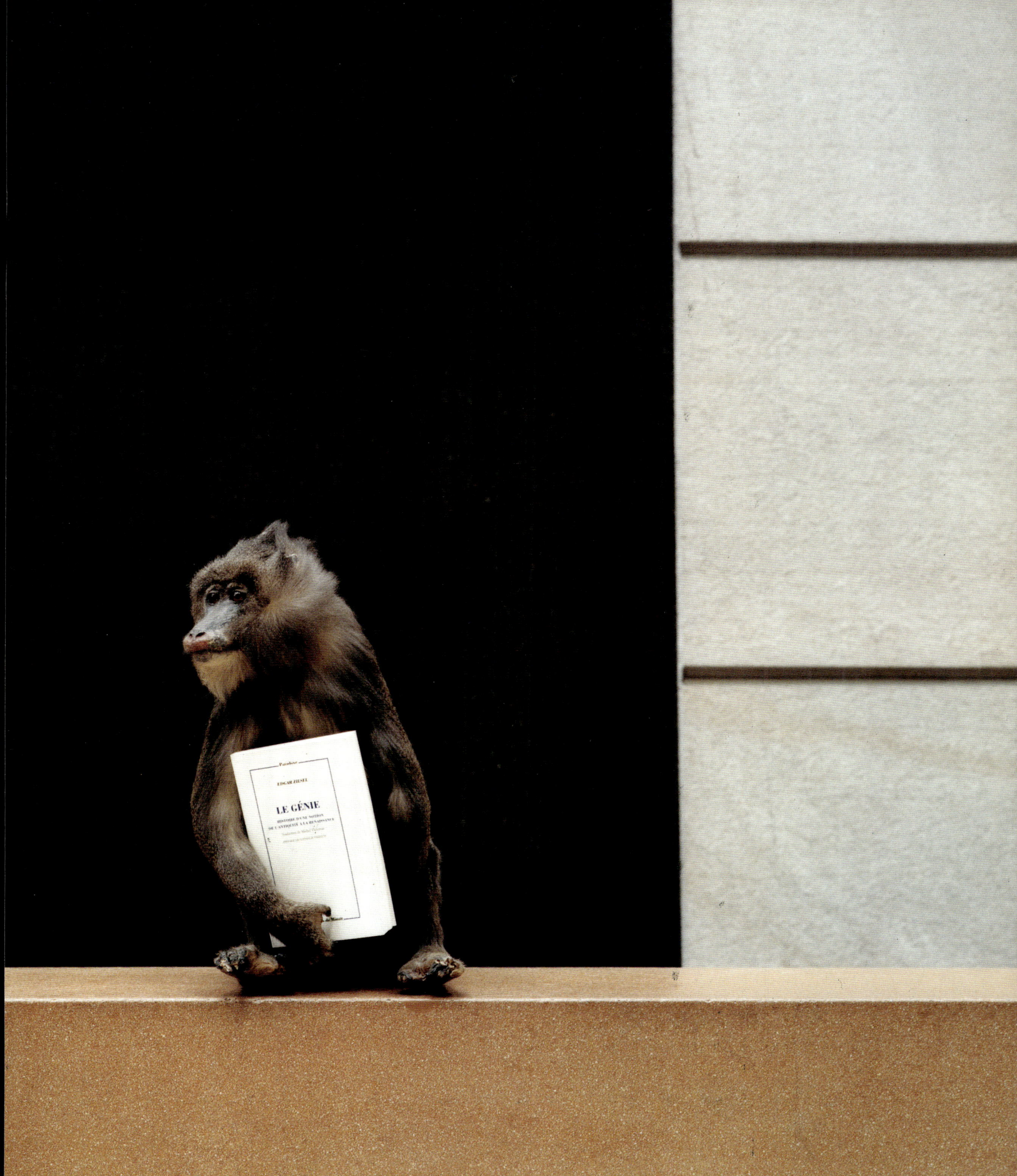
Paradoxe
EDGAR ZILSEL
LE GÉNIE
HISTOIRE D'UNE NOTION
DE L'ANTIQUITÉ À LA RENAISSANCE

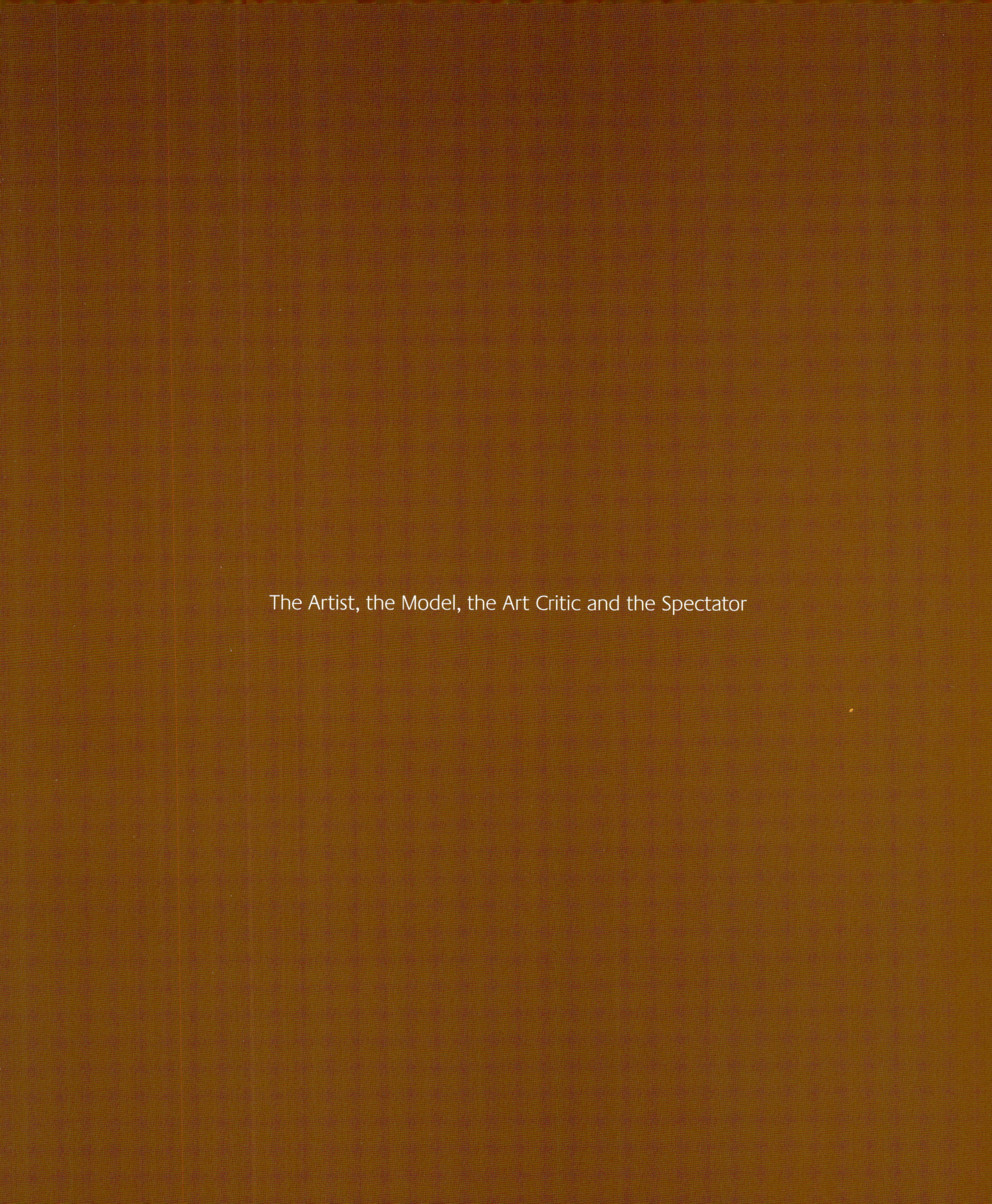

The Artist, the Model, the Art Critic and the Spectator

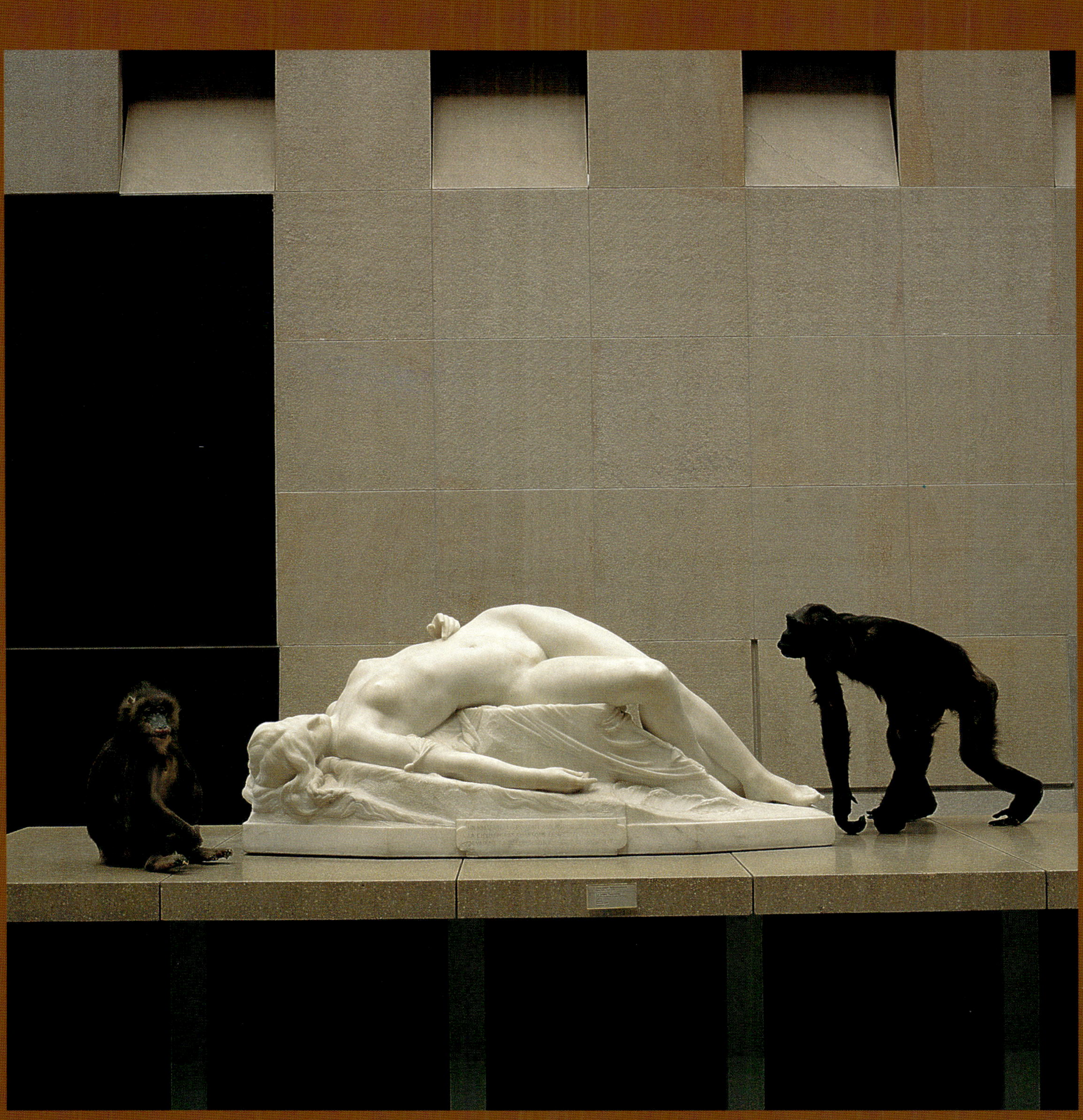

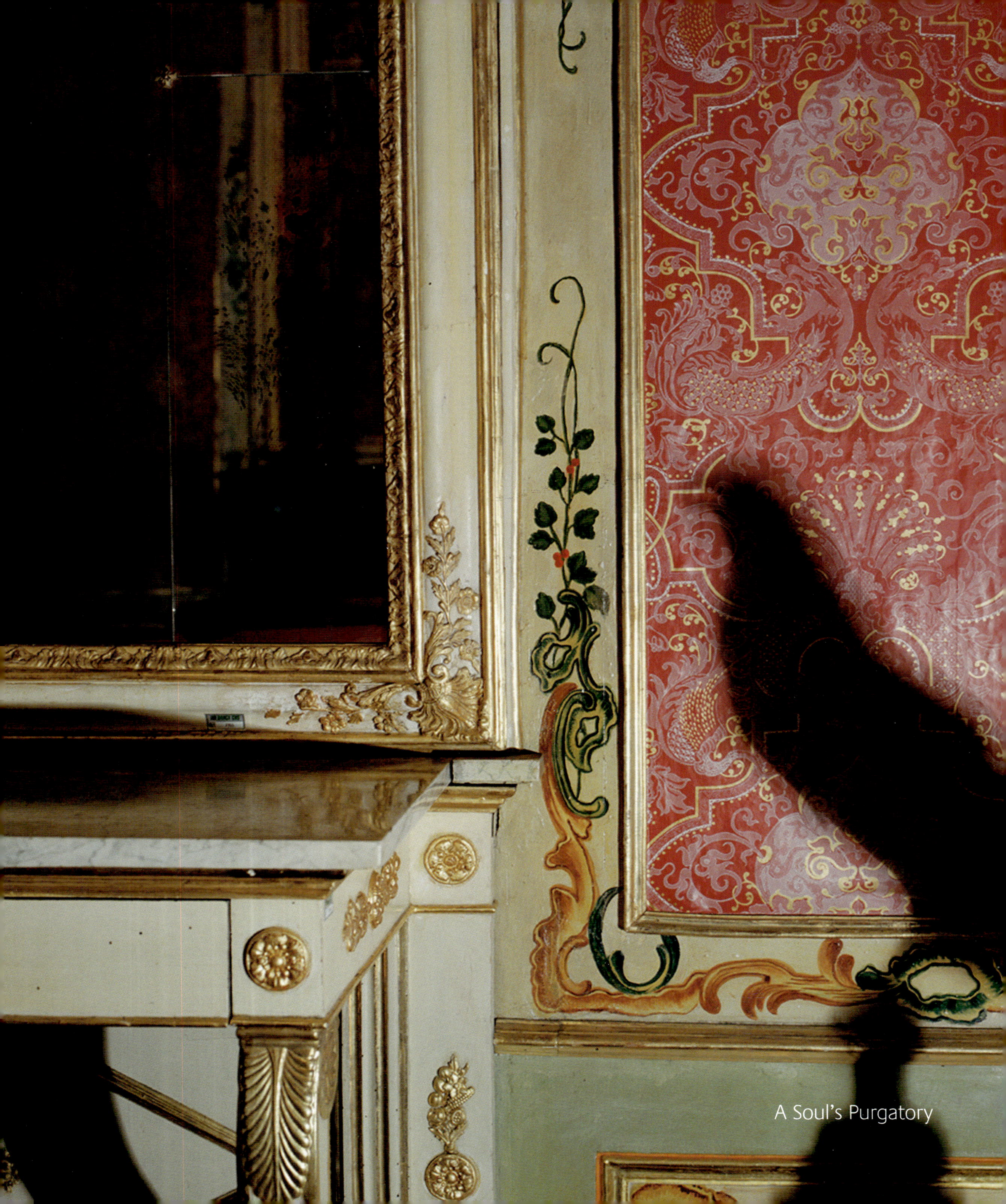

A Soul's Purgatory

VII

Spirits

Heaven on Earth

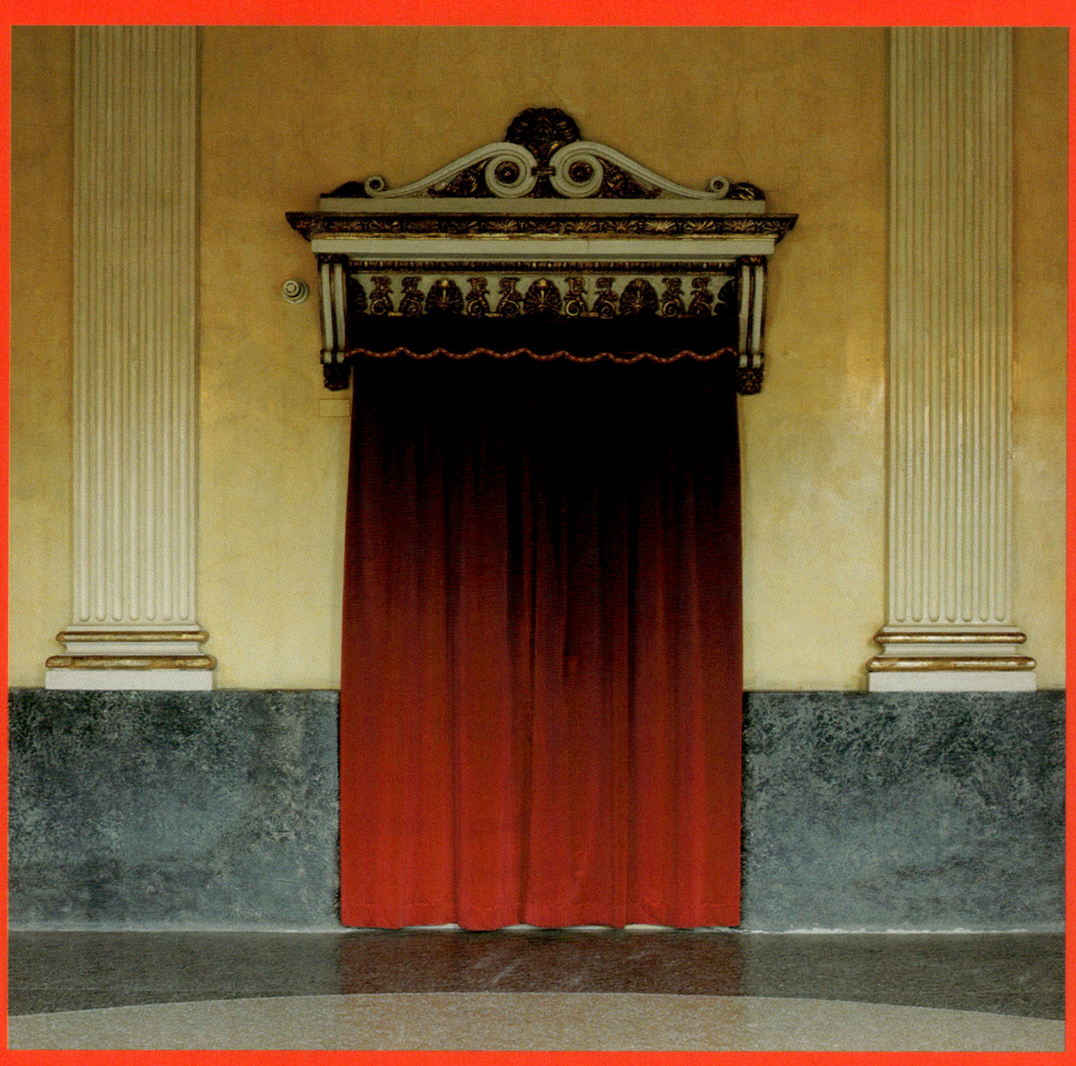

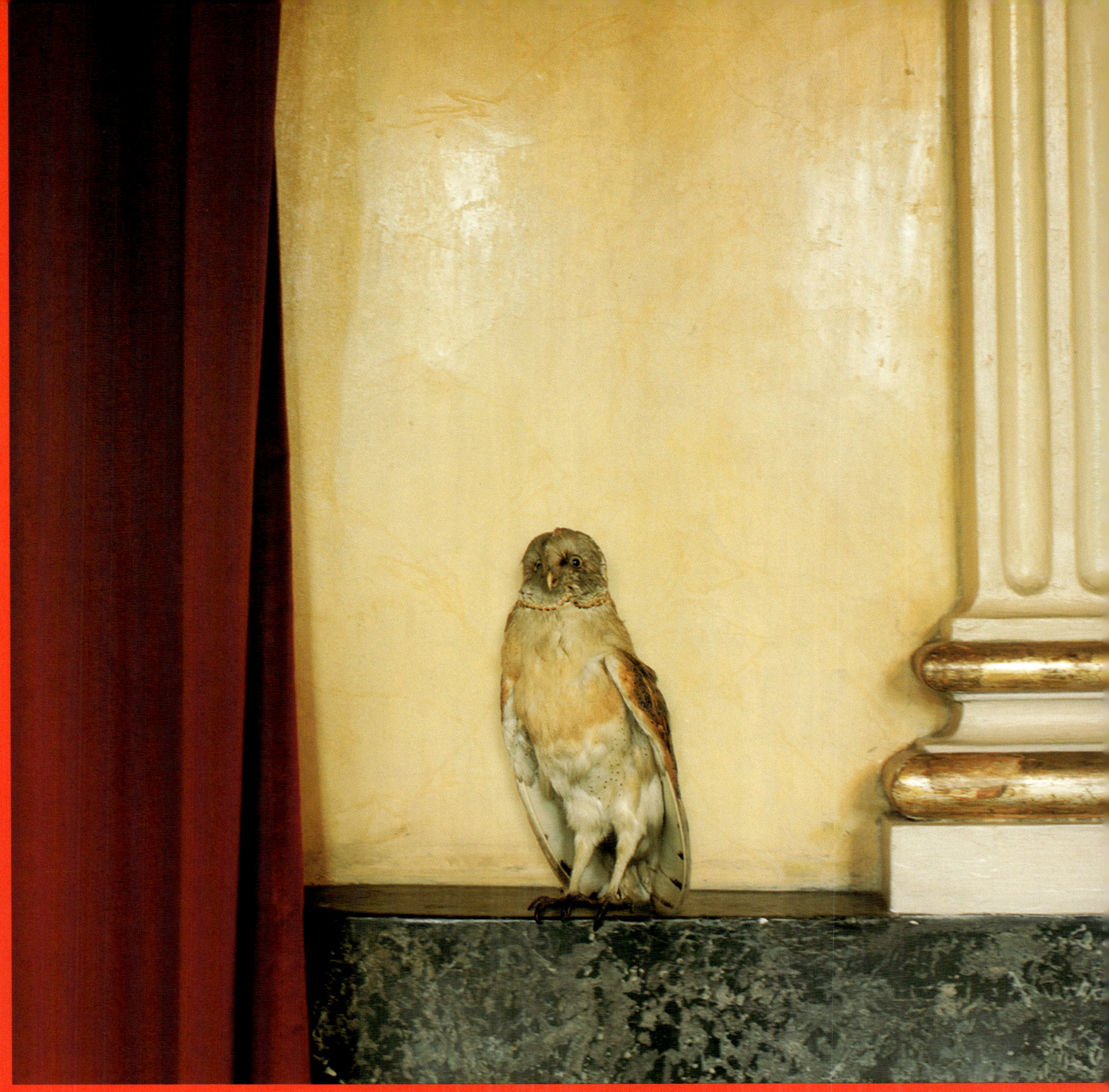

Annunciation

Transmigration of the Soul

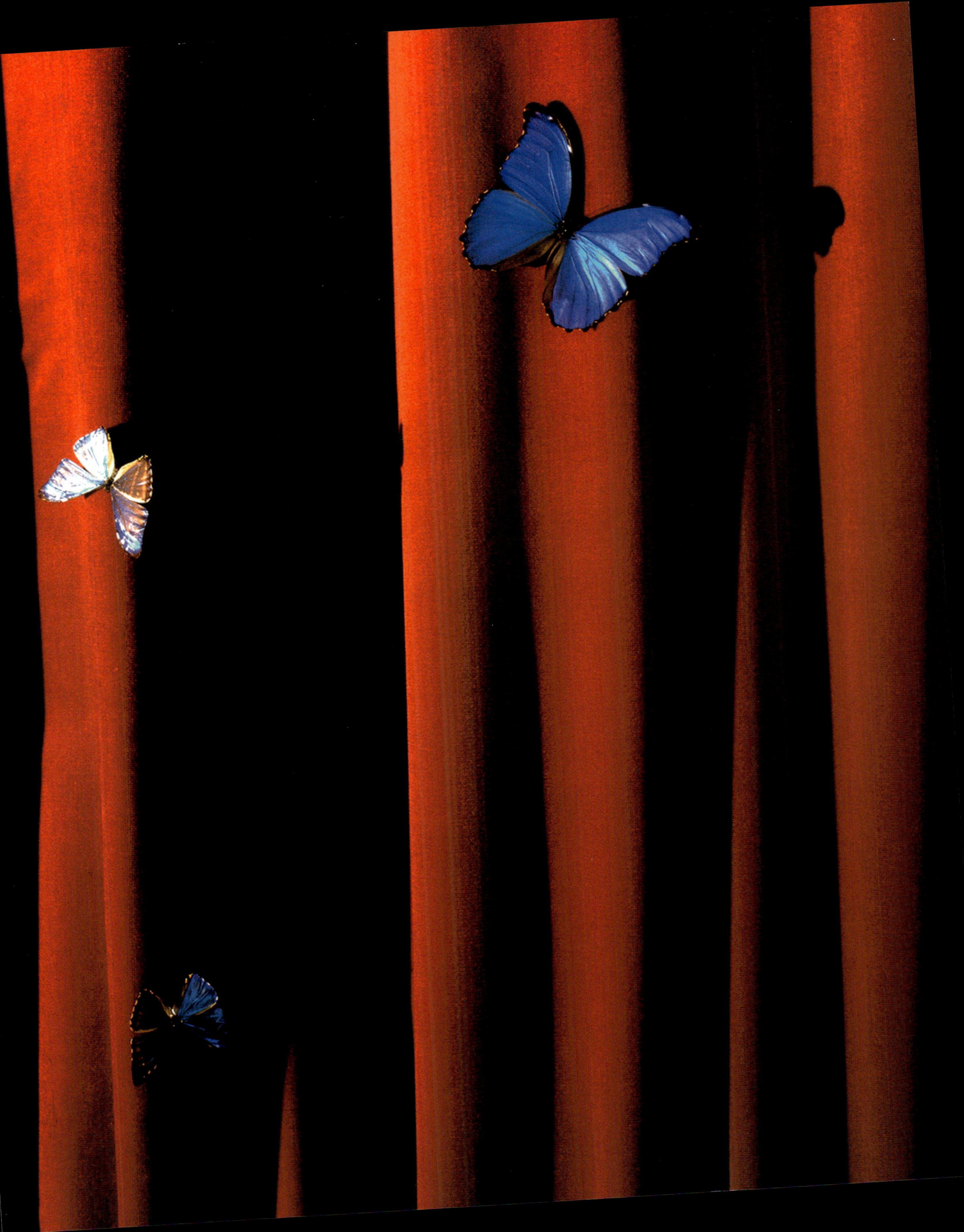

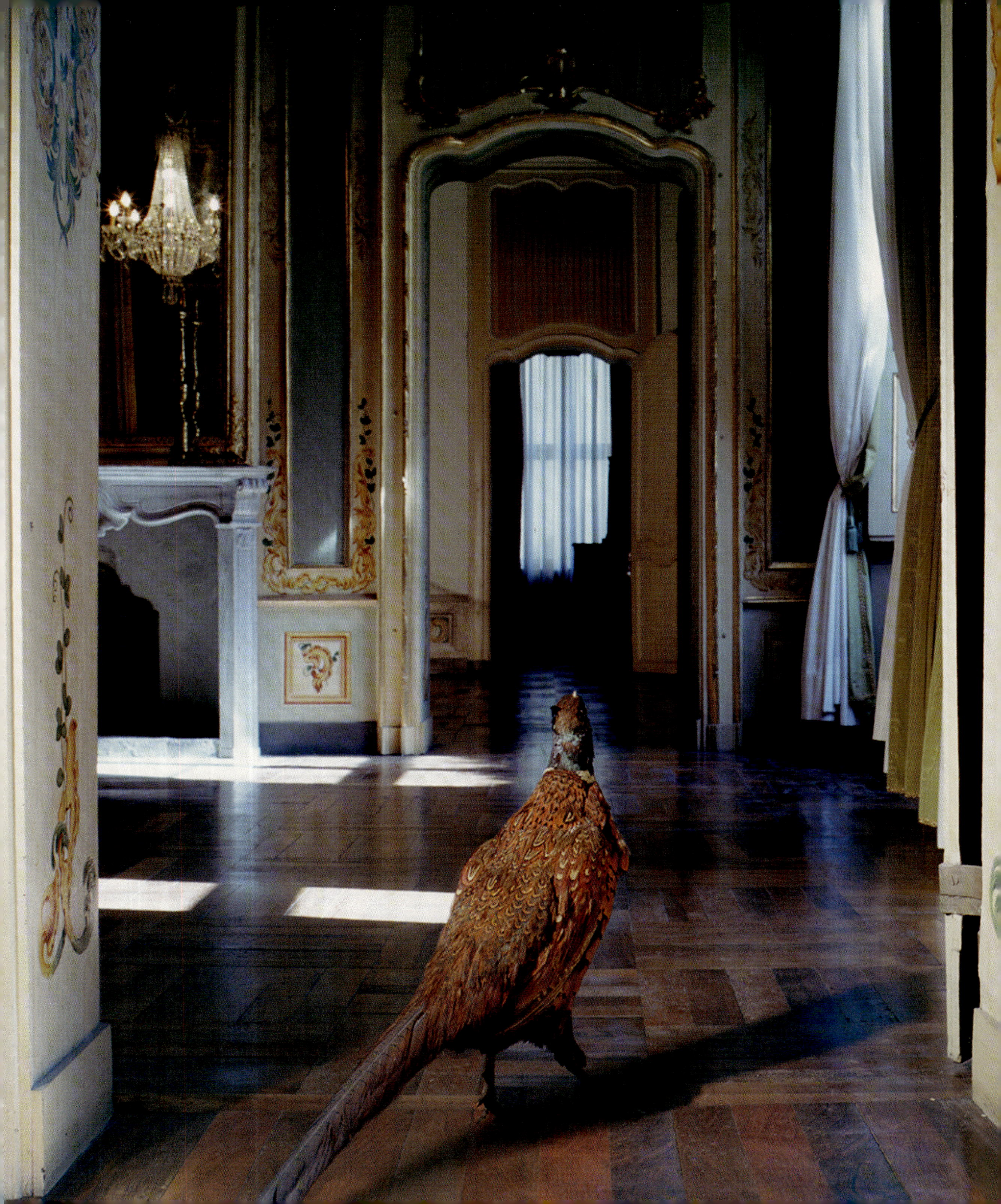

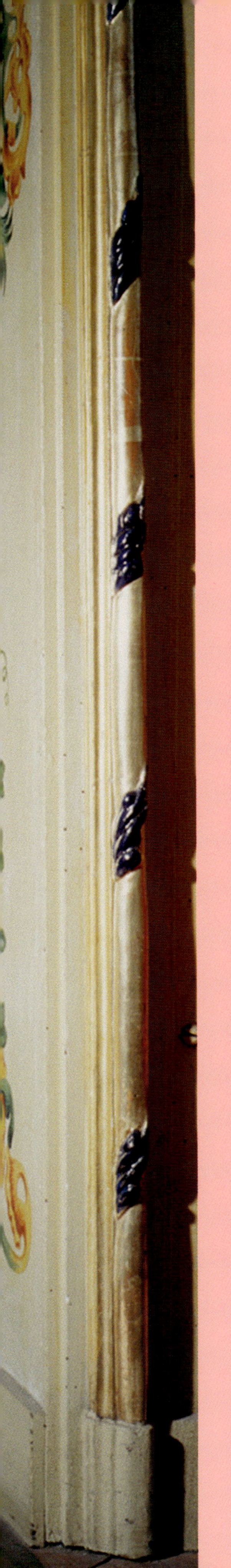

The Visitation

Rest on the Flight to Egypt

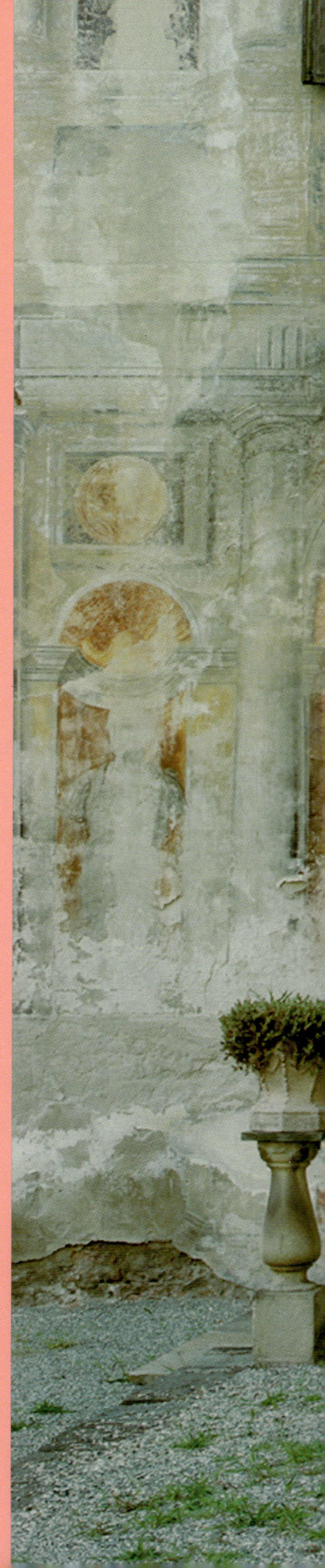

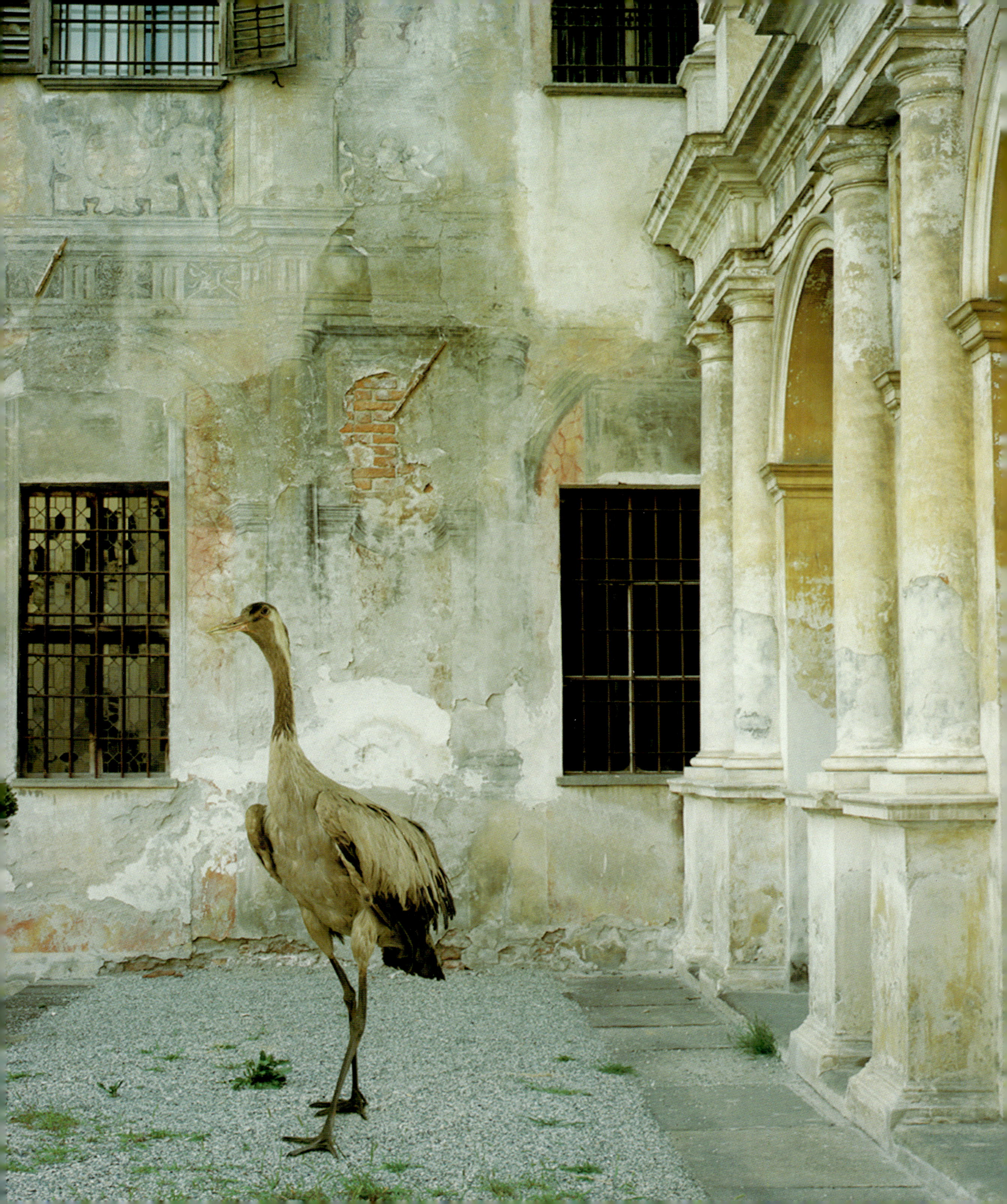

VIII

The Venery

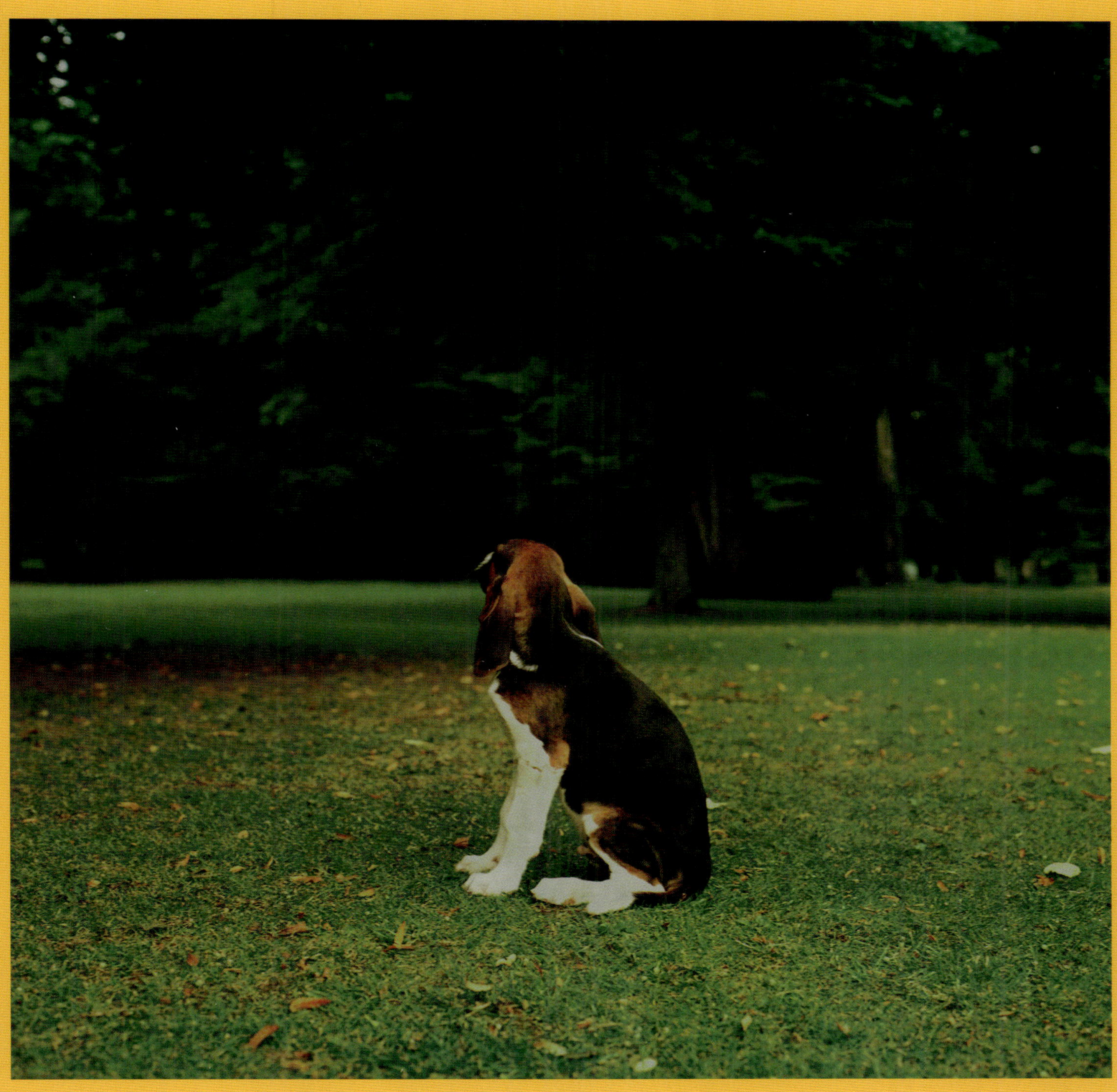

King Of The Forest

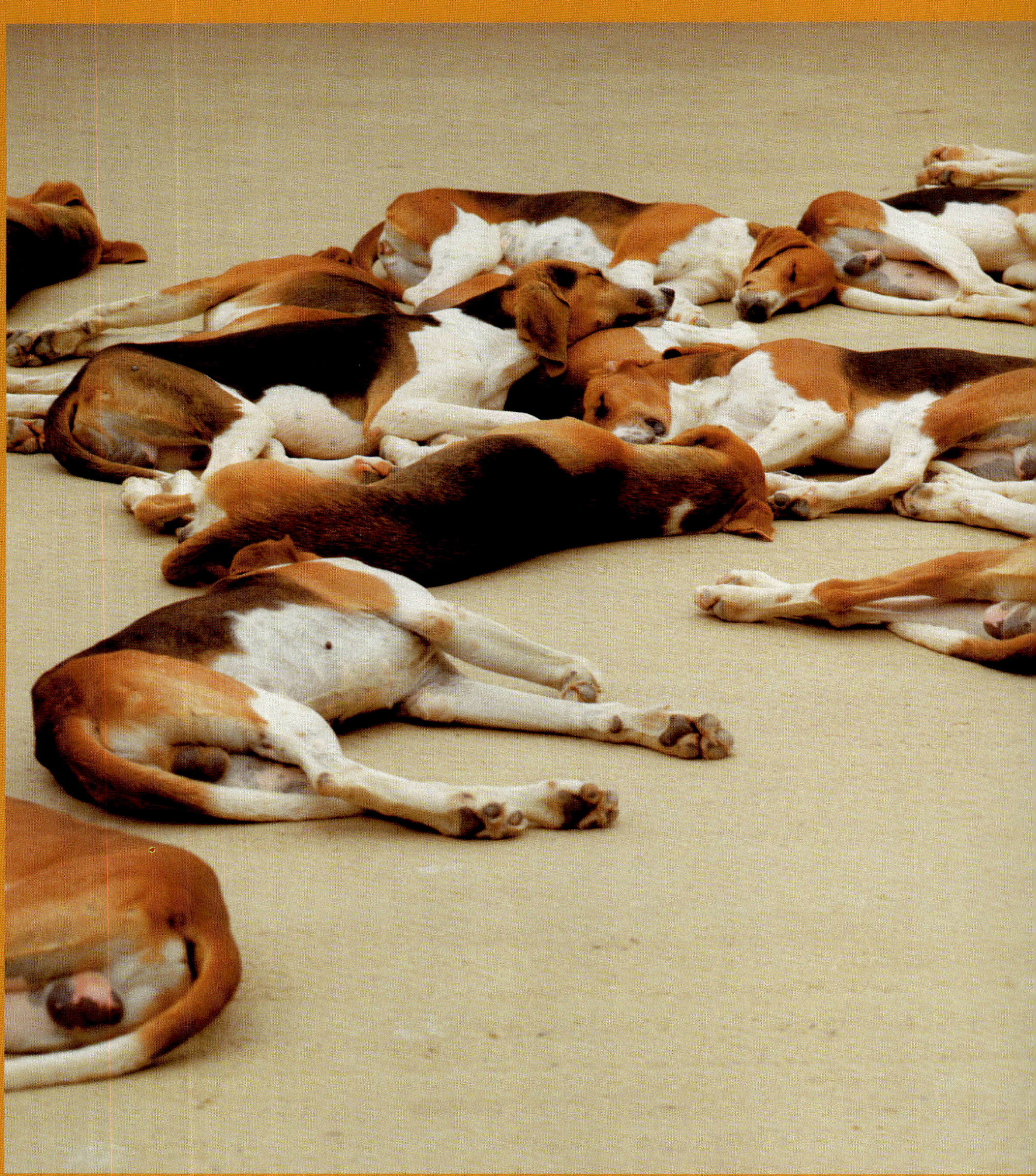

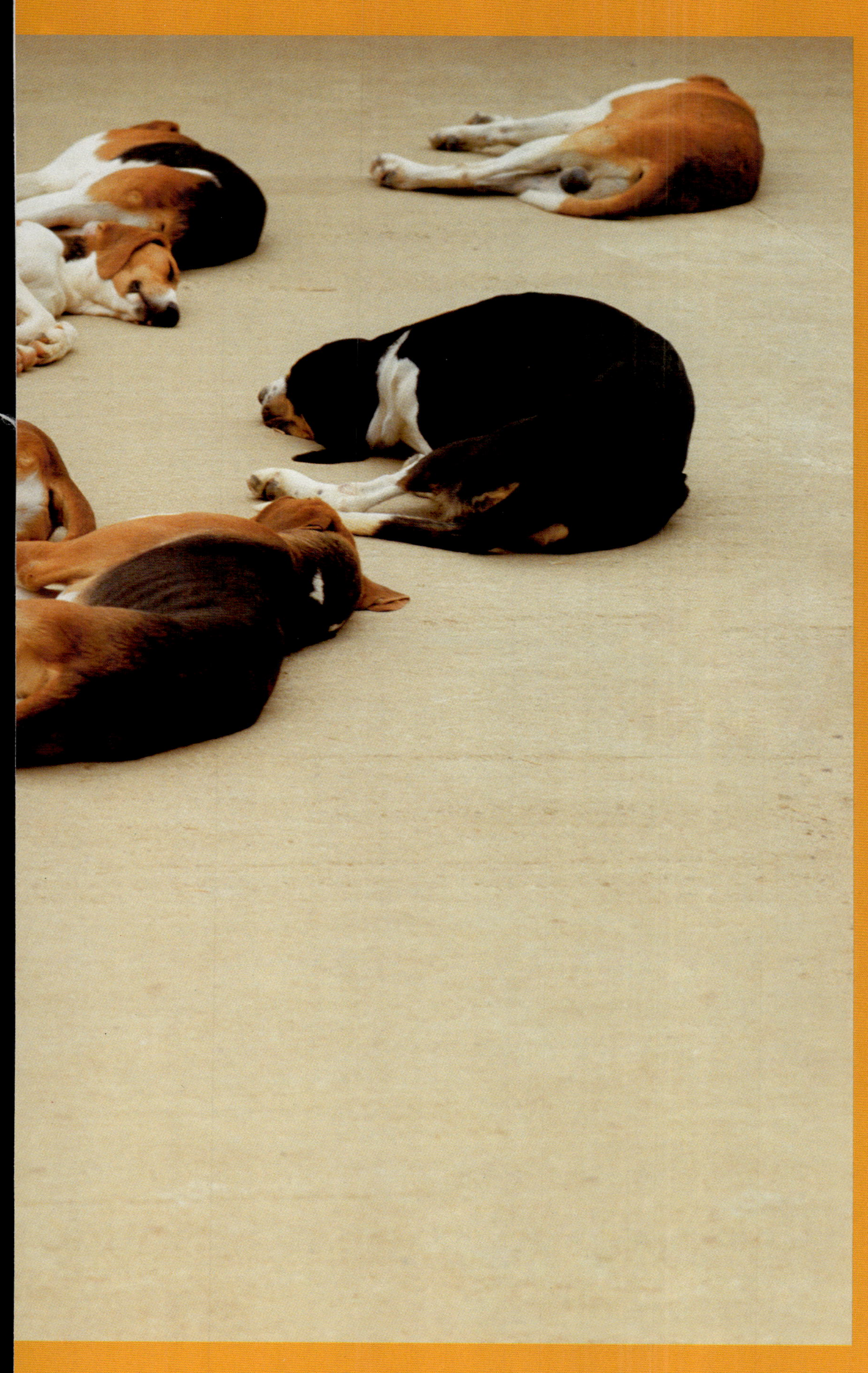

Dead Game